HIDDEN®
Florida Keys
& Everglades

"The guide provides a thorough rundown of the various sights and
activities in the Everglades and throughout the Keys."
—*Atlanta Journal Constitution*

"*Hidden Florida Keys and Everglades* covers a lot of ground, with
chapters on almost any subject the traveler can think of."
—*San Diego Union-Tribune*

"The new edition of this guidebook returns to favorite haunts
and reveals scores of new discoveries."
—*Fort Lauderdale Sun-Sentinel*

"This guide will lead the way to little pockets of natural wilderness that
have resisted encroachment by civilization."
—*Nashville Tennessean*

"Lets you discover Florida's greatest treasures."
—*Chevy Outdoors*

D1051483

HIDDEN®
Florida Keys
& Everglades

Candace Leslie

SIXTH EDITION

Ulysses Press®
BERKELEY, CALIFORNIA

Published by:
ULYSSES PRESS
P.O. Box 3440
Berkeley, CA 94703-3440
www.ulyssespress.com

ISSN 1524-5918
ISBN 1-56975-193-5

Printed in Canada by Transcontinental Printing

20 19 18 17 16 15 14 13 12 11 10 9

UPDATE AUTHOR: Ann Boese
MANAGING EDITOR: Claire Chun
PROJECT DIRECTOR: Lily Chou
COPY EDITOR: Steven Schwartz
EDITORIAL ASSOCIATES: Natasha Lay, Leslie Van Dyke
TYPESETTER: David Wells
CARTOGRAPHY: Robert Lettieri, Claire Chun
COVER DESIGN: Leslie Henriques
INDEXER: Sayre Van Young
COVER PHOTOGRAPHY:
    FRONT: Pat Canova (children playing in the water
    in the Florida Keys)
    CIRCLE: Andy Rouse/EarthWater Stock Photography
    (Florida panther, Everglades)
    BACK: Michael J. Pettypool/Dave G. Houser Stock
    Photography (Key West bed and breakfast)
ILLUSTRATOR: Norman Nicholson
CONTRIBUTING WRITER: Stacy Ritz

Distributed in the United States by Publishers Group
West, in Canada by Raincoast Books, and in Great
Britain and Europe by World Leisure Marketing

To Bob,
who always encourages

Write to us!

If in your travels you discover a spot that captures the spirit of the Florida Keys and Everglades, or if you live in the region and have a favorite place to share, or if you just feel like expressing your views, write to us and we'll pass your note along to the author.

We can't guarantee that the author will add your personal find to the next edition, but if the writer does use the suggestion, we'll acknowledge you in the credits and send you a free copy of the new edition.

ULYSSES PRESS
3286 Adeline Street, Suite 1
Berkeley, CA 94703
E-mail: ulysses@ulyssespress.com

＊

Ulysses Press would like to thank the following readers who took the time to write in with suggestions that were incorporated into this new edition of *Hidden Florida Keys & Everglades*:

Thomas Blackshear, e-mail from home.com; Catherine Collier of Manchester, England; David H. Owens of Ann Arbor, MI; Sally Prout of Norword, MA.

What's Hidden?

At different points throughout this book, you'll find special listings marked with a hidden symbol:

◄ HIDDEN

This means that you have come upon a place off the beaten tourist track, a spot that will carry you a step closer to the local people and natural environment of the Florida Keys and Everglades.

The goal of this guide is to lead you beyond the realm of everyday tourist facilities. While we include traditional sightseeing listings and popular attractions, we also offer alternative sights and adventure activities. Instead of filling this guide with reviews of standard hotels and chain restaurants, we concentrate on one-of-a-kind places and locally owned establishments.

Our authors seek out locales that are popular with residents but usually overlooked by visitors. Some are more hidden than others (and are marked accordingly), but all the listings in this book are intended to help you discover the true nature of the Florida Keys and Everglades and put you on the path of adventure.

Contents

Maps

OUTDOOR ADVENTURE SYMBOLS

The following symbols accompany national, state and regional park listings, as well as beach descriptions throughout the text.

▲	Camping		Windsurfing
	Hiking		Canoeing or Kayaking
	Biking		Boating
	Horseback Riding		Boat Ramps
	Swimming		Fishing
	Snorkeling or Scuba Diving		

ONE

Keys & Everglades Dreaming

The Everglades. The Keys. There are no places like them anywhere else on earth. The one is mysterious. The other romantic.
Though neighbors, they are alike mainly in their uniqueness.
Prominent on maps, they are fragile on the earth, homes to endangered species, dependent on the diligence of humankind for
their very survival. For the traveler, they are exotic worlds at the
tip of a colorful state long famous for its ability to beckon sojourn-
ers and settlers. As tourist destinations, they were late on the bandwagon, partly
because of their distance from the rest of the nation and partly because nature kept
them inaccessible for so long. But they have now emerged as South Florida's two
greatest treasures.

The Everglades, a great, broad and shallow, life-giving river, long kept its secrets
to itself in the dark reaches of cypress swamp and deep, watery grasses. In fact,
much of the vast wetlands is still inaccessible, and some of the more remote hammocks and islets remain unexplored. But not all. Today the traveler can easily enter
portions of this subtle, curious, jungly world, due to the skillfully designed roads
and paths provided by the planners and developers of the Everglades National Park.
What was once a shadowy wonderland has been partially exposed to the sun,
thanks to the Force Four winds of Hurricane Andrew, which blew through in 1992.
Today you can venture through once-impenetrable hardwood hammocks, walk
safely among alligators, count endangered wood storks on a tree branch, discover
brilliant snails on fragile plant stems, stoop down and observe clear, quiet water
ceaselessly flowing through tall saw grass, watch waterfowl winging their way
home, silhouetted against a brilliant sunset sky.

Animals and plants from both temperate and tropical zones inhabit this cross-
over environment. For those searching for hidden destinations, the Everglades is a
treasure trove. Even a short walk will introduce you to a host of secrets and likely
inspire you to probe ever more deeply. Whether on foot or paddling a canoe, you
can follow any of a host of well-designed trails that beckon you into the heart

and soul of the subtropics. The longer you stay and the deeper you explore, the greater will be your rewards.

The same can be said of a journey to the Keys, which appear like a sprinkling of afterthought on the tip of the Florida map. In reality, they are a chain of lush subtropical islands built on ancient coral reefs, floating like an emerald necklace that marks the meeting of the Atlantic Ocean and the Gulf of Mexico. Their history resounds with tales of pirate treasure and fortunes gleaned from ships tossed to bits on the still-living reefs that lie a few miles to the east out in the ocean. Long accessible only by boat, today 36 jewels of this necklace are joined by the great Overseas Highway. Fishing craft have replaced the pirate ships; scuba divers and snorkelers now explore the reefs where ships once met their dooms. Artists, adventurers and other free spirits call these isles home.

To the south and east of the Keys lies the Atlantic Ocean, usually as calm as a lake, held in check by the coral reef. On the other side, broad, shallow Florida Bay bounds the Upper Keys, opening into the Gulf of Mexico as the islands curve out beyond the tip of the state. Except in stormy weather, these waters to the north and west of the islands also lap the shore with a gentle touch. This lack of wave action means there are very few sandy beaches in the Keys, but water on both sides of the islands rivals the Caribbean in its clarity and its brilliant greens and blues.

Just driving down the Keys can be a thrill. There's something exciting about being able to view the sea on all sides from a bridge seven miles long, about finding tropical trees that grow nowhere else in the country, about visiting a house built in the Bahamas and delivered to Key West on a sailing ship. But with the thrill also comes a subtle slowing down, as if the farther out to sea you go, the less the clock matters. Keys folks are proud of this casual, laid-back lifestyle that is impossible to ignore. The best thing you can do is enter into its relaxing spirit by discarding your watch and letting the sun and sea rule your days and the moon and stars your nights. And, remember, surprises are here for the finding. If you look beyond the billboards, down side streets, over on the neighboring out-islands or under the sea, you'll be rewarded with plenty of hidden sights.

This book is designed to help you explore these very differing regions of South Florida. It takes you to countless popular spots and offers advice on how best to enjoy them. It leads you into some off-the-beaten-path locales, places you learn about by talking with folks at the neighborhood fish market or with someone who has lived in the area all his life. It acquaints you with the area's history, its natural habitats and its residents, both human and animal. It recommends sights that should not be missed. It suggests places to eat, to lodge, to play, to camp, always with consideration for varying interests, budgets and tastes.

The traveling part of this book begins with the Everglades, presenting in Chapter Two the main visitor accesses to this wild natural region as explored via the three entrances to the national park. Included in this chapter, too, are nearby destinations, both natural and manmade. Chapter Three heads down the Florida Keys, "the islands you can drive to," through Key Largo, Islamorada and Marathon, all the way to Big Pine and the Lower Keys. History and hype merge in Chapter Four, a guide to Key West, famous party town, arts center and ethnic village, whose romantic past and charm still color its life.

Where you go and what you choose to see is up to you—these areas include enough sights and activities to appeal to a very broad range of interests. This is verified by the numbers of retired people who return annually or settle down here, by the families who arrive each summer as soon as school is out, by the folks who come in their boats and tie up for a stay, as well as by the fanciers of the fast lane who come to live it up in Key West. For lovers of birds and wildlife and quiet, breathtaking beauty, there are few places as rewarding as the Everglades. For those who fish and dive or simply love the sea, the Keys offer all you could wish for.

These are southern Florida's two great gems. May they hold for you all kinds of hidden, and even not-so-hidden, rewards.

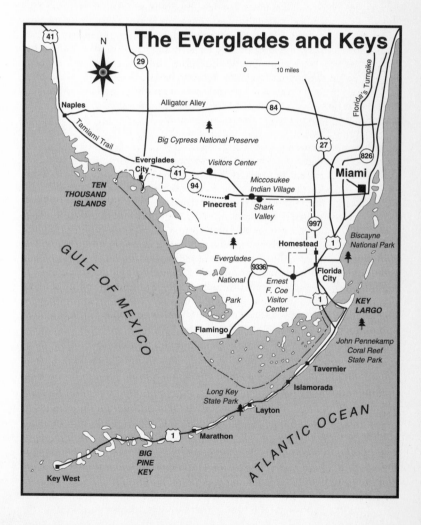

The Story of the Keys and Everglades

GEOLOGY

As land masses go, all of Florida is a mere child, having emerged from the sea as recently as 20 to 30 million years ago. For eons its bedrock base lay beneath the warm waters of the southern sea. Slowly it collected sediment, building limestone deposits that would eventually rise above the surface. As distant glaciers froze and melted, the seas rose and fell, forming and reforming the shores of Florida, depositing silt and bits of sea life.

The Everglades actually begin at Lake Okeechobee, and to learn their geology, one must look to this shallow lake whose rocky foundation lies only a few feet above sea level. Beneath the lake and extending down into the northern part of the Everglades, the rock is a limestone composed of alternating layers of hardened sea bottom and of freshwater peats and muds. Farther south, it becomes a more porous limestone known as oolite. The surface of this spongy layer often becomes full of holes that have been receptacles for decaying vegetation, fresh water, sand and shells.

Beneath these relatively "young" limestone formations lies the oldest rock in southern Florida, the impervious *Tamiami* formation. Like a giant underground cistern, it collects and holds the rainwater that falls on the spongy Everglades limestones and on Big Cypress Swamp. Nearby cities such as Miami and Palm Beach, as well as the Florida Keys, depend on this life-giving reservoir for their survival. The force and power of this giant aquifer also keep the seawater at bay. Scientists believe that without the Everglades, this reservoir would become salt, and southern Florida as we know it would be no more.

Though it is hardly discernable to the traveler, altitude also plays an important role in the structure of South Florida. From Lake Okeechobee southward, the surface rock slopes like an ever-so-slightly tilting tray to the tip of the state, dropping about a foot every dozen miles. It is down along this crucial slope that the freshwater Everglades "river," as wide as 50 miles and only a few inches deep, flows through saw grass from the rain-fed lake to the sea. Here and there, scattered limestone outcroppings form the "high-altitude" regions of the Everglades, occasionally attaining a barely noticeable few feet. Through the ages these little hillocks have gathered humus and eventually vegetation, including hardwood trees, to become water-surrounded islands known as hammocks.

To the south of the Everglades, the limestone bed continues under the shallow waters of Florida Bay, where the centuries have covered it with an overlay of fine mudlike marl. To the west are the Ten Thousand Islands, an ever-changing archipelago of mangrove islets seated on the tops of old sunken sand dunes of the Gulf of Mexico.

The Florida Keys, like the Everglades, lie on a thick layer of limestone. The rock is covered by an ancient coral reef. In the lower islands, the porous Miami oolite, with its rich vegetation, appears once again. Low-lying islands with slight variations in elevation, the Keys boast a high point of 18 feet, on Windley Key. For the most part, however, they are very flat.

To the east of the Florida Keys lies the only living coral reef in the continental United States. It is located between four and seven miles offshore, running parallel to the Keys from Key Largo to the Dry Tortugas. This living marine marvel, rising as high as a few feet below the surface of the water and descending to dark depths near the Gulf Stream, protects the Keys from the waves of the pounding Atlantic surf and hence from the development of sand beaches, a great surprise to many first-time visitors.

THE EVERGLADES STORY Although it took millions of years for the Everglades to evolve, and American Indians probably wandered into some of the mysterious interiors for a century or two, the real history of the unique region belongs mainly to the century just drawing to a close. The story of the Everglades is a microcosm of the global story of the interdependence and tensions between humans and nature, full of despair and promise, of lessons ignored and lessons learned, of life sources and of life itself hanging by a tenuous thread.

Some of the early Indians who roamed coastal portions of the Everglades left a few artifacts and their discarded shells in scattered mounds, but little is known about exactly how they fared in the mosquito-infested, watery environment. Nor is there much evidence that European explorers felt attracted to the marshy tip of Florida, so lacking in solid land and so hostile to travelers. To the casual observer as well as to the ambitious developer, the Everglades long seemed no more than a swamp to be drained and put to better use than nature obviously had in mind. Even as early as 1848, Army and Navy officers chasing Seminole Indians through the muck and swamps returned home stating that the land should be drained for cattle raising and for growing rice, sugar cane, fruits and vegetables. In 1865, a reporter sent to check out post–Civil War conditions in southern Florida commented on the need to get the water out of Lake Okeechobee and the Everglades.

Draining seemed a logical idea at the time and was attempted in little fits and starts as early as the 1880s. But the Everglades were not to be conquered easily. Early attempts were challenged by opponents of taxes and, hence, by lack of money. And whatever progress was made, the task always proved to be much more challenging than originally assumed. In 1905, the state's first comprehensive drainage law was passed, intending to construct a system of canals that would "reclaim" swamp and flood lands. Florida governor Napoleon Bonaparte Broward, convinced that if enough of the Everglades was drained, the state could grow sufficient sugar to supply the whole country, threw government efforts into the project. By 1909, a canal connecting Lake Okeechobee to Miami was completed, smaller waterways were constructed and drainage for farmland was underway in earnest.

There are over 800 islands in the Keys large enough to appear on government charts, though many other tiny mangrove islets exist. About 30 of the Keys are inhabited.

But even this early in the game, occasional critics warned that crucial studies had not been done, that water tables might be threatened, that not enough money was available to fulfill the dreams. But for many years the promises outweighed the criticisms. Southern Florida land sales boomed. Farming got underway. Then World War I put a damper on most of the enterprises. In the 1920s, a couple of devastating hurricanes, several serious fires in the peat-rich regions and, finally, the collapse of the Florida land boom brought a temporary end to state efforts to conquer the mighty Everglades.

At the end of the decade, the Army Corps of Engineers constructed Hoover Dike around Lake Okeechobee, hoping to end the threat of flooding. But again, in 1947, a hurricane caused floods to wipe out farm and grazing lands, proving once again that man-made canals and dikes could not always hold the waters in check. By then, some people began to realize that, though millions of dollars had been spent for drainage and flood control, effective reclamation of the wetlands had still not been achieved. And new problems were appearing as well. Salt began seeping into freshwater sources as water tables were lowered. Fires in the peatlike soils created clouds of smoke that could make eyes water as far north as Tallahassee. Thin layers of soil in land that had been successfully drained and farmed began to disappear. Dry summers pointed out the need for irrigation as well as drainage. A water management district was established in hopes of solving some of the problems.

At about the same time as these immediately practical problems were being examined, concerns of a new kind began to be heard. What was all this tampering with nature doing to wildlife, to plant life, to life in general? "Pollution" entered the vocabulary of the concerned, chief of whom was Marjorie Stoneman Douglas, who published her immediate classic, *The Everglades: River of Grass*, in 1947. The good news was that in the same year President Harry Truman dedicated 2000 square miles of the southernmost Everglades as a national park. Here, at last, was an area that could not be touched.

But as fine as the establishment of that important park was, the problems were not over. All the water feeding into the region was, by then, controlled by artificial means. The complex food chain of the Everglades that had always been dependent on natural cycles of rain and drought was now at the mercy of those who manned the pipes and dikes to meet the demands of Florida's evergrowing human population. Two major causeway-style highways, re-markable feats of wetland engineering, now cut across the once-pristine, free-flowing river of grass. Fertilizers and insecticides, so important to farmers but so deadly to many creatures of the wild, also threatened to further upset the fragile balance of nature.

As the problems arose, so did the champions of the preservation of the delicately balanced environment of the Everglades. Sometimes they lost their battles. Sometimes they won, as when they prevented the draining of Big Cypress Swamp, upon which the Everglades is dependent for much of its life, for a mammoth airport. After energetic and skillful protest, the region was turned into a national preserve in the 1970s. But not all the problems have been solved; tensions continue to this very moment.

Hurricanes pose another, ongoing problem for the Everglades, and in August of 1992, Hurricane Andrew underscored that threat. Driving rain and winds gusting to 175 miles per hour bowled through the middle of Everglades National Park and southern Dade County, toppling trees, trailers, homes and anything else in its path. By the time its last raindrop fell, Hurricane Andrew had caused more than $35 billion in damage, destroyed almost 126,000 houses and apartments, displaced 160,000 people and taken 38 lives. Dade County relief agencies mobilized with the help of 20,000 federal troops and recovery was astoundingly rapid. New underground power lines were planted, housing erected and Everglades National Park reopened in December, just four months after the storm. Little evidence remains of the storm today.

In spite of preservation efforts, some say the Everglades will disappear, that it is too late to turn things around. When the Everglades die, some say, so will all of Florida—Miami, the wildlife, the farms, the Keys and all who are dependent on the irreplaceable water tables that may one day turn to salt. But even with this forecast of doom, tireless efforts continue in search of the perfect balance between humankind and the natural world on which all survival depends.

AMERICAN INDIANS When the first Spanish explorers approached the Florida shores in the 16th century, a number of native tribes had long resided throughout the peninsula and on its surrounding islands. The southernmost regions were dominated by the Tequestas and the Calusas, who thrived on the abundance provided by the sea and the rich coastal lands. Though the two tribes may have merged from time to time, probably in the Cape Sable region at the tip of the mainland, they were essentially separated by the Everglades. The Tequestas roamed the region from present-day Pompano Beach southward; the Calusas dominated the westward regions from the tip of the peninsula as far north as Tampa Bay and roamed portions of the Florida Keys.

The Tequestas were thought to number only about 800 at the beginning of the historical period. They were great fishermen, usually living near the mouths of streams and enhancing their seafood diet with such varied fare as palmetto berries, sea grapes, palm nuts, prickly pears and venison and turtle meat. They made a flour from the starchy arrowroot plant known as coontie. The Calusas, whose number may have been triple that of the Tequestas, lived principally off the conch, clams, oysters and other shellfish abundant in the Ten Thousand Islands region on the western edge of the Everglades. Though they were not agricultural, some of the early natives often lived in villages and developed a high social structure, thanks to the bounties of nature within their reach. They used wood for ceremonial and practical implements, such as masks, bowls and boats. They made spears and bows and arrows; they designed tools and ornaments from bone and shell.

Like the other early Florida tribes, the Tequestas and Calusas eventually disappeared with the coming of Western civilization and its accompanying diseases and conquering spirit. Some of the void was filled, though, by other natives, Creek Indians who slowly moved into the Spanish Florida territory and down the peninsula from what are now the southern states. They were neither welcomed nor beloved by the European and American settlers. They came to be called "Seminoles," a name perhaps corrupted from the Spanish word *cimarrón*, meaning "wild" or from the Creek words *ishti semoli*, meaning "wildmen" or "outlanders" or "separatists."

By the time Spain finally relinquished Florida to the United States in 1821, one war had already been fought against the Seminoles in an attempt to rid the land of Indians for good. But the Indian "problem" did not go away, so Andrew Jackson, the territory's first governor, declared a second Seminole War in 1835, hoping to quickly remove the annoying offenders to Indian territory west of the Mississippi. The Seminoles proved to be a formidable enemy; the war lasted almost seven years and exacted a great price in dollars and lives. Patrols pushed the Seminoles deeper and deeper into the Everglades. Bounties were offered for the capture of live Indians—$500 for a man, $250 for a woman, $100 for a child. Finally, after seven years of fighting, the backbone of resistance was broken. Following the death of their great leader, Osceola, most of the surviving Seminoles allowed themselves to be "escorted" out of Florida.

But not all of the Indians left. Several hundred disappeared into the Everglades and Big Cypress Swamp, where they spent the remainder of the century living a nomadic life in the wet, lonely region. Like their prehistoric cousins, they lived off the land and sea. They built adaptable stilt houses, called "chickees," safe above the ever rising and falling waters. They developed unrivaled skills of survival in the difficult environment. Their secluded life continued until the building of the Tamiami Trail in the 1920s, when the outside world began to delve into the region.

Not until 1962 did the Seminoles finally resume official relations with the United States, a century-and-a-quarter after their self-imposed independence. Today their descendants, numbering about 2000, live in two separate groups on reservations. Fifteen hundred Seminoles, the Muskogee-speakers, live near Alligator Alley (Route 84) midway between Fort Lauderdale and Naples. A smaller tribe, the Hichiti-speaking Miccosukees, live in a series of little villages along the Tamiami Trail (Route 41) on the northern edge of Everglades National Park, still carrying out remnants of the Everglades lifestyle. Once considered enemies of settlers, these descendants of the Creeks are now accepted as a vital part of southern Florida's rich tapestry.

EARLY KEYS SETTLEMENT   Though they are neighbors, the Everglades and the Keys have very different histories. It helps to remember that in the early days of exploration, the former appeared as an impenetrable swampland, and the latter a collection of isolated islands accessible only by boat.

Spanish explorers first sighted the Keys early in the 16th century as they searched for rumored gold and eternal youth. One contemporary chronicler of explorer Ponce de León, observing the chain of islands on the horizon, said they appeared as men who were suffering; hence they were given the name *Los Mártires* or "the martyrs." No one knows exactly when the first European set foot on one of the Keys, but as exploration and shipping increased, the islands became prominent on nautical maps. The nearby treacherous coral reefs claimed many actual seafaring "martyrs" from the time of early recorded history. The chain was eventually called "keys," also attributed to the Spanish, from *cayos*, meaning "small islands."

In 1763, the Spanish ceded Florida to the British in a trade for the port of Havana. The treaty was unclear as to the status of the Keys. An agent of the king of Spain claimed that the islands, rich in fish, turtles and mahogany for shipbuilding, were part of Cuba, fearing that the English might build fortresses and dominate the shipping lanes. The British also realized the treaty was ambiguous, but declared that the Keys should be occupied and defended as part of Florida. The British claim was never officially contested. Ironically, the British gave the islands back to Spain in 1783, to keep them out of the hands of the United States, but in 1821 all of Florida, including the necklace of islands, officially became American territory.

Though most of the Florida Keys remained remote and inaccessible until well into the 20th century, their history glitters with romantic tales of pirates, fortunes gleaned from unfortunate shipwrecks, brief heydays for several island cities, struggling pioneer farmers and occasional military occupation. It also holds its share of tragedy resulting from settlers' encounters with hostile Indians, yellow fever–bearing mosquitoes, dangerous hurricanes and unpredictable seas.

PROTECTION AND PROSPERITY By the time of the territorial period, Key West was already recognized as a place with assets. Its proximity to the Florida reef made it a perfect center for the sometimes legitimate, sometimes dubious business of marine salvage. Its deep channels with protected anchorage made it a perfect location for a recoaling station for steamers and a strategic site for a naval base. In 1821, John Simonton bought the island for $2000 from its original Spanish land-grant owner, and the first permanent residents moved in. But by then, pirates had long been reaping great harvests from unfortunate ships in the Gulf of Mexico and West Indies. Pirate history being a colorful blending of fact and myth, in the Keys it rings with names and tales of Black Caesar, Jean Laffite, Blackbeard and other nefarious characters who frightened seafarers and buried as yet unearthed treasures throughout the islands.

In 1822, Lieutenant Matthew C. Perry was ordered to take possession of Key West for the United States and to go after the pirates. By the end of the year, 21 American ships cruised the waters in search of pirates, engaging in occasional confrontations. After one fight in which an American lieutenant was killed, a naval base was established at Key West and the fleet enlarged.

But an even more formidable enemy than pirates was yellow fever. In July of 1823 it took the lives of 68 men, causing the Navy to declare the base unfit from July to October. By 1826, the main operations were moved to Pensacola, leaving only coal and supply depots at Key West. However, the region was still considered to be important militarily, a "Gibraltar of the Gulf." In 1845 the War Department announced the building of fortifications at Key West and in the Dry Tortugas; these would become Fort Taylor and Fort Jefferson. Lighthouses had already been sending their beacons from these strategic points for several decades.

Meanwhile, Key West was on its way to its brief heyday as the wealthiest city in Florida. The chief industry was wrecking and salvage. Many 19th-century entrepreneurs were English Bahamians who brought the distinctive speech and architectural styles that would one day become known as "conch," named for the serviceable mollusk that resided in the surrounding waters. Bahamians also profited from the lucrative harvesting of fish and, along with Greek immigrants, of high-quality sponges. Cuban migrants arrived with their culture and cigar-making skills; by 1860 a million cigars a year were being rolled in over 150 Key West factories. The salt manufacturing business also achieved high success in the years before the Civil War.

Prosperity was thriving farther up the Keys as well. At the 1836 Constitutional Convention, when Florida became a state, Dade County was established to take in the vast area from Lake Okeechobee to Bahia Honda Key. The inauspicious island of Indian Key was named county seat. Located halfway between Miami and Key West, it was the prime location for wreckers and salvagers, some of whom were purported to be working outside the law, even perhaps luring ships to their dooms on the treacherous reefs. Like Key West, Indian Key boomed.

> Whether honest or dishonest, most wreckers did very well and often provided a much needed service to unfortunate captains, crews and shipowners.

But it all came to a tragic halt when, on an August morning in 1840, Indians piloting 17 canoes raided the island, looted and burned crucial stores and buildings and killed several prominent citizens. Four years later, Miami became the county seat, though it would be some time before it reached the former prominence of Indian Key. The final death knell for the wrecking business was the placement of a string of lighthouses to warn sea captains of the dangers of the treacherous reefs.

CIVIL WAR   During the Civil War, though much of Key West's population was loyal to the South, both the city and Fort Jefferson in the Dry Tortugas remained in Union hands. As early as November 1860, a captain of the United States Army of Engineers urged reinforcements so that these two strategic areas of defense would not be lost in case of secession. As the war began, the commanding officer at Key West, determined not to let unfinished Fort Taylor fall into secessionist hands, stealthily led his small force of 44 through a sleeping city to the fort in the dark of night. They set up a defense that the Confederates were never able to capture. Neither of the forts saw any serious action for the duration of the war, though individual blockade runners are thought to have darted about in the waters off the Keys.

Though Fort Taylor and Fort Jefferson became obsolete with the invention of the rifled cannon, the former was noted for the construction of a 7000-gallon-a-day seawater distilling plant and the latter as a dreary wartime and postwar prison.

Life apparently went on in the Keys with less distress than in the northern regions of the state. Just after the Civil War, a New York newspaperman was sent to southern Florida to check on postwar conditions. He observed that Key West, Florida's largest town, had grown during the conflict. He said that he had to remind himself that it was an American city, so rich was it in tropical plants and foreign tongues. Later in 1865 observers noted that people living on the Keys had a passion for liquor and wrecking, but they also recorded many citizens engaged in fishing, sponging, turtling and harvesting oranges, lemons, limes, coconuts and grapes.

THE SPANISH-AMERICAN WAR With its proximity to Havana, Key West and other southern Florida coastal cities took on great importance during the war for Cuban independence from Spain. American sympathy for Cuban patriots was flamed by the publication of a Spanish letter disparaging President William McKinley and by the mysterious sinking of the U.S. battleship *Maine* in Havana harbor on February 15, 1898. The United States demanded that Spain withdraw from Cuba, and, on April 24, Spain declared war. Volunteers, both American and Cuban, signed up to join in the fighting.

Dr. Samuel H. Mudd was interned at Fort Jefferson for four years because he had unknowingly set the broken leg of Lincoln's assassin, John Wilkes Booth.

The War Department first assumed that Key West would be the principal base for American forces, so civilian, Army and Navy activity increased in the busy city. But Key West lacked sufficient storage space, and its harbor needed improvements such as deepened channels for larger ships; Tampa became the main center of military activity. However, the Navy yard at Key West proved important to the invasion of Cuba. Only 90 miles from Havana, the harbor bustled with freight and passenger boats, newspaper dispatch craft, hospital services, Navy coaling and repair work and Spanish prisoner reception. Forts Taylor and Jefferson were reactivated. Newly installed condensers at the distilling plant were designed to increase freshwater supplies.

The war ended on August 12, but the Army and Navy stayed on to complete important projects in Key West. Improved facilities, beefed-up defenses and deeper channels contributed to both base and harbor.

HENRY FLAGLER'S RAILROAD By 1896, dreamer, entrepreneur and tycoon Henry Flagler had extended his Florida East Coast Railroad to Miami. In the first years of the new century, homesteaders began settling into the regions surrounding the ever-creeping rails. A town, appropriately named Homestead, sprang up where the railroad stopped in 1904. But Flagler's dream kept steaming forward. In 1905, work began on his remarkable "railroad that went to the sea," an incredible line that traversed islands, spanned inlets and ascended bridges, one of them almost seven miles long, down through the Keys and over the ocean to Key West. On January 22, 1912, the first train rolled into town. Flagler believed that Key West would become a terminal from which passengers and freight would set out across the sea to the south and west. In reality, it became just the end of the line.

Though tourists came to the Keys in impressive numbers and the economy picked up, the glory days were not to last. Key West's great boom began to bust with the beginning of World War I. Tourism was halted. The armed forces were eventually reduced to a garrison. Cigar makers began moving to Tampa. Blight and storm wiped out the sponge beds. Florida's pre-Depression land boom had little effect on the islands, but the ensuing Depression years almost destroyed them. Key West's population declined; debts rose. The government declared a state of emergency.

But the railroad had revealed the potential of the Keys as a tourist attraction. The Federal Emergency Relief Administration of the New Deal undertook to rehabilitate the city. Citizens rallied, many learning to make crafts and novelties from local products or organizing fetes and pageants for tourists. Artists on relief decorated walls and buildings with distinctive murals and other works. The influx of thousands of visitors promised great rewards. But the success was again short-lived.

On Labor Day 1935, one of the severest hurricanes on record destroyed the overseas railroad. Winds raged between 200 and 250 miles per hour, 75 miles per hour faster than the strongest winds of Hurricane Andrew. The barometer dropped lower than it had ever registered anywhere before. Near Islamorada, the storm overturned rescue cars with over 400 passengers on board. A camp full of war veterans was destroyed. Whole families disappeared into the sea. Many people predicted this terrible tragedy would mark the end of prosperity for the Keys and moved away. But some long-term residents stayed, determined to rebuild from the rubble of the Depression and storm.

MODERN TIMES   When it was discovered that Henry Flagler's railroad had been built on very sound footings, a new dream emerged. Bridges and trestles, undamaged by the storm, became the underpinnings for what would become the Overseas Highway. Old track was recycled as new guard rails for bridges. Flagler's vision of a route across the sea would still be realized, only now the thoroughfare would carry automobiles instead of trains. The first wheels rolled across its new pavement in 1938. Tourists began returning.

Once again, however, the vision of thousands of annual visitors flocking to the tropical islands was dashed, this time with the coming of World War II. But the war did bring the Navy and more improvements to the Keys. A submarine base was built at Key West. A water main, like a new lifeline, began carrying fresh water into the Keys from the mainland. Population again began to grow.

President Harry Truman fell in love with Key West and established his "Little White House" there for regular visits. After the war, artists and writers again began lauding the inspirational ambience of Key West, following such luminaries as Ernest Hemingway, Tennessee Williams and Elizabeth Bishop. Tourists began returning in earnest, attracted by sunsets, seafood, colorful history, beautiful seas and general good times. Gays found the town a comfortable place to establish residency.

The 1962 Cuban missile crisis briefly marred the Keys' positive image, but even that brought a little more military prosperity before most of the Navy finally left Key West for good. In 1980, the Mariel Boat Lift, bringing refugees of assorted backgrounds from Cuba, thrust Key West again into the public eye.

Today, the once-isolated Florida Keys are a tourist and retirement haven, popular with divers and sport fishermen and folks who love the climate and beauty of the place, and who thrive on its relaxed ambience. Though boasting a genuinely slowed-down lifestyle far from big-city hassle and northeastern work ethics, the Keys are no longer free from the influence of the outside world. Drugs and their attendant dynamics, particularly in a region of open southern seas and myriad uninhabited islands, are, and will probably long be, a challenge to law enforcement both on land and in the surrounding waters. Crime happens, as it will, in towns where a comfortable climate makes it easy to live in the streets. And some folks wonder just when the next hurricane will come.

But the mainstay of the Florida Keys is a booming, cheerful tourism. From the retired couple that settles in for the winter with their small RV to the former president of the United States, George Bush, who battles bonefish with his longtime Keys' friends, the visitors come year-round. They fish, they scuba dive, they sightsee, they eat seafood, they party, they relax, and some of them stay for good. The Overseas Highway is dotted here and there with clusters of chain eateries and motels that make it look like any-strip-U.S.A. But no matter what kind of resorts are built and how many hamburger places go up, the very nature and location of the Florida Keys will keep them as distinctive from their mainland neighbor as when the Spanish first spotted them across the water.

FLORA

One would need a whole book, or maybe several, to deal fairly with the flora of the Everglades and Keys. Fortunately, both the national park and the state parks, as well as bookstores, provide generous amounts of information to those who are captivated by the plants they discover in these botanically rich environments. The brief entries below can only provide a tantalizing mention of a few of the particular plants that one notices at first glance.

Though many plants are distinctive to the Everglades, one dominates above all others—the finely toothed, one- to two-foot bladed sedge commonly known as "saw grass." It is saw grass that makes so much of the Everglades appear as a broad prairie, concealing the shallow freshwater river that runs through it.

But though the saw grass dominates, the Everglades are rich in tropical and subtropical plant life, some found nowhere else on earth. Throughout the vast region, limestone ridges called hammocks rise like little islands in the river of grass, allowing trees to establish themselves above the water line and nourishing a wide variety of flora. Here grow the gumbo-limbo trees, royal palms, wild coffee, mastic, strangler fig, rare paurotis palms and huge mahogany trees. Air plants, including more than a dozen types of bromeliads, thrive among the trees of the hardwood hammocks. So do more than 20 species of wild orchids, some quite rare, and numerous species of exotic ferns and assorted vines.

Green in all but very dry winter months, saw grass is one of the oldest plant species on earth.

It is the dwarf cypress, draped with ghostlike Spanish moss, that contributes to the mysterious aura of the Everglades. Despite their stunted size, some of these wispy trees are over a century old. They lose their leaves in the winter, making them appear dead, but they are the hardy survivors of the wetlands. The Everglades also contain forests of tall slash pines that are dependent on the natural, lightning-caused fires to keep their floors clear of undergrowth that might inhibit the young trees. Still, as many as 200 types of plants, including 30 found only here, thrive on the floor of some of the pine forests. Most common is the saw palmetto, accompanied by hardwood seedlings fighting for footings among the pines.

In 1992, Hurricane Andrew changed the habitat in much of the Everglades. The hurricane's high winds sheared off the leafy treetops, exposing the forest floor, which had been shaded from the blazing Florida sun. Low-lying plants such as orchids and ferns are slowly adapting to the sun, while fallen trees are regenerating from their remaining planted roots. This is an interesting time in the Everglades, a time of transition for much of its tropical life.

Along the coastal regions of the Everglades and throughout the Keys reside some of Florida's true natives, the mangroves, or "walking trees." Best known is the red mangrove, with its arched reddish roots sprawling out like spider's legs where fresh and salt water meet. A little farther inland the black mangrove sends up its masses of tiny pneumatophores for breathing through the still brackish water. Behind them, the white mangrove and buttonwood thrive on hammocks with other tropical trees.

Mangroves reproduce in an unusual manner. Seeds sprout before they leave the tree to drop into the soft wet bottom or float on the tides to suitable locations where they catch hold and become the beginnings of new islands. Mangroves are useful as well as interesting, stabilizing fragile shorelines, catching the brunt of stormy waves, filtering water, serving as rookeries and shelter for birds and wildlife and supporting diverse marine life with their nutritious falling leaves.

The winds of Hurricane Andrew did the most damage to tall trees. The storm affected all of the large hammock trees, knocked down 20 to 40 percent of the slash pines and leveled 70,000 acres of mangrove forests. However, many of the fallen mangroves will survive, fed by the few roots that remain in the ground.

Plant life in the Keys, though much has succumbed to ever-growing development, has much in common with that of the Everglades. In the surviving natural regions grow gumbo-limbo trees, lignum vitae, West Indian mahogany, wild lime and tamarind, Jamaica dogwood and other tropical residents of the hardwood hammocks. Mangroves also abound, creating new keys and enlarging old ones. In the transition zones just above the mangroves can be found the evergreen sea grape, the toxic poisonwood tree, mahoe and cat claw. The slash pine forests of Big Pine Key gave the island its name.

Many of the plants and trees of the Everglades and Keys arrived from the West Indies and beyond, transported on the waves and currents of the sea. Other exotics were brought in by well-meaning (one assumes) settlers and residents. Most notorious of these transplants is the Australian pine (not a true pine) that, though lovely, especially when the wind sings through its branches, has crowded out many native plants and upset natural ecosystems. Many scientists are worried that Hurricane Andrew's winds brought in more exotic seedlings that will further overtake the native plants. Tropical fruits, as well as the vast but succulent vegetable farms, have also sometimes flourished at the expense of nature's balance, since they require chemical fertilizers and insecticides for their survival and our dining tables.

FAUNA

An abundance of wildlife resides in the unique subtropical environment of the Everglades. Some species here face extinction, the South Florida wetlands being their only remaining protected home. High on the endangered list is the Florida panther, a rare, seldom seen gray cougar whose number has been reduced to an estimated several dozen, due to the continued loss of habitat. Threatened, too, is the gentle manatee—the harmless, bulky "sea cow"—victim of motorboat propellers and abandoned fishing tackle. Though alligators are the most familiar and easily observed residents of the Everglades, their cousin, the crocodile, struggles for survival in a dwindling habitat (see "Alligators and Crocodiles" in Chapter Two). Facing uncertain futures, too, are the loggerhead and green sea turtles.

But many residents of the region thrive in healthy numbers. Winter's dry season, when they gather at shrinking water holes, is the best time to see them. Exceedingly common, especially around the campgrounds, are the opossum and the raccoon, a paler, smaller creature than his northern cousin. Bobcats appear with some regularity and can sometimes be heard howling on spring and summer nights. White-tailed deer roam freely. The nine-banded armadillo, a native of the Southwest and Central America, has found Florida, including the western Everglades, to be a comfortable home.

Many semiaquatic mammals thrive in the watery environment of the Everglades. Chief among these are the elusive river otter, the endangered Everglades mink, the protected round-tailed muskrat and the marsh rabbit, whose short-eared head is occasionally spied as he pops up on his hind legs on a raised piece of ground to survey his territory.

The princess of the hardwood hammocks may well be the harmless, showy golden orb weaver, a large female spider whose huge, spectacular webs are so strong that the silk was once used for cross hairs in guns and surveyor's instruments.

As one discovers with so much of this sub-tropical region, it is the visitor who takes plenty of time to explore and examine things closely who reaps the rewards. This certainly applies to those in search of wildlife, for a whole world of miniature creatures resides among the hammocks and prairies. Speedy little lizards of many varieties, colorful grasshoppers and the multi-hued *Liguus* tree snail, as different from one another as snowflakes, are only a sampling of the tiny animals who reside in this distinctive environment. The apple snail is another important resident, being the sole food of the Everglades kite. Photographers find the yellow-and-black zebra butterfly a photogenic delight.

Protected natural areas of the Keys are home to many of the creatures that also reside in the Everglades, but the Keys also claim some species unique to these isolated islands. It is believed that some are the genetically changed descendants of creatures who crossed the once low dry land that is now Florida Bay. When the water rose for the last time, they were isolated forever and slowly changed, adapting to their new environment.

Most famous is the tiny Key deer, a miniature subspecies of the mainland white-tailed deer. Residing mainly on Big Pine Key, where they are protected, they are also thinly scattered over more than a dozen other smaller islands. Distinctive, too, are the Lower Keys cotton rat, the Cudjoe Key rice rat, the Vaca Key raccoon, resident of the red mangrove hammocks, and the Key Largo wood rat and cotton mouse who, like the deer, are smaller than their mainland cousins. The endangered Schaus swallowtail butterfly appears occasionally on Key Largo.

Among the reptiles distinctive to the Keys are the mud turtle, the mangrove terrapin and the Florida Keys mole slink, a unique lizard. The Florida Keys ribbon snake, the Big Pine Key ringneck and several distinctive rat snakes also make their homes only on certain islands. A small family of alligators reside in the freshwater pool on Big Pine Key.

Some of the region's most interesting animals reside in the sea. Chief among these are the bottle-nosed dolphin (see "Days of the Dolphins" in Chapter Three) and many species of shark, one of the oldest creatures on earth. Manatees, once abundant in the Keys, are still spotted occasionally. Thirty mollusks, including the two-color crown conch, are among the endemic invertebrates of the Keys. The great reef that lies beneath the waters of the Atlantic Ocean, parallel to the Keys, is also made up of innumerable animals. For divers and snorkelers and passengers of glass-bottom boats, the reef presents a whole distinctive world of wildlife (see "Kingdoms Under the Sea" in Chapter Three).

BIRDS

More than 300 species of birds, natives of both the temperate and tropical zones, take up either temporary or permanent residence in the Everglades/Keys region each year. If, as we are sometimes told, 90 percent of the birds in the region are gone, entering the Everglades must have once been an incredible experience, for even the remaining ten percent that soar through the air, perch in the trees and stalk the shallow waters guarantee rewards for even the most casual birdwatcher. In cooler months, one can observe a wide variety without leaving paved paths and roads. Even the uncommon and beautiful roseate spoonbill can sometimes be seen near Flamingo Lodge on the southern tip of the Everglades or among the mangrove shallows beside Route 1 on Key Largo.

In winter, the prime season for birdwatching, endangered wood storks gather in trees along the Everglades park road and in Big Cypress to fish in the muddy shallows. With binoculars, visitors occasionally observe nesting bald eagles on little islands in Florida Bay and in the Lower Keys. White pelicans ride the winter waves in congenial groups near the Everglades shore.

Peregrine falcons may be spotted along the coasts in spring and fall on their long migrations between the Arctic and South America. Snail kites still nest in the park, and the Cape Sable seaside sparrow makes its exclusive home in the marshes of Big Cypress and the Everglades. And, of course, sea gulls and their assorted relatives, as well as brown pelicans, are part of the coastal scenery year-round.

FOR THE BIRDS

Though the bird population in the Everglades/Keys region is impressive indeed, it hardly rivals the flocks that caused John James Audubon to feel so astonished, a century-and-a-half ago, that he and his party "could for a while scarcely believe our eyes." Later visitors who crossed the state following the opening of the Tamiami Trail still recall having to wash their cars at the end of the trip, so thick were the birds overhead. Sadly, a big decrease in bird population came about when trendsetters convinced ladies that it was high fashion to wear bird feathers on their bonnets. Flamingos and great white herons and snowy egrets were slaughtered mercilessly; even pelicans and least terns could not escape.

The most visually exotic birds of the region are those that wade in the shallow waters, standing like beautiful sculptures for hours or stalking their prey with nary a ripple. Most impressive are the great white egrets and the great blue herons, elegant three- to four-foot-tall fishermen. Other easy-to-identify waders include the little blue heron, Louisiana heron, limpkin and the rarer reddish egret. White ibis are common and easy to identify as they bob their bills in and out of the shallows like needles on sewing machines. Magnificent frigate birds nest on the Marquesas Keys in early winter.

Easy to view, too, are many of the water birds, such as purple gallinules, grebes, bitterns, moorhens and marsh hawks. As if they know they are expected to be there, anhingas slice through the water for fish, then hang themselves out to dry in the trees along Anhinga Trail in the Everglades. Cormorants, too, are expert underwater fishermen, darting through the water in great haste and disappearing below the surface for remarkably long periods. On Bush Key, east of Fort Jefferson in the Dry Tortugas, nesting sooty terns from the Caribbean Sea and West Africa are joined by brown noddies and other exotic species in one of the nation's great wildlife spectacles.

Birds of prey include the endangered eagles and snail kites, as well as the swallow-tailed kite and several varieties of hawks, falcons and vultures. Ospreys are especially accommodating to bird-watchers, often building their bulky nests and raising their families on the tops of power poles beside busy Route 1 in the Keys.

Migratory birds, including numerous songbirds, make regularly scheduled visits to the Keys and Everglades. For example, indigo buntings, bobolinks and redstarts appear in the spring. Wintering raptors move in around October. Red-breasted mergansers drop in for their winter stay around November. Prairie warblers, cardinals and common yellowthroats reside in the hardwood hammocks year-round.

Most parks and wildlife refuges provide complete bird lists detailing which species one can expect to observe in a particular region each season of the year. A good bird book is a handy tool for anyone visiting this unique region where one can spot so many species seldom found anywhere else in the country.

NATURAL HABITATS

The Everglades and the Florida Keys contain a variety of habitats, some shared and some distinctive to each region. In this flat, low-lying world, very slight differences in elevation, even an inch or two, can create a dramatic contrast between one area and another. So can other infinitesimal changes, such as water salinity. In this region, human-designed changes—particularly those affecting water supplies—have had devastating effects on the homes and habits of resident wildlife.

The casual visitor to this portion of South Florida can easily learn to recognize a variety of basic habitats:

Pinelands are located on slightly elevated limestone outcroppings of the Everglades and on Big Pine Key and nearby islands. These slash pine forests are dependent on occasional fires to keep them clear of competing undergrowth.

Saw Grass Prairies, dominating the Everglades, consist of hundreds of thousands of acres of grasslike sedge and many other grasses through which the freshwater "river of grass" flows almost imperceptibly from Lake Okeechobee and other northern water sources to the sea.

Hardwood Hammocks, rising to as much as three feet, are islands in the "river of grass" on which thrive jungly collections of mahogany, strangler figs, gumbo-limbo, various palms and other trees. This is also where animals find refuge in high-water times.

Heads, soggy leafy mounds that grow clumps of trees, are often named for their individual dominant tree, such as "coco heads" or "cypress heads."

Dwarf Cypress Forests are collections of small, hardy, moss-draped deciduous trees. These open areas of stunted, scattered bald cypress develop where marl and muds build up in solution holes, dissolved cavities in the limestone bed.

Coastal Prairies, appearing like deserts near the sea, are lowlands featuring salt-tolerant plants such as yucca, agave and varieties of cactus.

Mangrove Estuaries are found on the western edge of the Everglades, the Ten Thousand Islands, in Florida Bay and on many of the Florida Keys. These estuaries are ever-enlarging collections of salt-tolerant trees that serve as barriers against high seas, residences for microscopic life crucial to the food chain, and rookeries and homes for wildlife.

Freshwater Sloughs, slow-moving, marshy freshwater rivers, serve as reservoirs that are crucial to the region's animals and plants during the dry seasons.

Transition Zones, located between the tidal wetlands and hammocks, are dryland regions that, like the coastal prairies, grow only salt-tolerant vegetation. Beside cacti and unusual shrubs, the area is host to joewood, silver palm and various orchids and bromeliads.

Rockland Zones, found on a number of islands, are harsh coastal areas lying between the mangroves and the transition zones and home to buttonwood and saltwort and a few other hardy survivors.

Underwater habitats are an important part of South Florida. These include the following:

Marine Estuaries, crucial spawning grounds for many types of marine life, harbor abundant varieties of wildlife and, in the Everglades, can be best experienced by canoe.

Florida Bay, the shallow waters between the tip of the mainland and the Keys, contains about one-third of the national park, including many refuges for nesting and shore birds; manatees, dolphins, turtles, sharks and fish ply the waters.

Sea Grass Beds, highly productive areas of turtle, manatee and Cuban shoal grasses, serve as nursery and feeding grounds for numerous species of fish and invertebrates.

Mud Flats, lining the mangrove hammocks and rocky shores of many islands on both the ocean and bay sides, are flooded at high tide and exposed at low, attracting many shore and wading birds to dine on their supplies of worms, mollusks and fish.

Coral Reefs, considered one of the most complex of all ecosystems, are "underwater gardens" made up of soft animals with hard, stony skeletons. As they die, their skeletal remains become a three-dimensional habitat for thousands of animals and plants ranging from microscopic to gigantic (see "Kingdoms Under the Sea" in Chapter Three).

When to Go
SEASONS

The subtropical Everglades and Florida Keys are warm, aquatic lands with a climate much like the islands of the Caribbean. Winter low temperatures in South Florida average around 60°F with average highs in the upper 70s. Summer average high temperatures reach near 90°, with average lows in the comfortable mid-70s.

There are basically two seasons in this region of far South Florida—winter and summer, or "dry" and "wet." While the Keys, thanks to cooling ocean breezes, are reasonably comfortable year-round, the Everglades are chiefly a winter destination. Winter, the dry season, brings droughts of varying degrees to the Everglades. Mosquito populations drop to their lowest, and birds and wildlife gather at watering holes, to the delight of park rangers and visitors alike. Cold fronts from the north can bring occasional frosts to the Everglades, but generally the weather is mild and comfortable.

In summer, the rains come, completing the annual cycle of drought and flood so necessary to Everglades survival. Great storm clouds gather to drench the land in spectacular afternoon electrical storms that replenish the region and bring welcome relief from hot, humid, steamy days. Biting insects thrive, keeping all but the most hardy visitor from exploring the interior Everglades in summer.

Hurricanes, though they can be devastating, need not keep one away during the fall. Usually developing in September, hurricanes have also been known to occur much later. (Ironically, the worst storm in decades, Hurricane Andrew, which struck in 1992, occurred in August.) Unlike many other weather phenomena, hurricanes come with plenty of warning, allowing visitors either to batten down or depart for inland locations.

In the Keys, winter is usually balmy and dry. Key West has never seen a frost. Though the Keys can get hot on summer afternoons, sea breezes keep the region tolerably comfortable for visitors. Welcome summer rains also cool things off from time to time. Downpours begin and end quickly, with little warning, seldom stopping daily activity. The Keys, long a warm haven for winter-weary northerners, are becoming more and more a year-round destination.

CALENDAR OF EVENTS

JANUARY   **Islamorada**   The **Cheeca Lodge Annual Presidential Sailfish Tournament** is a fishing competition with an emphasis on the billfish-tagging program. It includes dinner and an awards banquet and is dedicated to preserving the environment of the Keys.
Marathon   Elizabethan days of yore are recalled at the **Florida Keys Renaissance Faire**, where lords, ladies, knights, jesters and jousting tournaments keep Fairegoers entertained in kingly fashion.
Key West   The **Key West Literary Seminar** celebrates the island's famous role as residence to American literary luminaries with a three-day event featuring a different theme each year. The **Annual Key West Craft Show** is a two-day street fair featuring craftspeople from all over the country. A three-month feast of events celebrating the island's rich heritage, **Old Island Days** features house and garden tours, concerts, plays, flower shows, sidewalk art festivals and other happenings from January to March.

FEBRUARY   **Everglades**   Thousands gather in Everglades City for the **Everglades Seafood Festival** featuring arts and crafts booths, country music entertainment and, of course, lots of tasty seafood.

MARCH   **Islamorada**   A giant visual-arts display includes original creations of more than 100 artists at the **Rain Barrel Arts Festival**.
Marathon   The **Original Marathon Seafood Festival** celebrates the wondrous variety of seafood cuisine. There are live bands and children's rides along with savory samples of oysters, shrimps, lobsters and crab legs. The **Annual Save-A-Turtle Barbecue and Fundraiser** is a one-day event held in Pigeon Key dedicated to protecting the turtle population in the Keys. You'll find plenty of food, live music, prizes and games.
Key West   Shell blowers participate in the **Conch Shell Blowing Contest**.

Marathon and Key West Runners set out for a "marathon" dash over the sea in the annual **Seven Mile Bridge Run**, with fun and frivolity following in Key West at the Conch Republic Independence Celebration.

Lower Keys and Key West The annual **Key West Fishing Tournament** is an eight-month-long event with nine divisions and is held throughout the Lower Keys and off Key West, attracting several thousand anglers annually.

Key West The **Conch Republic Independence Celebration** includes such tongue-in-cheek events as raising conch colors at Fort Zachary Taylor State Historic Site, swearing in dolphins as citizens at Sugarloaf Sanctuary, crafts show and food fest, pedicab races and nasty-natives party.

APRIL

Marathon Transforming the Florida Keys' tradition of laid-back angling into a fishing frenzy, the **Marathon Dolphin Scramble** annually assaults the "world dolphin speed-fishing record." Under the dark of the moon, anglers from all walks of life compete in the **Annual Marathon International Tarpon Tournament**.

Key West The **Tarpon PrideFest** showcases the depth and diversity of talent in the gay community—tea dances, plays, films, performance art and musical events.

MAY

Islamorada A large group of women showcase their flyfishing techniques at the **Women's World Invitational Fly Championship**.

JUNE

Everglades South Florida ethnic groups join together at the Miccosukee Indian Village for the **Miccosukee Annual International Crafts & Music Festival**.

Key Largo Anglers ply the Gulf of Mexico and the Atlantic waters in search of dolphin in the **Key Largo Dolphin Derby**, supporting the area's children.

Lower Keys Divers glide among the coral heads at Looe Key National Marine Sanctuary while listening to an underwater broadcast of classical, semiclassical and contemporary music at the **Underwater Music Festival** benefitting marine preservation.

Key West Storytelling, arm-wrestling, fishing tournaments and look-alike contests highlight the week-long **Hemingway Days**, honoring the memory and the works of the island's most famous literary figure.

JULY

Key Largo Underwater photographers compete in the week-long **Nikonos Shootout**.

AUGUST

Key West **WomenFest**, one of the largest lesbian events in the world, draws more than 10,000 women to an activity-packed week of tea dances, wine-tasting dinners, book signings and more.

SEPTEMBER

OCTOBER   **Islamorada** Complimentary boat rides whisk visitors back 150 years during the **Indian Key Festival** for tours of the little island townsite destroyed by Indians in 1840.
Marathon Stalking the elusive bonefish in his shallow-water haunts draws anglers to the **Marathon International Bonefish Tournament**.
Key West Acclaimed for color, creativity and more than just a touch of satire, the ten-day-long **Fantasy Fest** is Key West's answer to Rio's Carnaval and New Orleans' Mardi Gras. **Key West Theatre Festival** offers a number of new plays, readings and workshops.

NOVEMBER   **Islamorada** Everyday fishermen team up with film stars, sports figures and famous fishing guides during the **Islamorada Redbone Fishing Tournament** for a weekend of redfish and bonefish angling and social events benefitting the Cystic Fibrosis Foundation.

DECEMBER   **Lower Keys** Local and national artists exhibit their talents at the **Annual Island Art Fair** on Big Pine Key.

▼▼▼▼▼▼▼▼▼▼▼▼
Before You Go

VISITORS CENTERS

Each chapter of this book lists the chambers of commerce and/or visitors centers that provide tourist and travel information. You can obtain materials on the **Everglades National Park** by writing: Information, Everglades National Park, 40001 State Road 9336, Homestead, FL 33034; 305-242-7700; www.nps.gov/ever.

If you require information on the **Florida Keys**, you can call 800-352-5397; www.fla-keys.com.

For a free copy of the *Florida Vacation Guide*, call 888-735-2872 or check the web site www.flausa.com.

PACKING   Unless you plan to spend your time in South Florida dining in ultra-deluxe restaurants, you'll need much less in your suitcase than you might think. For most trips, all you'll have to pack in the way of clothing are some shorts, lightweight shirts or tops, cool slacks or skirts, a hat for protection from the sun, a pair of quality sunglasses, a couple of bathing suits and coverups, and something *very casual* for any special event that might call for dressing up.

The rest of your luggage space can be devoted to a few essentials that should not be forgotten (unless you prefer to shop on arrival). These include good sunscreens and some insect repellent, especially if you are traveling in the summer or heading into the Everglades, even in winter. If stinging jellyfish are a concern, take along a small container of a papain-type meat tenderizer. It won't keep them away, but it will ease the pain should you fall victim.

In summer especially, be sure to take along an umbrella or light raincoat for the sudden showers that can pop out of nowhere. In winter, a sweater or light jacket can be welcome on occasional cool evenings.

Good soft, comfortable, lightweight shoes for sightseeing are a must. Despite its tropical gentleness, South Florida terrain doesn't treat bare feet well except on rare sandy shores or beside a pool. Sturdy sandals will do well unless you are hiking into the Everglades and other wilderness areas. For these forays, you may need lightweight boots or canvas shoes that you don't mind wading in.

Serious scuba divers and snorkelers will probably want to bring their own gear, but it's certainly not essential. Underwater equipment of all sorts is available for rent throughout the Keys. Fishing gear is also often available for rent.

Campers will need basic cooking equipment and can make out fine with only a lightweight sleeping bag or cot and a tent with bug-proof screens and a ground cloth. Because soil is sparse in many campgrounds, stakes that can penetrate rock are a must. A canteen, first-aid kit, insect repellent, flashlight and other routine camping gear should be brought along.

Be sure to take along a camera; South Florida sunsets are sensational. Binoculars and a magnifying glass enhance any exploration of natural areas. If you plan to take night walks any distance from the lodge in the Everglades National Park, you will need a flashlight. And don't, for heaven's sake, forget your copy of *Hidden Florida Keys and Everglades*.

LODGING

Lodgings in South Florida run the gamut from tiny old-fashioned cabins to glistening highrise hotels. Bed and breakfasts are scarce, except in Key West and a few other isolated locations. Chain motels line most main thoroughfares in populous areas, and mom-and-pop enterprises still successfully vie for lodgers in every region. Large hotels with names you'd know anywhere appear in the few centers of size. Schmaltziest of all are the upscale resorts. Here one can drop in almost from the sky and never have to leave the grounds. In fact, you can take in all the sports, dining, nightlife, shopping and entertainment needed to make a vacation complete, although you may miss a fair amount of authentic South Florida.

Other lodgings, such as historic inns that haven't been too spruced up or guest houses where you can eat breakfast with the handful of other visitors, offer plenty of local personality. A few guest houses in Key West cater exclusively to gays. Whatever your preference and budget, you can probably find something to suit your taste with the help of the regional chapters of this book. Remember, rooms are scarce and prices are high in the winter tourist season. Summer rates are often drastically reduced in many places, allowing for a week's, or even a month's stay to be a real bargain. If you'd like some help with lodging reservations, contact the **Florida Hotel Network**. This resource offers bookings throughout the state including the Keys and Everglades. ~ 305-538-3616, 800-538-3616, fax 305-538-5858; www.floridahotels. com, e-mail info@floridahotels.com. Whatever you do, plan ahead and *make reservations*, especially in the prime tourist seasons.

Accommodations in this book are organized by region and classified according to price. Rates referred to are for the high season, so if you are looking for low-season bargains, it's good to inquire. *Budget* lodgings generally are less than $80 per night for a standard double and are satisfactory but modest. *Moderately* priced lodgings run from $80 to $120; what they have to offer in the way of luxury will depend on where they are located. At *deluxe*-priced accommodations, you can expect to spend between $120 and $200 for a homey bed and breakfast or a double in a hotel or resort. In hotels of this price you'll generally find spacious rooms with a dressing room, a fashionable lobby, a restaurant and often a bar or nightclub. *Ultra-deluxe* facilities begin at $200 for a double and are a region's finest, offering plenty of extras.

If you crave a room facing the sea, ask specifically. Be forewarned that "waterfront" can mean bay, lake, inlet or even a channel. If you are trying to save money, lodgings a block or so from the water often offer lower rates than those on the edge of the sea.

DINING   Eating places in South Florida are abundant and fish is often the highlight. Whether catfish from the Everglades or yellowfin tuna from the Atlantic, you can almost always count on its being fresh and well prepared. Each season has its specialties, each region its ethnic influences and its gourmet newcomers.

Within a particular chapter, restaurants are categorized geographically, with each restaurant entry describing the establishment according to price. Dinner entrées at *budget* restaurants usually cost $10 or less. The ambience is informal, service usually speedy. *Moderate*-priced eateries charge between $10 and $20 for dinner; surroundings are casual but pleasant, the menu offers more variety and the pace is usually slower. *Deluxe* establishments tab their entrées above $20; cuisines may be simple or sophisticated, depending on the location, but the service is more personalized. *Ultra-deluxe* dining rooms, where entrées begin at $30, are often the gourmet places; menus may be large or small, though the ambience is almost always casual.

Some restaurants change hands often and are occasionally closed in low season. Efforts have been made in this book to include places with established reputations for good eating. Breakfast and lunch menus vary less in price from restaurant to restaurant than evening dinners. Even deluxe establishments often offer light breakfasts and lunch specialties that place them in or near the budget range.

Plenty of family adventures are available in South Florida, from manmade attractions to experiences in the wild. A few guidelines will help in making travel with children a pleasure. Book reservations in advance, making sure that those places accept children. If you need a crib or extra cot, arrange for it ahead of time. A travel agent can be of help here, as well as with most other travel plans. **TRAVELING WITH CHILDREN**

If you are traveling by air, try to reserve bulkhead seats where there is plenty of room. Take along extras you may need, such as diapers, changes of clothing, snacks and toys or small games. If your child has a favorite stuffed animal or blanket, keep it handy.

When traveling by car, be sure to take along the extras, too. Make sure you have plenty of water and juices to drink; dehydration can be a subtle problem, especially in a subtropical climate. Often a simple picnic or a fast-food place with a playground works best at lunch or suppertime, so children can run and stretch their legs. Restaurant dining can turn into a hassle after long hours in the car; it's better to let them have a romp with a peanut butter sandwich in hand.

A first-aid kit is a must for any trip. Along with adhesive bandages, antiseptic cream and something to stop itching, include any medicines your pediatrician might recommend to treat allergies, colds, diarrhea or any chronic problems your child may have.

If you plan to spend much time at the beach, take extra care the first few days. Children's skin is usually tenderer than adults', and severe sunburn can happen before you realize it. A hat is a good idea, along with a reliable sunblock. And be sure to keep a constant eye on children who are near any water.

For parents' night out, many hotels provide a dependable list of babysitters. In some areas you may find drop-in child care centers; look in the *Yellow Pages* for these, and make sure you choose ones that are licensed.

Many towns, parks and attractions offer special activities designed just for children. Consult local newspapers and/or phone the numbers in this guide to see what's happening when you're there.

As millions have discovered, South Florida is an ideal place for older vacationers, many of whom turn into part-time or full-time residents. The climate is mild, the terrain level, and many places **SENIOR TRAVELERS**

Text continued on page 30.

Keys and Everglades Cuisine

With saltwater on three sides of the Everglades and all sides of the Keys, seafood certainly tops the list of South Florida foods. Add to the saltwater fare freshwater delights from the meandering streams, dark ponds and canals of the Everglades and your fish and shellfish menu has expanded beyond all expectations. Grouper, yellowfin tuna, dolphin (mahimahi), shrimp, spiny lobster and stone crab are only a sampling of the fruits of local seas that offer particular specialties in every season. From freshwater sources come largemouth bass, catfish and delicate panfish of all sorts.

Each cook seems to prepare seafood dishes in his own way. Heaping fried or broiled platters of seafood are found almost everywhere, but creative chefs also try out unusual seafood recipes with the fervor of marathon competitors. Each region, too, has its own particular specialties, such as fried alligator tail, soft-shell terrapin and frogs' legs in the Everglades and spicy conch chowder and fritters down through the Keys.

No matter where you live, you may have partaken of South Florida's abundant winter produce. Fat red strawberries, long green beans, prize-winning peppers and tomatoes grow in abundance in the Homestead area. You can often stop at a roadside stand or go into the fields for a pick-your-own sale of whatever is left over from the great quantities shipped across the country. Citrus fruits, from easily peeled tangerines to sweet grapefruit, are abundant in the winter months. Exotic fruits also join the list of South Florida produce, familiar ones such as mangos, avocados and papayas and lesser-known zapotes, lychees and guavas. Coconuts grow in backyards here in the subtropics. Swamp cabbage yields its heart as the chief delicacy in "hearts of palm" salad.

Everywhere you dine, you will have an opportunity to eat Key lime pie. It's a simple dessert—a traditional baked pastry pie shell filled with a creamy tart-sweet yellow filling. But how to prepare this cool delicacy is a hot topic. Purists simply use the juice of the little yellow native limes, a few eggs and some condensed milk. Some say the tradition began when milk had to be canned before the days of refrigeration in the Keys. The limes "cook" the eggs, which may be whole or just yolks. Whether the pie should include meringue is still a debatable issue, as are green coloring, gelatin and crumb crusts. Many visitors have fun trying to locate the restaurant or bakery that serves up "the best Key lime pie."

Conch chowder also has its experts and its history. Queen conchs were once abundant in the Keys and used in all sorts of dishes. Though conchs are now imported, conch chowder is still wonderful, varying from thin and mild to thick and spicy, each cook possessing a favorite secret recipe. Conch is also prepared raw, marinated, in fritters or "cracked" (pounded, dredged in cracker meal and fried).

American Indian and ethnic foods have also influenced dining throughout the Everglades and Keys. The Miccosukee Indians along the Tamiami Trail serve pumpkin and fry breads and special Indian burgers and tacos. The Keys' Cuban heritage is reflected in such popular dishes as black beans and rice, *picadillo* (a ground beef dish with capers and raisins), *lechón* (roast pork prepared with garlic and citrus fruits) and *plátanos* (fried bananas).

Lately, inventive young chefs have been using local fruits and other tropical ingredients to create a new style of cooking. Seafood, chicken, lamb and beef get tropical treatments, and are often grilled, smoked or blackened. Some call it "tropical fusion," while others deem it "new Florida cuisine." Whatever its name, one thing is certain: This brand of cooking is marvelously adventurous. After all, where else can you find Key lime pasta or grilled grouper with mango salsa, plantains and purple potatoes?

offer significant discounts for seniors. Off-season rates make the Florida Keys exceedingly attractive for travelers on limited incomes. Florida residents over 65 can benefit from reduced rates at most state parks, and the Golden Age Passport, which must be applied for in person, allows free admission to national parks and monuments for anyone 62 or older.

The **American Association of Retired Persons** (AARP) offers membership to anyone over 50. AARP's benefits include travel discounts with a number of firms. ~ 601 E Street NW, Washington, DC 20049; 800-424-3410; www.aarp.org, e-mail member@aarp.org.

Elderhostel offers reasonably priced, all-inclusive educational programs in a variety of Florida locations—including Homestead, Key Largo and Key West—throughout the year. ~ 75 Federal Street, Boston, MA 02110; 877-426-8056, fax 617-426-0701; www.elderhostel.org.

Be extra careful about health matters. Bring along any medications you ordinarily use, together with the prescriptions for obtaining more. Consider carrying a medical record with you—including your medical history and current medical status as well as your doctor's name, phone number and address. Make sure that your insurance covers you away from home.

DISABLED TRAVELERS

The state of Florida is striving to make more destinations fully accessible to travelers with disabilities.

Everglades National Park (see Chapter Two) has many facilities, including short trails, that are accessible to travelers with disabilities.

There are several places to find more information, including the **Travel Disabilities Information Service**. ~ 1200 West Tabor Road, Philadelphia, PA 19141; 215-456-9600; www.mossresourcenet.org. The **Society for the Advancement of Travel for the Handicapped** is another organization that can provide information. ~ 347 5th Avenue #610, New York, NY 10016; 212-447-7284, fax 212-725-8253; www.sath.org, e-mail sathtravel@aol.com. Or try **Flying Wheels Travel**. ~ P.O. Box 382, Owatonna, MN 55060; 800-535-6790, fax 507-451-1685; e-mail thq@LL.net. **Travelin' Talk**, a networking organization, also provides information. ~ P.O. Box 1796, Wheat Ridge, CO 80034; 303-232-2979; www.travelintalk.net, e-mail info@travelintalk.net. **Access-Able Travel Source** has worldwide information online. ~ 303-232-2979; www.access-able.com.

WOMEN TRAVELING ALONE

Traveling solo grants an independence and freedom different from that of traveling with a partner, but single travelers are more vulnerable to crime and should take additional precautions.

It's unwise to hitchhike and probably best to avoid inexpensive accommodations on the outskirts of town; the money saved does not outweigh the risk. Bed and breakfasts, youth hostels and YWCAs are generally your safest bet for lodging, and they also foster an environment ideal for bonding with fellow travelers.

Keep all valuables well-hidden and clutch cameras and purses tightly. Avoid late-night treks or strolls through undesirable parts of town, but if you find yourself in this situation, continue walking with a confident air until you reach a safe haven. A fierce scowl never hurts.

These hints should by no means deter you from seeking out adventure. Wherever you go, stay alert, use your common sense and trust your instincts. If you are hassled or threatened in some way, never be afraid to call for assistance. It's also a good idea to carry change for a phone call and to know a number to call in case of emergency.

For more helpful hints, get a copy of *Safety and Security for Women Who Travel* (Travelers' Tales, 1998).

If you are hassled or threatened in some way, never be afraid to scream for assistance. In Key West, the 24-hour **Helpline, Inc.** can provide information and referrals. ~ 305-296-4357, 800-273-4558; e-mail teenline1@aol.com.

GAY & LESBIAN TRAVELERS

At the tip of Florida floats the island of Key West, a casual, comfortable getaway. The gay community lent a big hand in reviving the historic district here. Old Town is the center of this gay scene, replete with guesthouses, restaurants, stores and nightspots. (See "Key West Gay Scene" in Chapter Four.)

Numerous resource centers and publications in these areas are ready to help gay and lesbian travelers tap into the local happenings. For a weekly rundown on the trendiest nightspots in Florida, pick up *Contax* at any gay club; it serves the entire state (and other states, too). ~ 305-757-6333. *Hotspots* covers weekly nightlife and entertainment in Key West, South Beach, Fort Lauderdale, Tampa and West Palm Beach. ~ 954-772-0001; www.hotspotsmagazine.com.

In Miami, the **Lesbian, Gay & Bisexual Community Center** offers counseling, support groups and bulletin boards loaded with postings and literature about Miami and Key West. ~ 6445 Northeast 7th Avenue, Miami Beach; 305-759-5210. *The Fountain*, which comes out monthly, serves the gay, lesbian and bisexual community. Look for it at guesthouses, restaurants and clubs in Key West. ~ 2632 Hollywood Boulevard, Hollywood.

TWN (*The Weekly News*) focuses on the South Florida scene (including the Keys). In it you'll find news and features pertaining to the gay community. Can't think of anything to do? They also have a comprehensive events listing. You can pick up a copy at many Key West guesthouses. ~ 901 Northeast 79th Street, Miami; 305-757-6333.

In Key West, **Helpline, Inc.** is a 24-hour crisis and general information line benefitting the Keys area. ~ 305-296-4357, 800-273-4558; e-mail teenline1@aol.com. A monthly complete guide to gay Key West, *Southern Exposure* includes a map of Old Town and a calendar of events. ~ 819 Peacock Plaza, Suite 575, Key West; 305-294-6303. For help booking a variety of accommodations, call the **Florida Hotel Network**. ~ 305-538-3616, 800-538-3616, fax 305-538-5858; www.floridahotels.com, e-mail info@floridahotels.com.

FOREIGN TRAVELERS   **Passports and Visas**   Most foreign visitors need a passport and tourist visa to enter the United States. Contact your nearest United States Embassy or Consulate well in advance to obtain a visa and to check on any other entry requirements.

Customs Requirements   Foreign travelers are allowed to carry in the following: 200 cigarettes (1 carton), 50 cigars or 2 kilograms (4.4 pounds) of smoking tobacco; one liter of alcohol for personal use only (you must be 21 years of age to bring in alcohol); and US$100 worth of duty-free gifts that can include an additional quantity of 100 cigars. You may bring in any amount of currency, but must fill out a form if you bring in over US$10,000. Carry any prescription drugs in clearly marked containers. (You may have to produce a written prescription or doctor's statement for the custom's officer.) Meat or meat products, seeds, plants, fruits and narcotics are not allowed to be brought into the United States. Contact the **United States Customs Service** for further information. ~ 1300 Pennsylvania Avenue NW, Washington, DC 20229; 202-927-6724; www.customs.treas.gov.

Driving   If you plan to rent a car, an international driver's license should be obtained before arriving in the United States. Some car rental agencies require both a foreign license and an international driver's license. Many also require a lessee to be at least 25 years of age; all require a major credit card. Seat belts are mandatory for the driver and all passengers. Children under the age of five or under 40 pounds should be in the back seat in approved child-safety restraints.

Currency   United States money is based on the dollar. Bills come in denominations of $1, $5, $10, $20, $50 and $100. Every dollar is divided into 100 cents. Coins are the penny (1 cent), nickel (5 cents), dime (10 cents) and quarter (25 cents). Half-dollar and dollar coins are rarely used. You may not use foreign currency to purchase goods and services in the United States. Consider buying traveler's checks in dollar amounts. You may also use credit cards affiliated with an American company such as Interbank, Barclay Card and American Express.

Electricity and Electronics   Electric outlets use currents of 110 volts, 60 cycles. To operate appliances made for other electrical systems, you need a transformer or other adapter. Travelers who use laptop computers for telecommunication should be aware that modem configurations for U.S. telephone systems may be different from their European counterparts. Similarly, the U.S. format for videotapes is different from that in Europe; National Park Service visitors centers and other stores that sell souvenir videos often have them available in European format on request.

Weights and Measures   The United States uses the English system of weights and measures. American units and their metric equivalents are: 1 inch = 2.5 centimeters; 1 foot (12 inches) = 0.3 meter; 1 yard (3 feet) = 0.9 meter; 1 mile (5280 feet) = 1.6 kilometers; 1 ounce = 28 grams; 1 pound (16 ounces) = 0.45 kilogram; 1 quart (liquid) = 0.9 liter.

▼▼▼▼▼▼▼▼▼▼▼▼▼
Outdoor Adventures

CAMPING

South Florida offers a wide variety of camping opportunities, from primitive camping in wilderness areas to recreational vehicle parks that resemble fashionable resorts without the condos. Campgrounds in the Florida Keys are often crowded, with sites very close together. For a listing of all the state parks and recreation areas, with information on making reservations, send for the *Florida State Park Guide* and *Florida State Parks Camping Reservation Procedures*. ~ Department of Environmental Protection, Division of Recreation and Parks, 3900 Commonwealth Boulevard, Tallahassee, FL 32399-3000; 850-488-9872, fax 850-922-4925; www.dep.state.fl.us/parks.

Everglades National Park will send you information on both developed and wilderness camping within the park. ~ 40001 State Road 9336, Homestead, FL 33034; 305-242-7700; www.nps.gov/ever. **Big Cypress National Preserve** has information on primitive camping opportunities within the preserve. ~ HCR61 Box 110, Ochopee, FL 34141; 941-695-4111; www.nps.gov/bicy. Permits are required for some of the primitive campsites located on keys within **Biscayne National Park**. ~ P.O. Box 1369, Homestead, FL 33090; 305-230-7275; www.nps.gov/bisc.

The **Florida Association of RV Parks and Campgrounds** puts out an annual *Florida Camping Directory* of over 200 private campgrounds and RV parks in the state. Local chambers of commerce will also have information on private campgrounds in the area. ~ 1340 Vickers Drive, Tallahassee, FL 32303; 850-562-7151, fax 850-562-7179; www.florida-camping.com, e-mail flaarvc@aol.com.

An excellent book for visitors planning to camp in the state is *Florida Parks*, by Gerald Grow (Longleaf Publications).

PERMITS   Backcountry campsites in the **Everglades National Park** are accessible by boat, bicycle or foot. ~ 40001 State Road 9336, Homestead, FL 33034; 305-242-7700; www.nps.gov/ever/visit/backcoun.htm. A free permit, issued on a first-come, first-served basis no more than 24 hours before the start of your trip, is required and may be obtained at the visitors centers. Permits for wilderness exploration in **Big Cypress National Preserve**, **Biscayne National Park** and certain state parks may be obtained by contacting the individual sites, as found in the "Beaches & Parks" sections of the regional chapters of this book.

BOATING   From paddleboat to cruise ship, just about every imaginable method of ploughing the waters is available in South Florida. You can bring your own boat if you wish and travel the Intracoastal Waterway or laze away the day on a quiet inlet with a fishing pole. And if you have no boat, you can rent or charter a craft of just about any size or speed. Each chapter in this book offers suggestions on how to go about finding the vessel of your choice. Most marinas and other rental agencies will arm you with maps and advice. Boating regulations and safety information may be obtained from the **Florida Fish and Wildlife Conservation Commission.** ~ Office of Enforcement Planning and Policy, 620 South Meridian Street, Tallahassee, FL 32399; 850-488-5600, fax 850-488-9284; www.state.fl.us/fwc.

Houseboating is a lazy, leisurely way to experience the watery wilds in luxury; rentals are available in several regions.

Canoeing is a popular sport in the western and southern Everglades and in several areas of the Keys. To obtain the *Florida Recreational Trails System–Canoe Trails* brochure, contact the **Office of Greenways and Trails.** ~ 325 John Knox Road, Building 500, Tallahassee, FL 32303; 850-487-4784, fax 850-414-0177. Individual state and national parks also provide canoe trail information.

Because many interesting destinations are located offshore, tour boats and cruises are also available in numerous regions.

WATER SAFETY   Few places match South Florida for the variety of water sports available. Swimming, scuba diving, snorkeling or just basking on a float are options wherever you can get to the shore. Drownings do occur now and then, but they can be avoided as long as one respects the power of the water, heeds appropriate warnings and uses good sense.

Wherever you swim or dive, never do it alone. Though the surf is seldom high in this region, should the wind whip up incoming waves, keep your face toward them. They can bring unpleasant surprises even to the initiated. If you get caught in a rip current or any tow that makes you feel out of control, don't try to swim against it. Head with it or across it, paralleling the shore. Respect signs warning of undertows.

If you dive or snorkel, practice all the proper techniques and emergency procedures with an expert before starting out. Even professionals consider training updates to be essential for under-water safety. Always display a "Diver Down" flag when in the water, and avoid wearing shiny objects that might attract un-wanted sea creatures. Check all equipment prior to any dive, and always dive into the current so it can help you on your return to your boat.

Jellyfish stings are commonly treated with papain-type meat tenderizers. If you go lobstering or crabbing or wading around in murky waters and where shellfish dwell, wear canvas shoes to protect your feet.

Remember, you are a guest in the sea. All rights belong to the creatures who dwell there, including sharks. Though they are rarely seen and seldom attack, they should be respected. A wise swimmer or diver simply heads unobtrusively for the shore or boat. On the other hand, if dolphins are cavorting in your area, don't worry. Dolphins are equipped so as not to run into things, even you, and they may put on quite a show.

Life jackets are a must if you want your boating trip to end happily. This goes for canoes and kayaks as well as larger and faster craft. Don't mix alcohol and water; excessive drinking is involved in over 50 percent of all drownings and boating acci-dents. Learn boating rules and obey them; collisions resulting from operator error and high speeds are the primary cause of boating injury.

When swimming and boating, keep your eye on the weather. When there are electrical storms and high winds approaching, it's time to head for dry land.

And never, never take your eyes off a child who is near the water, no matter how calm conditions may appear.

Surrounded by so much water in South Florida, the best pro-tection is to know how to swim, and to use your good sense.

WILDER-NESS SAFETY

Certain precautions should be taken whenever leaving the main roads and heading into wilderness regions, especially in the Ever-glades and Big Cypress. First of all, be sure to let someone know your planned route and schedule before setting out. The biggest problem will likely be biting insects, especially mosquitoes, in all but the coolest winter months. Plenty of insect repellent, long-sleeved shirts, long pants and head covers are the best protection.

Learn to recognize poisonous plants, such as poison ivy, poi-sonwood and machineel, so they can be avoided. Coral snakes, water moccasins and diamondback and pygmy rattlesnakes do reside in South Florida; by being alert and looking before exploring, you can usually avoid unpleasant encounters. When hiking off the trails, be careful of your footing. Sharp-edged rock, mucky soil and hidden holes can make walking tricky. Check with the individual parks and preserves concerning rules for fires and use of off-road vehicles.

FISHING   No matter what the season of the year, the Everglades and Keys are an angler's paradise. How you approach the sport is up to you. You can dangle a hook from a cane pole into a sluggish slough or chase bonefish off Islamorada or wrestle with a tarpon on the edge of the Gulf Stream. You can even harvest great rewards by casting your line off an abandoned bridge of the Overseas Highway.

Popular fishing of the Everglades includes both inland waters, where freshwater canals and ponds harbor impressive largemouth bass, black crappie, catfish and bream and other panfish, and the coastal waters of the Gulf of Mexico and Florida Bay. The most sought-after saltwater species here are trout, redfish and snapper. For information on freshwater and saltwater options, contact the **Office of Informational Services**. ~ Florida Fish and Wildlife Conservation Commission, Bryant Building, Tallahassee, FL 32301; 850-488-1960; www.state.fl.us/fwc. Some areas of the national park are closed to fishing, so it is important to obtain a copy of the regulations from a visitors center or ranger station before dropping a hook.

Saltwater fishing in the Keys can be roughly divided into three types; reef fishing, offshore fishing (on the oceanside, beyond the reef and out into the Gulf Stream, or westward out on the Tortugas Banks) and inshore and "backcountry" fishing in the Gulf and Florida Bay. A monthly publication, *Florida Sportsman*, found at marinas and bait-and-tackle shops, features seasonal information and in-depth fishing articles.

Habitual area fishermen will tell you that there is enough variety in this region to keep you busy and learning for a lifetime, as well as something to catch every day of the year. In the spring, permit, tarpon and bonefish are abundant in the flats, and sharks move into shallow waters to spawn. Spring is also a good time for yellowfin tuna, white marlin, swordfish and snapper. The calm days of summer promise good catches of dolphin (mahi-mahi). As fall days get cooler, action on the reef for snapper and grouper improves; permit, marlin, tuna, wahoo and the challenging bonefish are some autumn rewards. Kingfish show in big schools in the winter; grouper and mackerel fishing also gets underway then. Barracuda and Atlantic sailfish, along with many other species, can be found all year round.

Numerous crustaceans are also harvested from the coastal waters of Florida. Perhaps the most popular is the spiny lobster, resident of both bay and ocean. Also delectable is the pugnacious blue crab. Stone crabs are harvested for the meat of their tasty claws, which they graciously grow back after being returned to the water. Shrimp are an important commercial fruit of the sea. Be sure to check on the legal seasons and sizes before taking any of these creatures.

If you'd like to try a kind of fishing that is new to you, you will find guide services available just about everywhere boats are rented and bait is sold. Charter fishing is the costliest way to go out to sea; party boats take a crowd but are less expensive and usually great fun. In the ponds and streams of the Everglades region and in the backcountry of Florida Bay, guides can show you the best place to throw your hook or skim a fly. Whatever your pleasure, in saltwater or fresh, a good guide will save you both time and grief and increase the likelihood of a full string or a handsome trophy. For those who wish to go it alone in their own boats, there are a number of public access landings throughout the region.

If you go freshwater fishing, you will need a license, and you will have to get it through the local county tax collector. It's easy to do, though, because most fish camps, bait-and-tackle shops and sporting goods stores act as agents. Just look for signs that say "Fishing License for Sale."

For information on freshwater and saltwater licenses, check at a local marina or with the **Florida Fish and Wildlife Conservation Commission**. ~ Bureau of Licensing and Permitting, 620 South Meridian Street, Tallahassee, FL 32399; 850-488-3641, fax 850-414-8212; www.state.fl.us/fwc. The **Florida Marine Patrol** nearest the area you are fishing can also provide you with the latest saltwater fishing facts on licenses, closed seasons and bag and size limits. ~ 1275 Northeast 79th Street, Miami, FL 33138, 305-795-2145, or 2796 Overseas Highway, Marathon, FL 33050, 305-289-2320.

There are also fish just to be viewed in the seas of South Florida, especially wherever the living reefs thrive. (See "Kingdoms Under the Sea" in Chapter Three.) Vivid yellows, reds, blues and greens characterize the reef fish, some of which take on almost electric hues. A face mask, with or without a snorkel, will open up an undersea world of incredible beauty and surprises, whether it be along the shore or out among the reefs. In fact, colorful tropical fish may well be some of Florida's loveliest hidden treasures.

TWO

The Everglades

From the air, it seems a vast, mysterious world of land and water at whose edge civilization suddenly stops, a place where no one dwells. From the highway, it appears an endless prairie above which birds fly in winter and clouds build into towering summer storms that flash and crash and deluge the land in torrents. Both impressions are right, but, like the seasonal breezes in this subtropical land, they skim the surface only. For here in the Everglades, perhaps more than anywhere else in the country, the old cliché rings true: there is far more than meets the eye.

In the Everglades, life teems, water flows, creatures struggle for survival in miraculous cycles that have repeated themselves over and over again since prehistoric times. Only today there is one difference. Now the cycles have been altered by humans, who have tamed the waters and channeled the streams and, as a result, now hold the survival of this beautiful, fragile region in their hands.

An understanding and appreciation of the Everglades has come only in recent decades, far too long after the waters that once spilled out of Lake Okeechobee and gently fed this region were diked and rechanneled. For decades, dreamers, developers and farmers were unconcerned about the devastating effects of the changes they so drastically wrought on the natural world of South Florida. To most of them, the Everglades were simply a vast swamp that could be drained and tamed for building and for growing food.

Then, in 1947, Marjorie Stoneman Douglas wrote a book that acclaimed the treasures of this subtropical wilderness, once inhabited by American Indians and home to myriad creatures and plants found nowhere else in the United States. She also struck at the consciences of those who were doing irreparable damage to a region whose existence contributed to the life of the whole peninsula. "There are no other Everglades in the world," she began *The Everglades: River of Grass.* "They are, they have always been, one of the unique regions of the earth, remote, never wholly known."

In the same year, President Truman dedicated Everglades National Park. The region has also been designated both an International Biosphere Reserve and a

World Heritage Site in recognition of its value as a crucial natural wonder of the world. Although the Everglades actually extend far beyond the park's 1.5 million acres, it is in this protected region that visitors can explore the wonders of this world.

Next to human beings, hurricanes are the most powerful force in the Everglades. While only a couple have hit the area in the last 30 years, their devastating winds have had dramatic effects on the landscape. Hurricane Andrew, the most recent to strike (1992), leveled groves of trees, stripped the forest canopies of their leaves and exposed the delicate forest floor to the sun. Slowly the forests have been rebuilding themselves. But the storm has changed certain parts of the Everglades forever.

At first glance, much of the Everglades looks like inviting prairie that visitors could easily hike through on a nice day. But looks are deceiving. Most of this plain is actually a shallow, gently flowing river, hidden beneath the tall saw grass and reeds. Except in the pinelands and hardwood hammocks, there is water everywhere. Luckily for visitors, well-designed roads, trails and boardwalks keep feet dry while allowing travel through remote areas. And for those who want to explore watery pathways, a number of canoe trails offer adventure into spots accessible only by boat. Bicycling along park roads also lets visitors get closer to nature and discover places that might be missed while traveling in a car.

Four visitor areas lie in Everglades National Park, and each shows a different side of the region's rich character. Shark Valley, the northeastern entrance off the Tamiami Trail, offers tours into the saw grass prairie, abundant in birdlife and alligators. The northwest area at Everglades City is a jumping-off place to the Ten Thousand Islands, a mangrove estuary popular with anglers and vacationers. The main visitor area, southwest of Homestead, marks the beginning of a 38-mile park road that meanders through saw grass prairie, hardwood hammock, cypress swamps and lake regions, ending at Flamingo on the edge of Florida Bay. This main road offers access to numerous Everglades habitats via a variety of short and long trails.

Winter is the time to visit the Everglades, the only season when mosquitoes won't eat you alive. In winter you can leave your car, walk the trails, canoe the streams and contemplate the subtle beauty of the place. There are no breathtaking panoramas in this region, where the altitude seldom rises above three feet, but rich rewards await those who take the time to explore. Slumbering alligators lie like half-sunken logs in shallow ponds. Comical anhingas gather on low branches, hanging their wings out to dry after fishing forays. Bird populations are spectacular and diverse, including such easily recognized favorites as roseate spoonbills, osprey, brown pelicans and bald eagles. Subtly colored snails and wild orchids adorn the woods in season. Endangered and rare animals such as the gentle manatee, the Florida panther and the American crocodile, though seldom seen, reside deep within the watery world of the Everglades.

Although well-placed signs explain where to go and what to see, the Everglades are also a region of hidden treasures that will reward all who are willing to quietly search, to wait and watch.

It is almost impossible to visit the Everglades without coming away caring about what happens to this wondrous wet world where life cycles begin and the flow of fresh water keeps the salt of the sea in balance so that life can survive. One cannot forget Douglas's words: "There are no other Everglades in the world."

▼▼▼▼▼▼▼▼▼▼▼▼▼▼
Tamiami Trail Area

Heading westward from Miami, Route 41, known as the Tamiami Trail, provides an almost straight shot from the Atlantic to the Gulf Coast. For many years, until the building of the faster, wider parallel Route 84 to the north, this was the only route across southern Florida. Route 41 plunges through the heart of the Everglades, skirting the northern edge of Everglades National Park and cutting through the southern portion of the Big Cypress National Preserve. Though not wildly scenic, it is an intriguing road, traveling through miles and miles of what the American Indians called *pa-hay-okee*, or "grassy water." Sometimes the narrow highway is paralleled by canals, their banks busy with people fishing with cane poles. But mostly the landscape is saw grass prairie, with the great, wide— almost hidden—life-giving river running imperceptibly through it. Drivers are instructed to travel this road with lights on at all times, a safeguard against possible tedium and the strange effect the region seems to have on one's depth perception when contemplating passing.

SIGHTS

A few entrepreneurs have set up shop along the Tamiami Trail, mostly in the business of airboat rides, which environmentalists frown upon. For the most part, however, the highway, while a masterful engineering feat in its day, is a lonely one, blessedly short on billboards and long on Everglades mystique.

Part of that mystique is conveyed by the region's only human inhabitants, the Miccosukee Indians. Although they trace their ancestry back to centuries before the United States became a nation, they were not recognized as a tribe by the federal government until 1962. About 500 of them now live on a reservation along Route 1. They are descendants of a group which successfully hid in the Everglades during the period when Florida's American Indians were being captured and forcibly sent west. You can visit the designed-for-tourists **Miccosukee Indian Village** for a guided or self-guided tour that includes a museum, cooking and living chickees (palm-thatched native houses), a nature walk, craft areas and an arena where you can watch alligator shows. Admission. ~ Route 41, about 25 miles west of Florida's Turnpike; 305-223-8388, fax 305-223-1011; www.miccosukee tribe.com. Also in the Indian village, the **Miccosukee Airboat Rides** offer noisy, environmentally questionable trips over the saw grass deeper into the Everglades. It includes a stop at an old hammock-style American Indian camp.

The 15-mile, two-hour tram tours offered in the **Shark Valley** section of the Everglades National Park acquaint visitors with the heart of the saw grass region. Stops are made along the way to spot birds or alligators, and for lessons on the park's hydrology, geology, vegetation and wildlife. Time is also allowed for climbing the 65-foot observation tower, which provides excellent views of the vast wetlands. Sightseers may also travel the tram road on foot or bicycles, which are rented at the entrance. Admission. ~ Route 41, about 25 miles west of Florida's Turnpike; 305-221-8455.

Where Route 41 veers northwestward, you can head straight and take a scenic detour on **Route 94**, which meanders deep into

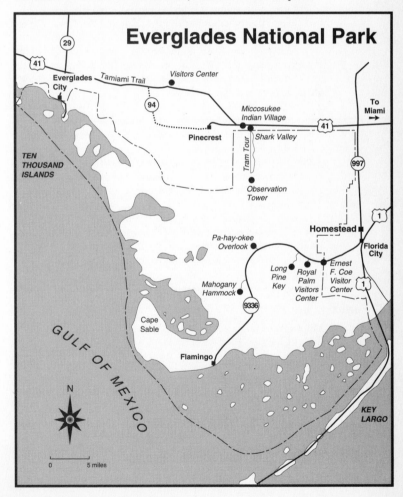

Everglades National Park

29

41

Everglades City

Tamiami Trail

Visitors Center

94

Miccosukee Indian Village

41

To Miami →

Pinecrest

Shark Valley

Tram Tour

997

TEN THOUSAND ISLANDS

Observation Tower

Pa-hay-okee Overlook

Homestead

1

Florida City

Long Pine Key

Royal Palm Visitors Center

Ernest F. Coe Visitor Center

1

Mahogany Hammock

9336

Cape Sable

Flamingo

GULF OF MEXICO

KEY LARGO

N

0   5 miles

cypress and pineland backcountry on its way out toward Pine-crest. This is called the "loop road," but unless you have a four-wheel-drive vehicle, you would do best to turn back when the road begins to deteriorate (about eight miles in), near an inter-pretive center.

Back on Route 41, slow down as you come up to the micro-scopic community of **Ochopee**, or you might miss "the smallest and most photographed post office in North America." You'll know it by the American flag, the blue letter box, the sign that reads **Post Office, Ochopee, FL** and all the tour buses disgorging passengers so that they can go into the tiny frame building and get their letters stamped. Closed Sunday. ~ 941-695-4131.

HIDDEN ▶

Soon you will enter **Big Cypress National Preserve**, 729,000 acres of subtropical Florida swampland vital to the preservation of the Everglades. To get an idea of Big Cypress' beauty and im-portance, stop at the **Big Cypress Visitor Center** and see the ex-cellent audiovisual introduction to this crucial region. ~ 941-695-4111; www.nps.gov/bicy.

Serious nature lovers can contact **Dragonfly Expeditions, Inc.** for a four-hour backwater trek through Big Cypress Swamp. Field biologists and naturalist guides lead the watery way through the subtropical landscape, searching for wading birds, otters and alligators. The tour price includes transportation, water gear, guide services and lunch. ~ 1825 Ponce de Leon Boulevard #369, Coral Gables; 305-774-9019, 888-992-6337; www.dragonfly expeditions.com.

Head south on Route 29 to **Everglades City**, the western edge of the Everglades National Park. You can stop at the **Everglades City Chamber of Commerce** to procure information about this little town and the neighboring region. ~ 32016 Tamiami Trail

▲▼

✔ CHECK THESE OUT

- Stop by the **Miccosukee Indian Village** in Everglades National Park, where you'll see chickees (palm-thatched houses), a crafts area, a museum and an alligator show. *page 40*
- Ride an airboat through the beautiful cypress swamps at **Big Cypress National Preserve** after catching the audio-visual show at the Big Cypress Visitor Center. *page 42*
- Search for sunken treasure or explore the continent's only living reef with a diving excursion in **Biscayne National Park**. *page 59*
- Stare down an alligator, and perhaps an ibis, while hiking the **Shark Valley Trail** in Everglades National Park. *page 64*

East, Everglades City; 941-695-3941, 800-941-6355, fax 941-695-3172.

At the privately owned **Eden of the Everglades** you can board a quiet jungle boat or airboat to observe some of the flora and fauna of the area in a natural setting. The service also operates an Everglades tram ride. Admission. ~ Route 41, a half mile west of Route 29, Everglades City; 941-695-2800, fax 941-695-4506.

Two thousand years of human habitation in the southwest Everglades are presented at the charming **Museum of the Everglades**. Housed in a restored 1927 laundry building where Tamiami Trail construction workers washed their dirty clothes, the museum covers American Indian and settler history, with an emphasis on Barron Collier's company town. Displays range from Seminole artifacts to early washing and dry-cleaning machines. Wheelchair accessible. Closed Sunday and Monday. ~ 105 West Broadway, Everglades City; 941-695-0008, fax 941-695-0036; www.colliermuseum.com.

Continue south to the **Everglades National Park Visitors Center**. Here you can obtain information about the western regions of the park, including the **Ten Thousand Islands** area, the largest mangrove forest in the world. This is a popular starting point for the 99-mile wilderness waterway, and canoe or kayak rentals are readily available from a number of vendors. ~ Gulf Coast Ranger Station, Route 29, south of Everglades City; 941-695-3311, fax 941-695-3621; e-mail gcrangers@aol.com.

The **Everglades National Park Boat Tours** cover portions of this territory on the Gulf of Mexico, informing visitors how the mangrove islands are formed and acquainting them with the resident wildlife, especially shore and wading birds like the roseate spoonbill. American bald eagles, gentle manatees and playful dolphins often reward the sharp-eyed explorer. Some of the tours make stops on a small Gulf island for shelling and a guided walk. ~ Ranger Station; 941-695-2591, 800-445-7724, fax 941-695-3919.

Nature expeditions by boat into the Ten Thousand Islands area are offered by **Captain Dan**. ~ P.O. Box 274, Chokoloskee Island, FL 34138; 941-695-4573. **Chokoloskee Island Charters** has nature trips especially geared to photographers and birdwatchers. ~ P.O. Box 460, Chokoloskee Island, FL 34138; phone/fax 941-695-0141, 941-695-2286. Frank and Georgia Garrett operate **Majestic Everglades Excursions**. City dropouts who have become dedicated conservationists, they share their very personal view of the western Everglades with groups of six through memorable half-day trips that include lunch or afternoon snack in their specially designed, covered boat. You're almost guaranteed osprey sightings, and groups of dolphins often gambol playfully around the boat through the shallow waters. Closed May through September. ~ P.O. Box 241, Everglades City, FL 34139; 941-695-2777; www.majesticexcursions.com, e-mail gladestour@aol.com.

HIDDEN ►   **Chokoloskee,** a small island filled with motor homes, cottages and little motels, is a popular spot for visitors wishing to fish the Ten Thousand Islands region. It also has the distinction of being built on a gigantic shell mound created by early Colusa Indians. ~ Route 29, across the causeway south of Everglades City.

After you leave the park's western area, you can travel seven miles north on Route 29 to get to **Fakahatchee Strand State Preserve,** the major drainage slough of the Big Cypress Swamp (see the "Parks" section below). You can walk the boardwalk through the tall, dense, swamp forest of royal palm and bald cypress and admire the numerous orchidlike air plants that are said to grow only here. From November through February rangers conduct weekend "wet" walks into the swamp to see other rare plant life. ~ 941-695-4593, fax 941-695-4947.

HIDDEN ►   The squeaky screen door at the **Historic Smallwood Store Museum,** built on stilts above the brackish waters of the Everglades, leads you back in time. In 1906, pioneer Ted Smallwood established this trading post, overlooking a serene section of the bay. Seminole Indians and settlers exchanged hides, furs and produce for soap, coffee and flour in this cracker-style building. Placed on the National Register of Historic Places in 1974, this time capsule makes it easy to spend hours gazing at old pharmaceutical bottles, advertisements, tools, pelts, photos, books and other memorabilia. The gift shop sells video tapes of Everglades oral histories, hand-crafted Seminole dolls and clothing. Closed Wednesday and Thursday from May through November. Admission. ~ P.O. Box 367, Chokoloskee, FL 33925; 941-695-2989, fax 941-695-4454.

Collier-Seminole State Park offers a good introduction to the vegetation and wildlife of the western Everglades (see the "Beaches & Parks" section). Besides interpretations of the natural world of rare Florida royal palms, tropical hammocks, cypress swamps, mangroves, salt marshes and pine woods, there is a replica of a blockhouse used in the Second Seminole War and a display of a "walking dredge" used to build the Tamiami Trail. Admission. ~ Route 41, 20 miles northwest of Everglades City; 941-394-3397, fax 941-394-5113.

If your trip takes you northwest from Everglades City to Naples (via Route 41) or due north to Immokalee (via Route 29),

HIDDEN ►   detour to **Corkscrew Swamp Sanctuary** for another excellent and easy foray into the Everglades. The National Audubon Society saved this 11,000-acre reserve from foresters in the 1950s; it now serves to protect endangered wood storks and other species. A two-and-a-quarter-mile-long loop trail leads through lakes of lettuce fern and a broad variety of Everglades ecosystems. Admission. ~ Sanctuary Road off Route 846; 941-657-3771.

When an Everglades excursion is planned, the traditional starting point is always Miami. But Naples, on Florida's west coast, is actually much closer—less than 20 miles in some cases—to wilderness areas. And your Everglades education can begin in Naples itself. Founded in 1964, **The Conservancy of Southwest Florida** is dedicated to conserving the area's native ecosystems. Along with programs designed to inform the public, it organizes guided boat trips and nature walks, and welcomes visitors to a wildlife rehabilitation center where injured eagles, owls, hawks and other native wildlife are nursed back to health. Closed Sunday from April through December. Admission. ~ 1450 Merrihue Drive; 941-262-0304; www.conservancy.org, e-mail info@conservancy.org.

Everglades, The Story Behind the Scenery, by Jack de Golia is a beautifully illustrated, reasonably priced book that introduces many of the Everglades' hidden treasures. You can find it in most area bookstores and gift shops.

Somewhat more commercial is the safari-type half- and full-day trip offered by **Everglades Excursions**, which allows you see it all from an air-conditioned "Safari Wagon." You'll get a narrated nature tour through the saw grass prairies and mangrove wilderness, an Everglades luncheon that includes alligator meat and a visit to the Seminole Indian Village. If you've been burning to see a wrestling match where the 'gator takes a fall or to hold one of the scaly babies before its jaws become fearsome, this is your trip. ~ 1010 6th Avenue South, Suite 227A, Naples; 941-598-1050, 800-592-0848, fax 941-262-6967; www.everglades-excursions.com.

LODGING

If you prefer to stay close to the western park area, try the **Captain's Table Lodge and Villas**. This large resort offers hotel rooms and suites in its main lodge and one-bedroom villas, some featuring screened decks. There is a large pool and a boat ramp. Boat tours of the Ten Thousand Islands are available; good beaches are only five miles away—by boat. ~ Route 29, Everglades City; 941-695-4211, 800-741-6430, fax 941-695-2633. MODERATE.

◄ HIDDEN

The **Rod and Gun Club**, a 1868 hunting and fishing club, will be reopening eight rooms in the original lodge itself in January 2000. Over a scheduled three-year summer renovation plan, 25 of the 1940s antique-style rooms named after celebrated guests such as Ernest Hemingway, Gypsy Rose Lee, John Wayne and Burl Ives will once again welcome visitors. You can sit on its airy screened porch or admire the mounted game fish and red cypress paneling of the massive old lobby. Or stay in the cottages on the grounds, swim in the screened-in pool, play tennis and feast on the large waterfront veranda. Complete docking facilities alongside attract some pretty impressive boats. Strictly nonsmoking in the lodge, due to fire hazard. ~ 200 Riverside Drive, Everglades City; 941-695-2101. MODERATE.

Ivey House Bed and Breakfast is a shotgun-style residence built in 1928 with a large living room and library and ten twin- to queen-bedded rooms furnished in southern pine. You can also rent a two-bedroom cottage with a bath, a kitchen and a screened porch. Have a continental breakfast on one of the comfortable porches. There are daily guided canoeing/kayaking and boating excursions; half-day or overnight trips are offered. Complimentary bicycles are available for touring on your own. Non-smoking. Closed May through October. ~ 107 Camellia Street, Everglades City; 860-739-0791 in summer, 941-695-3299 in winter, fax 941-695-4155; www.iveyhouse.com, e-mail sandee@iveyhouse.com. BUDGET.

Outdoor Resorts is basically an RV park that takes up a goodly portion of this small island, but if you stay in one of their eight motel units or rent one of their RVs you can take advantage of all the resort amenities. The units are tiny and neat with modern kitchenettes; on the grounds are a health spa, pool and tennis courts; boat rentals are available. ~ Route 29, Chokoloskee Island; 941-695-2881, fax 941-695-3338. MODERATE.

If you are seeking the amenities of a full-service resort while exploring the western Everglades, try **Port of the Islands** about ten miles northwest of Everglades City. Residing on 500 acres and surrounded by parklands, the resort offers deluxe-priced hotel rooms and ultra-deluxe-priced efficiencies. You can keep yourself busy with skeet and trapshooting, swimming, dining, spa and health club activities, and nature cruises and guided fishing trips into the Ten Thousand Islands. The freshwater river that flows through the grounds feeds a harbor that has been designated a manatee sanctuary. ~ 25000 Tamiami Trail East/Route 41, Naples; 941-394-3101, 800-237-4173, fax 941-394-4335. DELUXE TO ULTRA-DELUXE.

DINING

HIDDEN ►

The **Miccosukee Restaurant** is a typical roadside restaurant with fried-fish fare. But the local American Indians who own and operate this place add their own special dishes to the menu—good things such as pumpkin bread, chili and fry bread, Miccosukee burgers and tacos, and hushpuppies and Everglades-caught catfish. It's the best place to eat while traveling the Tamiami Trail. Breakfast and lunch only. ~ Route 41, Miccosukee Indian Village; 305-223-8380. MODERATE.

Along with steak, chicken and the usual fried and broiled seafood, you can try grilled pompano and such delicacies as 'gator tail and lobster tail at the **Oyster House**. Ships' wheels and other nautical paraphernalia create a very pleasant, informal seaside atmosphere. ~ Route 29, Everglades City; 941-695-2073. MODERATE TO DELUXE.

The menu at the **Rod and Gun Club,** like so many area eateries, features frogs' legs, stone crab claws and native fish in season, but the ambience is unlike any other in far South Florida. You may dine in the massive, dark, cypress-paneled dining hall of this once-elegant old hunting and fishing lodge or be seated on the large, airy veranda where you can have a splendid view of the yachts and other fine boats that dock a stone's throw away. The selection of seafood, steak and chicken is small, but well prepared. ~ 200 Riverside Drive, Everglades City; 941-695-2101. MODERATE TO DELUXE.

Locals head to **PJ's Deli** for sandwiches, subs, burritos, ice cream and memorable Key lime tarts. Patio seating is available. ~ Glades Haven RV Park, 800 Southeast Copeland Avenue, Everglades City; 941-695-2746. BUDGET.

SHOPPING

Along with the usual souvenirs, you will find handcrafted baskets, beaded jewelry and the intricate, colorful patchwork clothing for which the Miccosukee Indian women are famous, at the **Miccosukee Indian Village Gift Shop**. ~ Route 41, 25 miles west of Florida's Turnpike; 305-223-8388.

◄ *HIDDEN*

If you've about given up on finding a souvenir of Florida that's truly Floridian and a work of art to boot, stop in at **Big Cypress Gallery**, where Clyde Butcher, photographer extraordinaire, produces and displays amazing black-and-white scenes of Florida, particularly its wetlands. Take home a wall-size limited-edition print, a poster or maybe even a T-shirt you might sooner frame than wear. The gallery's wilderness setting alone is worth the trip (45 miles west of the Turnpike and about 60 miles east of Naples) and mosquitoes are not a problem in the summer. ~ 52388 East Tamiami Trail, Ochopee; 941-695-2428, fax 941-695-2670.

If you are a souvenir hound, stop at **Wooten's** and you'll never have to go anywhere else for those plastic flamingos and vinyl alligators. ~ Route 41, Ochopee; 941-695-2781.

NIGHTLIFE

One Everglades City resident explained, "We don't have much nightlife here, and we like it that way!" So unless you can be contented with the dark, tropical night and the jungle sounds, you'll usually have to head up to Naples and beyond for bright lights.

"The Glassroom" at the **Oyster House** is great for private parties. The main bar of this father-and-son establishment has sports trophies on the wall, a jukebox and a pool table, all beside an 80-foot observation tower—the highest in the Everglades. There is dancing to live bands on weekends in the winter. ~ Route 29, Everglades City; 941-695-2073.

PARKS   **SHARK VALLEY/EVERGLADES NATIONAL PARK** 🚶 🚲 This public access to the park features a 15-mile loop road that delves deep into the saw grass expanses of the Everglades. Because no private vehicles are allowed in this protected region, you must visit either on foot, by bicycle or via one of the open-sided trams. There's an $8 per vehicle or $4 per person (walk-in or bike-in) fee. (See the "Tamiami Trail Area" section.) During the winter, there are ranger-led bicycle and hiking trips, including the "slough slog" wet hike through the freshwater marsh. Facilities include restrooms, vending machines, a hiking and biking trail, a nature trail, bicycle rentals and tram rides. ~ Off Route 41, 25 miles west of Florida's Turnpike; 305-221-8455, 305-221-8776, fax 305-221-1307; www.nps.gov/ever, e-mail ever_information@nps.gov.

EVERGLADES CITY/EVERGLADES NATIONAL PARK 🚣 🛶 🚤 🎣 This entrance to the park allows access to the vast, ever-changing Ten Thousand Islands, a mangrove archipelago that serves as both a nesting grounds for birds and a nursery for sea life. There's excellent fishing here for snapper, redfish and sea trout. Sportfishing is the region's greatest drawing card, but visitors can also take guided boat tours to observe dolphins, manatees and birds, and to learn of the American Indians who once fished these waters and left their shell middens behind. The 99-mile Wilderness Waterway, popular with experienced canoeists, twists through marine and estuarine areas all the way to Flamingo at the tip of the state. Several area rivers offer shorter canoeing opportunities. Swimming is not recommended, except on certain island locations accessible only by boat. There's a visitors center, restrooms, concession stand, boat tours and canoe and boat rentals. ~ The entrance is located on Route 29 off Route 41 at Everglades City; 941-695-3311, fax 941-695-3621; www.nps.gov/ever, e-mail gcrangers@aol.com.

▲ There are 22 free primitive sites on the Gulf Coast. They are accessible by boat only and require a backcountry permit (fee during winter months).

BIG CYPRESS NATIONAL PRESERVE 🚶 🚲 🐎 🛶 🚤 🎣 A 729,000-acre area of subtropical Florida known as Big Cypress Swamp makes up this preserve. Its establishment reflected a serious concern for the state's dwindling wetlands and watersheds, especially those affecting the Everglades National Park. Established in 1974, this preserved wilderness area of wet and dry prairies, coastal plains, marshes, mangrove forests, sandy pine woods and mixed hardwood hammocks has few facilities for visitors. It exists to protect the abundant wildlife living here and the watershed, which will be needed by future South Florida generations. There are picnic tables at several roadside parks, restrooms at the visitors center, bike trails and a hiking trail. Anglers can expect bass and gar. Off-road and all-terrain vehicles are allowed with a permit ($35). ~ The visitors center is on Route 41 between Shark Valley and Everglades City; 941-695-4111; www.nps.gov/bicy.

A There's primitive camping in the six campgrounds. Several campgrounds have sites that accommodate motor homes; however, there are no hookups or facilities. A dump station is located at Dona Drive. Free at all campgrounds.

FAKAHATCHEE STRAND STATE PRESERVE 🚶 🚴 ⚓ 🚣
This strand, the drainage slough for the Big Cypress Swamp, is the largest and most interesting of these natural channels cut by the flow of water into the limestone plain. The slough's tall, dense, swamp forest stands out on the horizon in contrast to the open terrain and saw grass plain around it. Its forest of royal palms, bald cypress trees and air plants is said to be unique on earth. Approximately 20 miles long and three to five miles wide, the preserve offers visitors views of some of its rare plant life, including numerous orchids. From November through February, rangers conduct "wet" walks every third Saturday of the month into the swamp at the preserve to see other unusual and endangered plant life. Reservations are required. The only facilities at the preserve are an interpretive trail and a boardwalk leading into the swamp. Canoeing is allowed south of Route 41, in East River only. ~ On Route 29, six miles north of Everglades City. The boardwalk is seven miles west of Route 29 on Route 41;. 941-695-4593, fax 941-695-4947.

COLLIER-SEMINOLE STATE PARK 🚶 ⚓ 🚤 🛥 🚣 The wildlife and vegetation of this park are representative of the Everglades region with tropical hammocks, salt marshes, cypress swamps, mangroves and pine flatwoods. A number of endangered species, such as West Indian manatees, Florida black bears, crocodiles and Florida panthers, are protected, and sometimes spotted, in this rich and diverse region. On display are a "walking dredge" used to build the Tamiami Trail and a replica of a blockhouse from the Second Seminole War. A limited number of visitors each day are allowed to canoe into the park's pristine mangrove swamp wilderness preserve, a 13.5-mile trip. There's saltwater fishing for mangrove snapper, redfish and snook. Facilities include a picnic area, restrooms, a nature trail, hiking trails, canoe rentals, a boat ramp, a concession stand and an interpretive center. Day-use fee, $3.25. ~ Located about 20 miles northwest of Everglades City on Route 41; 941-394-3397, fax 941-394-5113.

▲ There are 137 sites, 80 with electricity; $13 per night without hookups and $15 per night with hookups.

▼▼▼▼▼▼▼▼▼▼▼▼▼▼

Main Visitor Area

Early settlers came to Homestead to cultivate the rich land that was slowly "reclaimed" from the swampy Everglades. They planted and harvested vegetables and citrus and other tropical fruits suited to the far South Florida climate. Much of the area is still agricultural today, a winter fruit and vegetable basket that feeds people all across the country. The Homestead/Florida City area, which was hit harder by Hurricane Andrew than anywhere else in the state, is also a crossroads of sorts. Miami, to the north, is close enough that some of Homestead's street numbers are continuations of those in the big city, and crime is a problem from time to time. Head southeast and you are on your way to the Florida Keys. Due east is Biscayne National Park, a mostly underwater preserve of sea and reef and islands that are an upper continuation of the Keys but accessible only by boat. To the west is the main section of Everglades National Park where visitors can travel a 38-mile road all the way to Florida Bay and experience the many wonders of this exotic landscape.

SIGHTS

If you want to begin your exploration in the Florida City/Homestead area, don't forget to stop at the very fine **Tropical Everglades Visitors Association** in Florida City. Here you can obtain information about the main public portion of Everglades National Park as well as a number of other places to see and things to do in the Florida City/Homestead and Florida Keys areas. ~ 160 Route 1, Florida City; 305-245-9180, 800-388-9669; www.tropicaleverglades.com, e-mail tevisitor@cs.com.

There is a lot to be seen off the Atlantic coast east of Florida City in **Biscayne National Park**, most of it underwater (see the "Parks" section below). But even if you are not a snorkeler or scuba diver, you can get an excellent view of the nearby coral reef from the **glass-bottom boat** that departs from the Dante Fascell Visitor Center at Convoy Point. Daily trips to the reef, with occasional island cruises in the winter, are offered by **Biscayne National Underwater Park Tours Inc.** Reservations are required. ~ Biscayne National Park Headquarters, end of 328th Street, east of Florida City; 305-230-1100 (tours), 305-230-7275 (park), fax 305-230-1120; www.nps.gov.bisc, e-mail bisc_information@nps.gov.

Florida City is the hub of the most southern farming area in the continental United States. A drive northward on Krome Avenue or along any side road in the area will take you through vast truck gardens where you may see—and even pick from—great fields of tomatoes, corn, strawberries, okra, peppers and other fruits and vegetables. Large areas are also devoted to avocados, limes, mangos and papayas.

You can get an idea of how the early settlers lived in this fertile, challenging region between the eastern edge of the Everglades and the sea by visiting the **Florida Pioneer Museum**. The ◄ HIDDEN down-home collection consists mainly of fine old photographs and items from Florida family attics, and is housed in a caboose—a reconstructed railway station and an agent's house left over from the days of Henry Flagler's "railroad that went to the sea." Admission. ~ 826 North Krome Avenue, Florida City; 305-247-8221.

The **Coral Castle** is a strange place; some claim it's almost mystical. According to legend, this curious limestone mansion was built, between 1923 and 1940, because of an unrequited love. Its creator, a Latvian immigrant, claimed to know the secret of the construction of the pyramids. Perhaps he did, for he was able to move multi-ton pieces of local coral rock to the site and construct towers, massive stone furnishings, a nine-ton gate that swings open to the touch, a 5000-pound valentine heart and myriad other strange symbols of devotion to his mysterious lost love. Supposedly, no one has ever figured out the builder's secret, but you can go and give it a try, and marvel at this historic curiosity. Take the 35-minute self-guided audio tour (weekends only) in English, Spanish, French or German. Admission. ~ 28655 Route 1, Homestead; 305-248-6344, fax 305-248-6344; www.coralcastle.com.

North of Homestead, the **Preston B. Bird & Mary Heinlein Fruit & Spice Park** is a 30-acre random grove planted with over 500 varieties of fruit, spices and herbs from around the world. Visitors are invited to stop by the giftshop and stroll among the citrus, banana, lychee, mango, starfruit and other tropical trees. Admission. ~ 24801 Southwest 187th Avenue, Homestead; 305-247-5727, fax 305-245-3369; e-mail fsp@co.miami-dade.fl.us.

EVERGLADES NATIONAL PARK   South of Homestead, the cultivation suddenly stops—and Everglades National Park begins, almost like a boundary of uneasy truce between man and nature. You quickly forget that Miami is just up the road a piece or that tended gardens lie behind you. Before you lies the mysterious world of what some call "the real Florida," the home of the alligator, the panther, the royal palm and the flamingo.

There are a number of ways to tackle this area of the park. For help in designing your plan, stop at the **Ernest F. Coe Visitor Center**. Here park staff members will provide you with all sorts of helpful information, including weather, trail and insect conditions and listings of the season's varied and informative ranger-guided tours. A fine audiovisual presentation and a wide assortment of books provide good introductions to the area. All visitors centers in the park are wheelchair accessible. ~ 40001 State Road

Text continued on page 54.

Alligators
and Crocodiles

Stroll the boardwalk of Anhinga Trail, take the loop tour in Shark Valley or explore many of the other paths in the Everglades National Park and you will be certain to see the area's chief resident, the American alligator. Like dark, greenish-black, lifeless logs, they often lie basking motionless on the sunny banks of water holes or glide through ponds and sloughs with only their nostrils and eyes breaking the surface.

Once hunted for the stylish shoes, boots, luggage and pocketbooks produced from their tough hides, or for the slightly chewy, chicken-flavored tail meat, alligators are a now a success story of preservation. Classified as endangered and protected by law for several decades, their once perilously low population has recovered so well that alligators are once again a common sight in the Everglades. They appear in many other parts of Florida as well, occasionally to the distress of nearby human residents. While man's encroachment still takes its toll on this ancient creature, the comeback has been so dramatic that the alligator has been reclassified from endangered to threatened.

The American crocodile has not been so fortunate. Only a few hundred are believed to remain in Florida, and they are rarely seen. However, the sign along Route 1 on the way to Key Largo warning "Crocodile Crossing" can be believed. Regular drivers of this road claim to have occasionally spotted the reptiles, who make their homes in this marshy region. Lighter in color than alligators, crocodiles possess narrower, more pointed snouts than their cousins. They can also be identified by a long lower fourth tooth that protrudes impressively when the jaw is closed. Occasionally growing to lengths of 12 feet, they are considered to be more aggressive than alligators.

But one should not be misled by the seeming docility of the Everglades alligator. An active predator, the alligator roams freely in search of food and will eat anything from turtles to wading birds to unlucky mammals trespassing its territory. Females build impressive nests, piling up mud and grass and debris to as high as six or eight feet. Here they lay their eggs, which heat from the sun and decaying mulch will hatch after about nine weeks. The alligator is a good mother, staying nearby so she can care for her young as soon as the eggs hatch. Male alligators can measure up to 14 feet in length, though most adults average between six and ten feet.

Of particular importance is the alligator's role as the "Keeper of the Everglades." Getting ready for the region's annual dry season, the alligator prepares its own water reservoirs by cleaning out large solution holes, dissolved cavities in the limestone bed of the Everglades. As the rains decrease, these "'gator holes" become important oases for all manner of wildlife. Fish, snails, turtles and other freshwater creatures seek refuge in the pools. Here many will survive until the rains return, when they will leave to repopulate the Everglades. Others will serve as food and sustenance for resident mammals and birds, as well as for the accommodating, future-thinking alligator. This role has made the alligator's comeback particularly important to the continuing life cycles of the Everglades.

While alligators are generally not considered dangerous to humans, warnings for avoiding close contact should be taken seriously. Tragic accidents do happen from time to time, particularly when people carelessly trespass in an alligator's territory. These reptiles are known to be especially aggressive during the spring breeding season, and mothers remain protective of their young for quite some time.

But alligators are certainly the chief attraction of the Everglades, and the national park has designed a number of excellent observation points in a variety of habitats. A small family of alligators also reside at **Blue Hole** on Big Pine Key in the lower Florida Keys. ~ Key Deer Boulevard, two and a quarter miles north of Route 1.

Crocodile and alligator ancestry reaches back millions and millions of years. Viewing them, one is looking back into another time. Though their surroundings may have changed greatly, these creatures and their habits and habitats have not.

9336, ten miles southwest of Homestead; 305-242-7700, fax 305-242-7711; www.nps.gov/ever, e-mail ever_information@nps.gov.

Once you have paid your admission and entered the park, you are on the single park road that will eventually arrive at **Flamingo**, 38 miles away, at the tip of the state on the edge of Florida Bay. This winding, lonely road traverses the heart of the park, meandering among tall pines, through seemingly endless expanses of saw grass prairie and alongside mysterious dark ponds. Off this road lie a number of paths, trails, boardwalks and waterways designed to give the visitor as wide an Everglades experience as possible. Some of the trails require only short strolls of half a mile or less, but they reward with close-up views of a great range of environments and inhabitants. Because so much of the terrain is submerged in water, it is wise to stick to the paths unless you go exploring with a park ranger.

At some point during its existence, enterprising residents of the area that is now the Flamingo Visitors Center produced moonshine whiskey and gathered bird plumes for ladies' fashionwear.

About four miles inside the park entrance, watch for signs to the **Royal Palm Visitor Center** on your left. Even if you have already spent a good amount of time at the main center, you should take a stroll down each of the two half-mile trails that begin here. Close together but very different, each plunges into a distinctive Everglades environment. Interpretive signs help you notice things you might otherwise miss, such as how the strangler fig got its name or why alligators are so vital to the survival of the region. Ranger-led walks are offered here year-round. Most trails are wheelchair accessible.

The **Anhinga Trail** (.5 mile) travels a boardwalk across Taylor Slough, a marshy pool that attracts winter birds and other wildlife that assemble with apparent unconcern for the season's thousands of visitors with cameras and zoom lenses. This is a perfect spot for viewing alligators and numerous water birds, including anhingas. Here, too, you can gaze across broad vistas of saw grass prairie.

Nearby, the **Gumbo-Limbo Trail** (.5 mile) leads through a jungly tropical hardwood hammock rich in gumbo-limbo, strangler fig, wild coffee, royal palms and other tropical trees as well as numerous orchids and ferns. Air plants and butterflies often add to the beauty of this spot; interpretive signs help visitors get acquainted with the tropical flora that appears again and again throughout the park.

About six miles from the main entrance, the half-mile **Pinelands Trail**, near the Long Pine Key campground, circles through a section of slash pine forest. Here the ground is dry; occasional fires keep undergrowth in check so the pines can thrive without competition. This is a good place to get a look at the rock and solution holes formed in the shallow bed of limestone that lies under South Florida. Or just to picnic beside a quiet lake. For a view of pinelands closer to the park road, stop at the **Pinelands** sign about a mile farther on.

As you continue down the park road and gaze across the saw grass prairie, you'll notice stands of stunted trees that, during winter, appear dead or dying, since they are hung with moss from ghostlike grey branches. These are bald cypress, which thrive in watery terrain but remain dwarfed due to the peculiar conditions of the Everglades. In spring they put out lovely green needles. Some, though dwarfed, have been growing here for over a century.

About six miles beyond the Pinelands, you come to the **Pa-hay-okee Overlook** (.25 mile) named for the American Indian word for Everglades, meaning "grassy waters." Walk the short boardwalk and climb the observation tower for a wonderful panorama of the saw grass prairie dotted with collections of ancient dwarf cypress and small island hammocks of hardwoods. This is one of the best overviews in the park; it's a great place for birdwatching.

Some park rangers refer to hammocks as the "bedrooms of the Everglades," the places where so many wild creatures, large and small, find dry ground and shade from the tropical sun. About seven miles from Pa-hay-okee, you can explore one of these magnificent "highlands" that thrive just above the waterlines. The half-mile **Mahogany Hammock Trail** enters the cool, dark, jungly environment of a typical hardwood hammock, where you'll find rare paurotis palms and large mahogany trees, including one said to be the largest mahogany in the United States. Look and listen closely—barred owls, golden orb spiders, colorful *Liguus* tree snails and many other creatures make their homes in this humid "bedroom."

From Mahogany Hammock the park road heads due south through stands of pine and cypress and across more saw grass prairie. You are now nearing the coast and will begin to see the first mangrove trees, evidence of the mixing of saltwater from Florida Bay with the freshwater that flows from the north. You will pass several canoe-access spots along the road here, including the one at West Lake, about 11 miles from Mahogany Hammock.

Stop at the **West Lake Trail** for a good close-up look at mangroves. You can walk among the three varieties that thrive here along the half-mile boardwalk trail. With practice you will be able to identify them all—the predominant red mangroves with their arched, spidery prop roofs, black mangroves sending up fingerlike breathing tubes called "pneumatophores" from the mud and white mangroves and buttonwood on the higher, dryer shores of the swampy areas. The West Lake shoreline is one of many important spawning grounds for fish and shellfish that in turn attract raccoons and other wildlife who come to feed. You may see a gourmet diner or two if you walk quietly and keep your eyes open.

As you near the end of the park road, you'll pass **Mrazek Pond**, another lovely birdwatching spot, especially rewarding during the winter months. Roseate spoonbills often come to this quiet, glassy pond to feed, along with many other common and exotic waterfowl.

The road ends at the **Flamingo Visitors Center**, where a remote fishing village once stood. Early settlers could reach the area only by boat, and along with fishing, farming and the making of charcoal, all sorts of other activity, legal and not—went on here. The town is gone now, replaced by a marina, concessions, a motel and cabins, a gift shop and a visitors center. At Flamingo you can select from a variety of sightseeing opportunities, such as ranger-guided walks, wilderness canoe trips, campfire programs and hands-on activities. Offerings vary with the seasons; check at the visitors center for a schedule. ~ Located 38 miles from the main entrance; 941-695-2945, fax 941-695-3854; e-mail ever_flamingo_-_interp@nps.gov.

Sightseeing by boat is particularly enjoyable. Most boat tours in this region, including some backcountry explorations, are available year-round. Sunset cruises are a delight, offering views of spectacular skies as well as allowing close-ups of a wide variety of birds winging their way to shore. In winter, pelicans ride the gentle waves, and gulls soar up and around the boat. Some boat **HIDDEN ►** trips will take you to **Cape Sable**, the farthest-out point of southwestern Florida, where the Gulf of Mexico laps a broad, sandy beach.

For more birdwatching, especially in winter, take a short stroll from the visitors center to nearby **Eco Pond**. At dusk you may see ibis, egrets and other water birds winging in for the night to nest in nearby trees.

(For more information on exploring other regions of the park's main visitor area, see the "Canoeing & Kayaking" section in "Outdoor Adventures.")

LODGING   The usual chain motels line Route 1 in Homestead and Florida City. If you are looking for less expensive lodging, head into the downtown areas where you'll find rows of mom-and-pop motels along Krome Avenue. The **Super 8 Motel** is near several restaurants and offers plain but clean and roomy accommodations. A swimming pool, coconut palms and other tropical plants set this one somewhat apart. ~ 1202 North Krome Avenue, Florida City; 305-245-0311, 800-800-8000, fax 305-247-9136; www.super8. com. BUDGET.

The **Hampton Inn** offers comfortable accommodations near both Biscayne and Everglades national parks. The 123-unit facility is clean and modern, and has the obligatory swimming pool. A rarity for chain hotels, there's no charge for the breakfast bar and local calls. ~ 124 East Palm Drive, Florida City; 305-247-8833, 800-426-7866, fax 305-247-6456; www.hampton-inn.com. MODERATE.

To really experience the Everglades, stay at least a couple of nights in the **Flamingo Lodge**. This, the only accommodation in the park, is a plain old motel with window air conditioners and jalousies that can be opened to let in the intriguing watery smells of the 'glades and the shallow bay. Far from city lights and surrounded by jungle sounds, Flamingo Lodge lies in the heart of the Everglades. It offers a beautiful pool circled by tropical plants. Flamingo also offers rustic cottages with fully equipped kitchens and all motel amenities. Park entrance fee of $10 is not included in the rates. ~ State Route 9336, in Everglades National Park; 941-695-3101, 800-600-3813, fax 941-695-3921; www.flamingo lodge.com, e-mail everglad@ix.netcom.com. DELUXE TO ULTRA-DELUXE.

DINING

There is only one restaurant in Everglades National Park, but there are a variety of eating places in Homestead.

Though ultimately rural and a bit rough around the edges, Homestead has developed something of a tearoom culture in recent years. Locals, especially seniors, love lunching at a tearoom and then antiquing in downtown Homestead. The most popular place for tea and lunch is **White Lion Cafe**, folksy, friendly, and cluttered with pewter, baskets and other finds. Diners settle into well-worn wood booths for sandwiches like the "june buggy," with roast beef, horseradishes and green olives. At night, there's music by Katie P. Jones on the piano and "Blue Plate Specials." ~ 146 Northwest 7th Street, Homestead; 305-248-1076. MODERATE.

◄ HIDDEN

Tiffany's Cottage Dining offers more traditional tea fare: lots of crisp, cold salads, soups, quiche and finger sandwiches. They serve breakfast on Saturday and Sunday as well; if you're hungry, order the scrambled egg on country biscuit, otherwise, the cinnamon-walnut oatmeal is terrific. Tiffany's has lots of pink— pink lace, pink roses of silk, real pink carnations on deeply pink tablecloths. After lunch, everyone wanders into the adjacent boutiques filled with "Enchantables, Country to Victorian." ~ 22 Northeast 15th Street, Homestead; 305-246-0022. MODERATE.

The Friendship Garden Café is a French-style café specializing in traditional soups. Don't miss the sandwiches made on fresh baguettes and croissants, or the rich desserts. No lunch on Saturday; no dinner Monday through Thursday. Closed Sunday. ~ 30360 Old Dixie Highway, Homestead; 305-246-1633. BUDGET TO MODERATE.

Mexicans make up a substantial portion of Homestead's agricultural workforce. Thus, the town supports several Mexican restaurants, including some that aren't particularly tourist friendly. **El Toro Taco**, however, bustles with a mixed clientele. Tops with dining critics, this is a noisy, happy place. Decorated with terracotta tile, fake adobe and huge windows, El Toro Taco serves up terrific *carne gisada* (an authentic beef-and-potato stew), *mole de pollo* and *menudo* (tripe soup with lime and onion). Tacos, enchiladas and fabulous fajitas should sate the less adventurous. Try the spicy breakfasts. ~ 1 South Krome Avenue, Homestead; 305-245-8182. BUDGET TO MODERATE.

The Mexican fare at the light and airy **Casita Tejas** includes such Tex-Mex favorites as fajitas and chimichangas but also features genuine south-of-the-border dishes like *carne guisada* (spicy stewed beef and potatoes) and shrimp à la Mexicana (grilled shrimp with tomatoes, jalapeños and onions). The setting is fun and cheery, styled with wooden floors, woven blankets and glass tables. ~ 27 North Krome Avenue, Homestead; 305-248-8224. BUDGET TO MODERATE.

Although it's the only place to dine in the Everglades National Park, the **Flamingo Lodge Restaurant** is surprisingly good. The small but satisfactory menu features chicken, seafood and beef dishes. Located on the second floor of a small complex, the multilevel restaurant presents pretty views of Florida Bay. Tropical plants within and the dark night without remind you that while the menu is routine, the setting is quite exotic. Closed mid-April through October. ~ State Route 9336, in Everglades National Park; 941-695-3101, fax 941-695-3921; e-mail everglad@ ix.netcom.com. MODERATE.

SHOPPING   **Cauley Square** has a Miami address, but Homestead claims it, too. This restored area of historic homes and buildings encompasses a variety of shops, including an art gallery selling south Florida and Bahamian art and the Cauley Square Tearoom. ~ 22400 Old Dixie Highway, Goulds; 305-258-3543, fax 305-258-3546.

More than two dozen antique stores line Krome Avenue and sidestreets in downtown Homestead. Here you'll find items in varying degrees of restoration, from armoires and jukeboxes to vintage clothing, five-and-dime folk art, and even boat motors and gas pumps. The **Antique Mall**, home to half-a-dozen stores and a café, is a good place to start. ~ 115 Krome Avenue, Homestead.

The **Redland Fruit & Spice Park Gift Shop** is located on the grounds of the Preston B. Bird & Mary Heinlein Fruit & Spice Park. Here you can browse among shelves of imported and domestic dried and canned exotic fruits, unusual spices and seeds, and out-of-the-ordinary juices, jellies and jams. There's a good selection of cookbooks and reference books on tropical fruits. ~

24801 Southwest 187th Avenue, Homestead; 305-247-5727, fax
305-245-3369; e-mail fsp@co.miami-dade.fl.us.

The **Knaus Berry Farm** is owned and operated by a family of
German Baptists who wear quaint clothing while running the marvelous bakery and waiting on the customers. You can buy spectacular berries in season here, along with guava, strawberry and
other homemade jams to eat on the bakery's mouth-watering
breads. Closed May through November. ~ 15980 Southwest 248th
Street, five miles northeast of Homestead City; 305-247-0668.

On your drive to the main entrance of Everglades National
Park, you'll pass an old-fashioned, open-air produce stand known
as **Robert Is Here**. Robert has fresh fruit such as mangos, lychees,
monstera, tamarind and star fruit, and he has added sweet
onions, cabbage, broccoli and cauliflower to the array. His U-
Pick service for strawberries and snapdragons carries through the
growing season (Thanksgiving to Easter). He serves up Key lime
milkshakes and pies and sells an assortment of jellies and preserves. In addition, you may view his collection of giant tortoises
out back. ~ 19200 Southwest 344th Street, Homestead; 305-246-
1592, fax 305-245-6273; www.robertishere.com, e-mail fresh@
robertishere.com.

While the **Gift Shop at Flamingo Lodge** has lots of the usual
Florida souvenirs, they also have some interesting books on the
Everglades, along with high-quality shirts and stationery. Limited
hours from mid-April through October. ~ State Route 9336, in
Everglades National Park; 941-695-3101, fax 941-695-3921; e-
mail everglad@ix.netcom.com.

NIGHTLIFE

From the Florida City/Homestead area, it is less than an hour's
drive to the bright lights of Miami and Miami Beach.

In Homestead and Florida City, there is an assortment of roadside taverns, and some of the motels keep their lounges open and
provide occasional entertainment for late-night socializers. But most
folks will tell you that the sidewalks roll up early around here.

If you spend any nights in Flamingo, deep in the Everglades,
take time to walk outside (providing it's not mosquito time) away
from the lights of the lodge and marina. On a moonless night,
you'll experience a darkness that is ultimate and hear sounds made
nowhere else in the United States as the subtropical jungle creatures begin their night-long serenades.

PARKS

BISCAYNE NATIONAL PARK 🏃 🦌 🚤 🛶 ⛵ This 173,500-
acre marine park is one of the largest of its kind in the National
Park system, but most of it is hidden from the average traveler
since it lies beneath the waters of Biscayne Bay and the Atlantic
Ocean. The park includes a small area of mangrove shoreline
(which was hit hard by Hurricane Andrew), part of the bay, a

line of narrow islands of the northern Florida Keys and the northern part of the Florida Keys coral reef tract. Brown pelicans, little blue herons, snowy egrets and a few exotic fish can be seen by even the most casual stroller from the mainland jetty, but to fully appreciate the beauty of this unusual park you should take a glass-bottom boat tour or go snorkeling or scuba diving around the colorful reef. The park may also be explored by canoe or with a ranger on a guided trip. The little mangrove-fringed keys allow discovery of such tropical flora as gumbo-limbo trees, strangler fig and devil's potato. Birdlife abounds. This park features excellent saltwater fishing in open waters; fishing, however, is prohibited in harbors. Lobster may be taken east of the islands in season. Swimming is not recommended except on the tiny beaches of Elliott and Sands keys where care must be taken to avoid sharp coral rock and spiny sea urchins. Picnic areas, restrooms, showers, canoe rentals and boat tours can be found here. ~ Park headquarters are at Convoy Point, nine miles east of Homestead. The rest of the park is accessible by boat from Convoy Point; 305-230-7275, fax 305-230-1120; www.nps.gov/bisc, e-mail bisc_information@nps.gov.

▲ Tent camping is allowed on Elliott and Boca Chita keys, in about 30 sites, boat access only; $15 per night docking fee or $10 per night for camping only. Prepare for mosquitoes.

HOMESTEAD BAYFRONT PARK This is a next-door neighbor to the mainland part of Biscayne National Park (see above). It's a very popular spot enhanced by a small manmade beach, grassy areas and some shade offered by pines and palms. Entrance to the park is through a dense grove of mangroves, allowing a close look at these amazing island-building trees. There's good shore fishing for snapper. Swimming is pleasant and facilities include picnic areas, a playground, restrooms, showers and a marina. Day-use fee, $3.50 per vehicle. ~ Follow signs at Biscayne National Park (see above); 305-230-3034.

EVERGLADES NATIONAL PARK With an area of more than 1.5 million acres, this protected section of Florida's Everglades covers the southwestern end of the state and a vast section of shallow Florida Bay dotted with tiny keys. The main visitor area, with its 38-mile park road running from the Ernest F. Coe Visitor Center at the entrance to Flamingo at the tip of the state on Florida Bay, affords numerous opportunities to explore a wide variety of Everglades habitats, ecosystems, flora and fauna. Naturalists are available to offer advice on how best to explore the prairies, ponds, hammocks, inlets and bay. (See the "Main Visitor Area" section.) There's excellent inland fishing, especially for largemouth bass, and in coastal waters for snapper, redfish and trout. Facilities in the Flamingo area include picnic areas, restrooms, a restaurant, a motel, cabins, a grocery, a marina, interpretive trails, boat tours, boat rentals, canoe rentals and bike rentals. There's a $10 per vehicle or $5 per person (walk-in or bike-in) fee. ~ The main park entrance is off State Road 9336, ten miles southwest of Florida City; 305-242-7700, fax 305-242-7711; www.nps.gov/ever, e-mail ever_information@nps.gov.

▲ The Long Pine Key and Flamingo campgrounds have more than 300 tent/RV sites (no hookups); $14 per night. Wilderness camping (first-come, first-served) is allowed, with a permit, in designated areas; $10 to $30 per night, depending on the number of campers. Permits may be obtained, in person, at the Flamingo and Everglades City visitors centers. Reservations: 800-365-2267; reservations.nps.gov. There are also many privately owned camp-grounds outside of the park.

Chekika Recreation Area 🏃 ⛵ This 640-acre area allows easy exploration of some of the many Everglades terrains, including a tropical hammock, tree islands and the grassy waters flowing over honeycombed limestone surface rock. There's pleasant fishing in a natural lagoon. The small campground is located in the hardwood hammock, providing a pleasant and protected wilderness experience within an easy drive of Miami. Alligators make their home in the park and are to be respected. Facilities include a picnic area, restrooms, showers, a nature trail and a boardwalk; groceries and restaurants are in Homestead. Day-use fee, $8 per vehicle; $4 per walk- or bike-in. ~ Off Krome Avenue, 15 miles from Homestead; 305-242-7700, fax 305-242-7711; e-mail ever_information@nps.gov.

▲ There are 20 sites, some accommodate RVs (no hookups); $14 per night.

▼▼▼▼▼▼▼▼▼▼▼▼▼▼
Outdoor Adventures

FISHING

Tarpon, snook, redfish and trout are the four most popular fish that charter captains will help you locate in the western Everglades and Ten Thousand Islands region. Contact one of the following for a fishing trip: **Rod and Gun Club** will take you on a full- or half-day trip into the Ten Thousand Island backcountry. Box lunches can be provided. ~ Everglades City, 941-695-2101. **Captain Dan** will guide up to four people in the shallow water of the outer islands or around the oyster beds. ~ Chokoloskee, 941-695-4573. About 40 miles south of Naples, Captain Dave operates **Chokoloskee Island Outfitters**, taking up to three people out into the Everglades after the elusive snook and tarpon. ~ Chokoloskee; phone/fax 941-695-0141, 941-695-2286. Based in Key Largo, **Back Country Adventures** offers charters into Everglades National Park for snook, tarpon, trout and snapper. ~ 59 North Blackwater Lane near MM 105, Key Largo; 305-451-1247.

BOATING   **Majestic Everglades Excursions** offers a four-hour trip for up to six on a small boat through the Ten Thousand Islands. Light lunch and snacks are provided. Closed May through September. ~ Everglades City; 941-695-2777; www.majesticexcursions.com, e-mail gladestour@aol.com.

DIVING   For scuba and snorkeling excursions via glass-bottom boat to little-traveled, beautiful outer reefs and the patch reefs closer to shore, contact the **Biscayne National Underwater Park, Inc.** ~ Convoy Point, in the Dante Fascell Visitor Center building; 305-230-1100, fax 305-230-1120; www.nps.gov.bisc, e-mail bisc_information@nps.gov.

CANOEING   To explore the shoreline of Biscayne National Park by canoe,
& KAYAKING   contact the **Biscayne National Underwater Park, Inc.** ~ Convoy Point, east of Homestead; 305-230-1100, fax 305-230-1120; www.nps.gov.bisc, e-mail bisc_information@nps.gov. For kayak and canoe rentals, outfitting and guided trips in the northwestern Everglades, try **North American Canoe Tours**. Closed May through October. ~ Ivey House Bed & Breakfast, 107 Camellia Street, Everglades City; 941-695-3299 in winter, 860-928-2329 in summer; www.iveyhouse.com, e-mail sandee@iveyhouse.com. You can canoe the streams and ponds of the southern Everglades through the **Flamingo Marina**. ~ State Route 9336, Flamingo; 941-695-3101, fax 941-695-3921; e-mail everglad@ix.netcom.com. **Reflections Nature Tours** on Little Torch Key takes novice and experienced paddlers into the Everglades National Park. ~ 305-872-2896, 305-304-6785.

A limited number of canoes are allowed (and may be rented) each day for exploration of the **Collier-Seminole State Park**. ~ Route 41, 20 miles northwest of Everglades City, 941-394-3397, fax 941-394-5113.

Following are a number of popular canoe trails in Everglades National Park.

TAMIAMI TRAIL AREA   **Wilderness Waterway** (99 miles) extends through a well-marked mangrove forest in the Ten Thousand Islands region of the national park. The entire trip can take from several days to a week. Backcountry permits are required, and arrangements must be made in advance for pickup and canoe transport.

MAIN VISITOR AREA   All Flamingo canoe trails are accessible from the main park road. Check with rangers before you set out, as varying water levels may close portions of some trails in dry seasons. The park provides maps and guides for canoe trails.

Nine Mile Pond Trail (5.2 miles) travels through a shallow saw grass marsh and past islands of mangroves. It is the best summer trail in the park.

Noble Hammock Trail (2-mile loop) was once used by boot-leggers, whose old "cutting" markers are still on the trees. This trail meanders across open country and small alligator ponds through buttonwood, red mangrove and saw grass.

Hells Bay Trail (5.5 miles) travels through overgrown passageways of red mangrove and brackish water environments. A backcountry permit is recommended for this trip, even when not camping. There are campsites at the four- and eight-mile points.

West Lake Trail (8 miles) includes a long exposed crossing of the lake as well as a meandering trail through coastal lake country bordered by red and black mangrove and buttonwood trees and through the remains of a once-great living forest destroyed by hurricanes. Alligators and fish are numerous.

Believe it or not, the Everglades is really a river running 50 miles wide and a few inches deep. A close look into the tall saw grass reveals the area's true nature.

Mud Lake Loop (6.8 miles) crosses shallow Mud Lake, which has a prairie, mangrove and buttonwood shoreline, making it good for birdwatching. The trip continues to Coot Bay through what may have once been a Calusa Indian canal and returns via the Buttonwood Canal.

Canoeing is also possible in Florida Bay, depending on wind and weather conditions. There is good birding in the shallows; during the dry months, the bay is the only realistic way to reach the beach at Cape Sable. But be sure to check with rangers on tides and weather conditions before setting out. It's a hefty jaunt to the beautiful but isolated sandy beach area, and sudden winds could make the return trip very difficult.

To go houseboating in the southernmost Everglades and Florida Bay, contact Flamingo Lodge, which has four air-conditioned, 37-foot Gibsons that sleep six and four pontoons that sleep eight. There's a two-night minimum. Closed mid-April through October. ~ Flamingo; 941-695-3101, fax 941-695-3921; e-mail everglad@ ix.netcom.com.

HOUSE-BOATING

At Homestead, try the 18-hole course at the semi-private Redland Golf & Country Club. ~ 24451 Southwest 177th Avenue; 305-247-8503, fax 305-245-0642. At Key Colony Beach, near Marathon, the public may play at the nine-hole KCB. ~ MM 53.5; 305-289-1533.

GOLF

You can bike the paved roads of the visitor areas in Everglades National Park; the only specific bikeway is the 15-mile loop road at Shark Valley, which is shared with hikers and the sightseeing tram.

Bicycles are for rent for exploring the Shark Valley day-use area of the Everglades National Park at Shark Valley Tram Tours.

BIKING

~ Route 41, about 25 miles west of Florida's Turnpike; 305-221-8455.

HIKING   There are some intriguing trails into the Everglades suitable for both novice strollers and serious explorers. All distances for hiking trails are one way unless otherwise noted.

EVERGLADES AREA   Shark Valley Trail (15-mile loop) in Everglades National Park leads hikers and bicyclists across a saw grass waterway where they are sure to see alligators and a wide assortment of birds such as snail kites, wood storks and ibis. They may also observe deer, turtles, snakes and otters. About halfway is an observation tower that offers a good overview of the "river of grass." Because of a lack of shade and few facilities along this single-lane, paved walkway, only well-equipped, hardy hikers should attempt the entire 15-mile loop. A short nature trail is located near the entrance to Shark Valley.

Florida National Scenic Trail (South Section) (33 miles) is a trail that begins at the Big Cypress Visitor Center on Route 41 west of Shark Valley. This wilderness trail, for experienced hikers only, plunges deep into the Big Cypress Swamp (the trail is usually under water from May to November), which is actually a vast region of sandy pine islands, mixed hardwood hammocks, wet and dry prairies and mysterious marshes. Stunted bald cypress stand amid the grasses; wildlife is abundant. Bring your own drinking water.

Collier-Seminole State Park Hiking Trail (6.5 miles) explores a section of the northwestern edge of the Florida Everglades. This low-lying trail winds through pine flatwoods and cypress swamps where you can observe a variety of plants and wildlife, including a number of endangered species.

MAIN VISITOR AREA   A number of short interpretive trails, .5 mile or less, are accessible in the main section of the Everglades National Park from the park road (State Road 9336) between the main entrance and Flamingo. These short walks acquaint visitors with some of the varied flora, fauna and terrain of the huge park (see "Main Visitor Area" in this chapter).

Longer trails allow hikers to explore the coastal prairie and delve deeper into the mysteries of the Everglades. As they are sometimes under water, be sure to check at the ranger station or visitors center before starting out. Between April and October most trails are impassable. These trails include the following:

Long Pine Key Nature Trail (7 miles), beginning on the road to Long Pine Key, is a network of interconnecting trails running through an unusually diverse pineland forest. About 200 types of plants, including 30 found nowhere else on earth, grow here. Among the mammals you can spot along the trail are possums, white-tailed deer, raccoons and the seldom-seen, endangered Florida panther.

Snake Bight Trail (2 miles) commences about three miles northeast of Flamingo off the park road and heads due south to a boardwalk at Florida Bay. Two miles along, it is joined by **Rowdy Bend Trail** (2.6 miles). The two make a good loop hike through a variety of terrains and flora.

Old Ingraham Highway Trail (11 miles) begins at the Royal Palm Visitor Center and follows an old road through hammocks, saw grass prairie, and pine forest. This flat hike is ideal for bird-watching. Look for deer along the way.

Bear Lake Trail (1.6 miles) begins about three miles north of Flamingo's visitors center at the end of Bear Lake Road. This raised trail was made with fill dirt from the digging of the Homestead Canal and heads due west, skirting a canoe trail and the north shore of Bear Lake. Woodland birds are abundant here.

Christian Point Trail (1.8 miles), begins about one and a half miles northeast of Flamingo, travels across coastal prairie and winds through mangrove thickets to the shore of Florida Bay.

Coastal Prairie Trail (7.5 miles) follows an old road bed leading to Cape Sable. This trail can be quite demanding, depending on ground conditions, as it progresses through open salt marsh and tends to flood. The trail begins at Flamingo and ends at Clubhouse Beach on the edge of Florida Bay.

The sign at the beginning of **Everglades Trail** (24 miles) advises hikers to bring water, sunscreen, a cellphone, first-aid kit and bug repellent—it is, after all, 24 miles of asphalt, and there is not a speck of shade to be found. What you will find is a window on South Dade's farmland, views into the cabbage and corn patches, across tomato fields that bleed into the sunset (mountain biking and horseback riding are also recommended). And you will likely find solitude, as this new-in-1997 trail, which runs alongside a canal on the east side of the Everglades, is slowly discovered. The only access points to Everglades Trail are on either end: at Southwest 136th Street west of Krome Avenue, and at Route 9336, two miles east of the entrance to Everglades National Park.

BISCAYNE NATIONAL PARK   Beginning at Elliott Key harbor in Biscayne National Park, the **East-West Trail** (.5 mile) is a self-guided nature trail that leads through a tropical hardwood hammock of rare vines, flowers and trees. If you're up for a longer hike, the **Spite Highway** (about 7 miles) runs the full length of the island.

▼▼▼▼▼▼▼▼▼▼▼▼

Transportation

CAR

From Miami, **Route 41**, the Tamiami Trail, heads due west through the middle of the Everglades, skirting the northern boundary of Everglades National Park. **Route 1** and the almost-parallel **Florida Turnpike** head toward Homestead and Florida City, where **Route 27** branches off into the heart of Everglades National Park. If you prefer the road less traveled, start from Naples and head east along Route 41.

AIR

Many visitors to the Everglades arrive via Miami. **Miami International Airport** (Wilcox Field) is a megaport served by numerous domestic/international carriers, including American Airlines, Continental Airlines, Delta Air Lines, Northwest Airlines, Trans World Airlines, United Airlines and USAir.

There are even more international carriers: Aerolineas Argentinas, Aeromexico, AeroPeru, Air Canada, Air France, Air Jamaica, ALM, Aviateca, Bahamasair, British Airways, BWIA, Cayman Airways, El Al, Halisa, Iberia, LAB, Lacsa, Lan Chile, Lufthansa, Mexicana, TACA, Varig, Viasa and Virgin Atlantic.

BUS

Greyhound Bus Lines bring passengers from all over the country to the Miami area. The main Miami terminal is at 4111 Northwest 27th Street. The Homestead terminal is at 5 Northeast 3rd Road. ~ 800-231-2222.

Astro Tours offers daily shuttles between Miami and New York. ~ 2909 Northwest 7th Street, Miami; 305-643-6423. **Omnibus La Cubana** has daily service between Miami and Virginia, Philadelphia, New York and New Jersey. It also services Tampa, Orlando, Atlanta, South Carolina and North Carolina. ~ 1101 Northwest 22nd Avenue, Miami; 305-541-1700, 800-365-8001, fax 305-643-2165; www.lacubanabus.com.

TRAIN

Amtrak (800-872-7245) will bring you into Miami from the northeastern states on its "Silver Meteor" or "Silver Star." From the western United States, there are three trains to Miami by way of Chicago and Washington, D.C. The Miami station is at 8303 Northwest 37th Avenue. There is also a station in Homestead at 5 Northeast 3rd Road; 305-247-2040.

CAR RENTALS

Avis Rent A Car (800-331-1212), **Budget Rent A Car** (800-527-0700), **Dollar Rent A Car** (800-800-4000), **Hertz Rent A Car** (800-654-3131) and **National Interrent** (800-328-4567) are represented at both the Miami and South Florida airports.

Companies offering free airport pickup in Miami are **Quality Rent A Car** (305-871-3930), **Capital Rent A Car** (305-871-5050), **Alamo Rent A Car** (800-327-9633), **Biscayne Auto Rentals** (800-688-0721), **Enterprise Rent A Car** (800-325-8007), **Interamerican**

Car Rental (800-327-1278), Demo A Car (305-649-7012) and
Value Rent A Car (800-468-2583).

For an aerial view of the Ten Thousands Islands area on the
western side of Everglades National Park, consider a flightseeing
trip with **10,000 Islands Aero-Tours**. Low-level 15- to 60-minute
flightseeing tours buzz over 35 miles of the park with views of
sawgrass prairies, cypress forests and tiny islands dotting the waters. Kids 12 and under fly free. Closed May through October.
~ Everglades Airport, Route 29, Everglades City; 941-695-3296.

**AERIAL
TOURS**

THREE

The Keys

The Florida Keys are a narrow, gently curving chain of subtropical islands that mark the meeting of the Atlantic Ocean and the Gulf of Mexico off the tip of Florida. "Key" comes from the Spanish word *cayo*, meaning "small island," though it is said that the earliest explorers designated this particular group *Los Mártires*, for the land appeared to them as a succession of suffering martyrs lying low on the horizon.

Until early in this century, the Keys were accessible only by boat. Isolated bits of jungly land, they attracted only the hardiest of adventurers and those who, for whatever legal or illegal reasons, desired to get away from civilization. The Keys' relatively brief history is dotted with pirates, salvagers, smugglers, struggling farmers and fisherfolk. In contrast, today these islands are easy to get to and represent one of the country's prime travel destinations.

In 1912, developer Henry Flagler, spurred by dreams of carrying sportsmen to luxurious fishing camps and freight to ships sailing from Key West to Cuba and Central America, completed his greatest project, a railroad from Florida City to Key West. The remarkable line crossed three dozen islands over bridges spanning lengths from less than fifty feet to seven miles. The state's worst recorded hurricane destroyed the railroad in 1935, but its sturdy bridges and trestles became the links for the Overseas Highway, which would make these out-to-sea islands accessible to anyone who could drive, hike or bike the hundred-plus miles from the mainland to Key West.

Some of the Keys are so narrow that you can watch the sun rise over the Atlantic and see it set into the Gulf of Mexico just by strolling across the road. To the east of the chain lie the continental United States' only living coral reefs, popular with divers, snorkelers and passengers in glass-bottom boats. Because of these protective reefs, there is little surf, hence few sandy beaches in the Keys, a surprise to most visitors.

Time, folks claim, means little in the Keys. Visitors soon discover that slowing down is both easy and essential, especially if there's a traffic problem on the Overseas Highway (Route 1) or when the weather is too good to pass up, which it is most of the time. The Keys are basically vacation and retirement havens these days, now that wrecked sailing ships no longer yield up their booty on the rocky reefs, now that the sponge beds are gone and the commercial fishing industry has greatly dwindled. Romantics call these Keys "America's Caribbean Islands," "the islands you can drive to" and even "the last resort." Accommodations range from crowded RV and trailer parks to motels with a boat dock for each room to luxurious resorts. Dining runs the gamut from shrimp boils beside a dock to gourmet feasting in sedate restaurants. The basic fare, naturally, is seafood.

Fishing, boating and diving are the main sports of the Keys. Marinas lie on both sides of many of the islands; you can put out a rod for game fish from unused bridges as well as from classy yachts. Each of the centers of population claim to be the best of something, whether it be fishing, diving, relaxing, eating or partying.

Largest of all the islands, Key Largo is the gateway to the Keys and the beginning of the 113-mile journey to Key West. As Route 1 meanders out to sea, it passes through populated areas that could be anywhere in the country, with chain motels and restaurants, little shopping areas and ever-increasing development. But that's where the similarity ends, for this is a water-borne highway, heading into magnificent sunsets, bordered by sea or mangroves or marinas and even bits of surviving junglelike hammocks. Alongside it runs the vital viaduct, a huge pipe carrying water from the mainland. These dependent islands, though surrounded by the sea, once offered little but rainwater for drinking.

Closest Key to John Pennekamp Coral Reef State Park, Key Largo is the premier diving site of the Keys. Less than 20 miles farther along, Islamorada, on Upper Matecumbe Key, is centerpiece of a group known as the "purple isles," thanks to an explorer who probably named them for the violet sea snails that thrived there.

The region is famous for sportfishing and was once the prosperous headquarters for wreckers. The next good-sized center of population is the town of Marathon on Vaca Key. The whole area is a popular winter resort and choice fishing spot.

Crossing the famous Seven Mile Bridge, Route 1 enters the Lower Keys, whose population center is Big Pine Key. The flora and fauna here are different from much of the rest of the Keys. Big Pine is home to the endangered tiny Key deer. One of the Keys' few fine beaches is found on nearby Bahia Honda Key. From here on, the population thins out considerably until Route 1 approaches Key West (presented in detail in Chapter Four), almost the outermost region of the state. Only the Dry Tortugas lie beyond.

One might suspect that the Keys, being such a narrow chain of islands with a single highway running through them, could not provide any "hidden" sites to explore. But they are there for the finding, little pockets of natural wilderness that have so far survived the encroaching civilization, small restaurants away from the highway, quiet lodgings on out-of-the-way islands, bits of history and treasure out to sea. Though winter is the chief tourist season in the Keys, breezes keep the days pleasant and the mosquitoes down most of the year. Rates are considerably lower in the summer.

So, if you are planning a trip to the Keys, get ready to slow down, to relax, to veer away from the fast-food chains along Route 1, to enjoy some sunsets, do a little fishing and find out what hidden pleasures the Keys have in store.

Note: Mile markers, often called mile posts, can be seen each mile along Route 1 in the Keys. They appear on the right shoulder of the road as small green signs with white numbers, beginning with Mile Marker (MM) 126 just south of Florida City and ending at MM 0 in Key West. When asking for directions in the Keys, your answer will likely refer to a Mile Marker number. We use them throughout this chapter.

▼▼▼▼▼▼▼▼▼▼
Key Largo

Key Largo is the first of the Keys you will reach along the Great Overseas Highway, Route 1, when you head south from Florida City. Motels, resorts and campgrounds abound through much of this, the largest of the Keys. Both the island and its main town are called "Key Largo," a name made famous by the spellbinding 1948 film about crime and a hurricane. You'll still hear a lot about the movie today, and a few local spots claim to have been featured briefly.

The island's main thoroughfare, with its "any-strip-U.S.A." fast-food ambience, tends to disappoint some visitors who had expected a more subtle tropical-island feeling. But there's also the overwhelming assortment of dive shops, which point to something that makes Key Largo unique indeed: just a few miles offshore lies the country's only living coral reef outside Hawaii. The jewel of Key Largo is the John Pennekamp Coral Reef State Park, the only underwater state park in the continental United States. Here are facilities to introduce even the most confirmed landlubber to the sea kingdom and its living treasures.

Key Largo has a few other interesting sights, a couple of historic spots, plenty of shopping and eating opportunities and a wide variety of accommodations. Many visitors, especially city dwellers from Miami and environs, make Key Largo their sole Keys destination.

To get there, you can travel the busy, narrow Route 1, with its "crocodile crossing" warnings, or go via the slower Card Sound Road. The latter features a high toll bridge that affords good views of the mangrove swamps and a real feel for the early Keys, when fishermen lived in functional shacks and chain eateries were still to come.

Soon after arriving on the Key, you'll reach the hiking/biking path that begins at Mile Marker 106 and parallels Route 1 for about 20 miles. It ties in with a short nature trail, passes the John Pennekamp Coral Reef State Park, follows an old road to a county park and leads to some historic sites.

SIGHTS   For lots of good information on the Key Largo area, stop at the **Key Largo Chamber of Commerce**. ~ MM 106, Key Largo; 305-451-1414, 800-822-1088, fax 305-451-4726; keylargo.org, e-mail klchamber@aol.com.

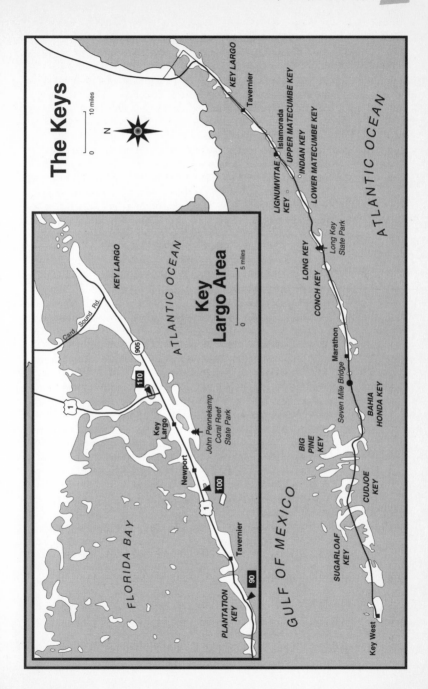

The Keys

N

0 _____ 10 miles

KEY LARGO
Tavernier
Islamorada
LIGNUMVITAE KEY
UPPER MATECUMBE KEY
INDIAN KEY
LOWER MATECUMBE KEY
LONG KEY
Long Key State Park
CONCH KEY
ATLANTIC OCEAN

Key Largo Area

0 _____ 5 miles

KEY LARGO
Card Sound Rd.
905
110
1
Key Largo
John Pennekamp Coral Reef State Park
Newport
100
1
Tavernier
90
PLANTATION KEY

ATLANTIC OCEAN

FLORIDA BAY

GULF OF MEXICO

BIG PINE KEY
Marathon
Seven Mile Bridge
BAHIA HONDA KEY
CUDJOE KEY
SUGARLOAF KEY
Key West

Island Smoke Shop is where Cuban master cigar rollers ply their craft, and the air is redolent as a result. A visit to the "humidor," the back room where the air is kept a constant 70°, refreshes the weary and keeps expensive stogies—each one lying in state in its own little sarcophagus—in peak condition. "El Original" is the shop's house brand; its creator, Santiago Cabana, frequently demonstrates the art of rolling. ~ In the Pink Plaza, MM 103.4, Key Largo; 305-453-4014, 800-680-9701, fax 305-453-0448; www.islandsmokeshop.com, e-mail info@islandsmokeshop.com.

Slow down as you approach the short bridge that crosses the **Marvin D. Adams Waterway**, a manmade cut that creates a channel all the way across a narrow section of Key Largo. The banks on either side of the cut are the one place you can really get a good look at the geological makeup of the Upper Keys. There are fine examples of petrified staghorn coral, coral heads and other pieces of the ancient coral reef on which the islands are built. ~ MM 103.

To observe treasures recovered from Florida's reefs, visit the **Maritime Museum of the Florida Keys**. Resembling a 15th-century castle, the "treasure castle" contains historical exhibits and glittering riches. The spoils on display include a jewel-studded gold medallion, Chinese "blue and white" porcelain, a collection of sea-salvaged coins and rotating exhibits of treasures from shipwrecked Spanish galleons in the Caribbean. If they are very strong, visitors may lift an 80-pound silver bar. Closed Sunday. Admission. ~ MM 102.6, Key Largo; 305-451-6444.

Whether or not you're a snorkeler or scuba diver, **John Pennekamp Coral Reef State Park** offers many ways to enjoy this underwater treasure (see the "Beaches & Parks" section below). An excellent visitors center features a giant reconstruction of a living patch reef in a circular aquarium and other exhibits of the undersea world, mangrove swamps and hardwood hammocks. Admission. ~ Route 1, MM 102.5, Key Largo; 305-451-1202; www.dep.state.fl.us/parks. Scuba and snorkeling tours, as well as glass-bottom boat tours, are offered daily. ~ 305-451-1621; www.pennekamppark.com.

HIDDEN ►   Hidden under the Atlantic waters, the **Christ of the Deep** statue is a favorite destination of divers in the state park. This nine-foot-high bronze statue, located in the Key Largo National Marine Sanctuary, was created by an Italian sculptor and given to the Underwater Society of America by the Florida Board of Historic Memorials. A duplicate of *Christ of the Abysses* in the Mediterranean Sea near Genoa, its uplifted arms are designed to be a welcome to "all who lived for the sea and who, in the name of the sea they so dearly loved, found their eternal peace."

Glass-bottom boat cruises to the reef are also available on the **Key Largo Princess**, which sails to Molasses Reef in the National

Marine Sanctuary. Choose from daily public cruises as well as sunset cruises with underwater lights. ~ MM 100, Holiday Inn docks, Key Largo; 305-451-4655, fax 305-453-9553.

Atlantic bottle-nosed dolphins can often be spotted swimming and cavorting in Key Largo area waters, especially on the bay side. For a closer experience with these delightful and intelligent sea mammals, make an appointment to visit **Dolphins Plus**, one of several places in the Keys where you can actually swim with dolphins (although you must be at least seven years old to swim). Basically a research center, Dolphins Plus studies how dolphins relate to human beings. They are also researching the dolphin's role in "zoo-therapy" with disabled individuals. Admission. ~ MM 99, Key Largo; 305-451-1993, fax 305-451-3710; www.dolphins plus.com.

◄ HIDDEN

The little town of **Tavernier** boasts a bit of history that local folks are hanging onto as best they can. Along with the Old Methodist Church on Route 1, a few **old frame houses** with big shutters for protection against hurricanes remain, mementos of the farming days before pizza parlors and gas stations. You can see them if you wander the few side streets and peer into the dense grove of tropical trees. ~ Around MM 92.

◄ HIDDEN

Watch for an unobtrusive entrance just south of Key Largo on the bay side. **Florida Keys Wild Bird Rehabilitation Center** is a nonprofit organization—it started with one caring woman and continues to grow with the help of some dedicated volunteers—that cares for ailing avians. Stop by and get close up and personal with wild birds that you would usually see only from very far away. You'll find it somewhat heartrending when you realize that much of the damage is done by man's inhumanity to his fellow creatures, but heartwarming at the same time to find that there are

◄ HIDDEN

✔ **CHECK THESE OUT—UNIQUE SIGHTS**
- Lend a hand—or a heart—at the **Florida Keys Wild Bird Rehabilitation Center**, a nonprofit organization that tends to ailing avians. *page 73*
- Learn about the tragic history of the ten-acre island of **Indian Key State Historic Site**, a town destroyed not by overpartying but by an Indian attack in 1840. *page 87*
- Cross from Marathon to the Sunshine Key via the newer **Seven Mile Bridge**, which is set parallel to the old bridge, the "longest fishing pier in the world." *page 107*
- Get up early and see if you can spot the three-feet-high Key deer, the world's tiniest, at the **National Key Deer Refuge**, 8500 acres set aside for this endangered species. *page 108*

still many people who care deeply. ~ MM 93.6, Key Largo; 305-852-4486, 888-826-3811, fax 305-852-3186; florida-keys.fl.us/flkeyswildbird.htm, e-mail fkwbc@reefnet.com.

For Everglades airboat rides and sightseeing tours, contact **Captain Ray Cramer** (said to be one of the best authorities on the region), an excellent guide and spinner of regional tales. Call for reservations and directions. ~ Key Largo; 305-852-5339, 305-221-9888; e-mail airboattours@aaof.com.

LODGING   Accommodations are numerous in the Keys, from small motels to condominiums to chain hotels to luxurious resorts. Almost all offer something special, from a dock for snorkeling to extensive dive and fishing charters. Lodging information may be obtained from the **Florida Keys Visitors Bureau**. ~ Mallory Square, 402 Wall Street, Key West; 305-294-2587, 800-352-5397, fax 305-294-7806; www.fla-keys.com, e-mail kwchamber@compuserve.com.

Calling itself the PADI "gold palm resort," **Kelly's On the Bay & the Aqua-Nuts Dive Resort** offers Caribbean-style charm where diving enthusiasts can almost roll out of bed and into the water. Right on the bay, on the sunset side of Key Largo, Kelly's has 32 comfortably furnished rooms and efficiencies, a dive center, a pool, a hot tub, two 42-foot dive boats and both PADI and NAUI scuba courses. Kayaks are provided free of charge to guests. Holidays require a three-day minimum stay. Breakfast is included. ~ MM 104.2, Key Largo; 305-451-1622, 800-226-0415, fax 305-451-4623; www.aqua-nuts.com, e-mail kellysmo@aol.com. MODERATE TO ULTRA-DELUXE.

The **Marriott Key Largo Bay Beach Resort** impresses with its rambling four-story sun-washed buildings, embellished with white wrought iron and coral rock pillars, and looking across a great sweep of shimmering bay. Along the bay is more fantasy design, including a suspension bridge and numerous peak-roofed gazebos, a swimming pool and a manmade beach with attendant lounge chairs. Only 20 of the 153 rooms do not command a bay view; most rooms feature plush surroundings that include white-washed oak and vibrant tropical patterns, as well as spacious balconies.

BOGIE'S BOAT

If you want a very small bit of nostalgia, you can usually see the original *African Queen* (the little boat in which Humphrey Bogart and Katharine Hepburn battled the jungle and found romance) on display at the Holiday Inn docks. If the ship's gone for the day, you can have a look at the *Thayer IV*, the boat seen in the Hepburn film *On Golden Pond*. ~ MM 100, Key Largo.

Amenities include a restaurant, café, tiki bar, nine-hole miniature golf course, tennis court, day spa, dive shop and exercise room. ~ MM 103.8, Key Largo; 305-453-0000, 800-932-9332, fax 305-453-0093; fla-keys.com/keylargo/marriott.htm, e-mail bay beach@reef.net. ULTRA-DELUXE.

Jules' Undersea Lodge is so hidden that you can't even see it   ◄ HIDDEN when you get there because it's 22 feet below the surface of a tropical lagoon. You don't have to be an advanced scuba diver to get into your air-conditioned quarters (there are two rooms for guests and an entertainment room); the staff will give you lessons. The reward is a unique underwater experience—with fish swimming by your 42-inch windows, no noise except the comforting reminder of the air support system and the knowledge that you are staying in the only underwater hotel in the world. All meals are included in the rate. ~ 51 Shoreland Drive, near MM 103.2, Key Largo; 305-451-2353, fax 305-451-4789; www.jul.com, e-mail info@jul.com. ULTRA-DELUXE.

Tropical trees, dense foliage, ibis in the yard and a nice little bayside beach reinforce the claim at **Largo Lodge** that "paradise can be reasonable." For the reasonable price you get one of six very nice, roomy apartments with a kitchen, a living room and a big screened porch. The place is beautifully maintained and the owner is delightful. Adults only. ~ MM 101.5, Key Largo; 305-451-0424, 800-468-4378; www.largolodge.com. DELUXE.

Marina del Mar Resort is one of those places with everything—lodging, marina, restaurant and nightclub, tennis courts, fitness center, pool and diving services. On the oceanside of the island, it is convenient to the popular nearby diving waters. The one- to three-bedroom suites are spacious and airy with tile floors; some have whirlpool tubs. There are also studios with full kitchens. Continental breakfast included. ~ MM 100, Key Largo; 305-451-4107, 800-451-3483, fax 305-451-1891; www.marinadel mar.com, e-mail marina-del-mar@msn.com. DELUXE TO ULTRA-DELUXE.

The **Sunset Cove Motel** is really a complex of small, old-time, plain but neat rooms and apartments. This modest spot has a real old Keys feel. It's set among life-sized carved panthers and pelicans and enhanced with talking parrots and wonderful, relaxing Jamaican swings in the shade of thatched chickees huts. Guests may catch sight of a manatee (if you're lucky!), watch the pelicans and use their paddleboats and canoes. ~ MM 99.5, Key Largo; 305-451-0705, fax 305-451-5609; www.digitalpark.com/suncove, e-mail suncove99@aol.com. MODERATE.

The gardens at bayfront **Kona Kai** are filled with fruit trees—jackfruit, breadfruit and Key lime—and there are stands of great old gumbo-limbos. Four low-slung buildings with tin roofs are tucked among the flora, their 11 suites tiled in pale ceramic and

furnished with rattan and tropically patterned fabrics. The feeling is very villagelike. And very new, thanks to an injection of $750,000 in 1996. A tennis court, heated pool and jacuzzi, fishing pier with dockage, a perfect little white sand beach—everything is here. The lobby doubles as an art gallery. ~ MM 97.8, Key Largo; 305-852-7200, 800-365-7829, fax 305-852-4629; www. konakairesort.com, e-mail konakai@aol.com. DELUXE TO ULTRA-DELUXE.

Select from motel rooms with refrigerators and microwaves, efficiencies, or fully equipped cottages at the modest and clean **Bay Harbor Lodge**. Shaded by palms, poincianas and frangipani, this lodging offers a small, swimmable sandy beach on Florida Bay, a heated pool, and free use of the dock and its canoes, kayaks and paddleboats. Pets welcome. ~ MM 97.8, Key Largo; phone/fax 305-852-5695, 800-385-0986; www.thefloridakeys.com/bayhar borlodge, e-mail harborkl@aol.com. MODERATE.

Here is a resort that reminds one of what the Keys used to look like. The **Westin Beach Resort Key Largo**, obscured as it is in hardwood hammock, offers a glimpse of a natural habitat. Footpaths wend along the property, and signs point to wild coffee plants and a mahogany tree—surely one of the few remaining in the Upper Keys. The 200 balconied rooms are far from woodsy, offering luxuries such as marble vanities with theater lighting, cushy carpets and coffee makers. Fourth-floor rooms, with views of the bay instead of the forest, are most coveted. Another plus: twin swimming pools—one for families, the other for adults. ~ MM 97, Key Largo; 305-852-5553, 800-826-1006, fax 305-852-8669; www.1800keylargo.com. ULTRA-DELUXE.

At the **Stone Ledge Hotel** you'll have access to a nice dock, a small bayside beach, a shady yard and a pleasant motel room, ef-

●◆

✔ CHECK THESE OUT—UNIQUE LODGING

- *Moderate:* Picnic beneath the coconut palms at **Hidden Harbor Motel**, which boasts its own aquarium. *page 102*
- *Moderate to ultra-deluxe:* Pick an assortment of bananas, figs and papayas for breakfast at **Hopp-Inn Guest House**, one of the few bed and breakfasts in the Keys. *page 99*
- *Deluxe to ultra-deluxe:* Experience the villagelike aura of **Kona Kai**, where you can wander the gardens and do a little fishing just steps away from your suite. *page 75*
- *Ultra-deluxe:* Re-create your favorite pose at **The Moorings**, a lodge sought out by fashion magazines for its tropical-safari chic. *page 90*

Budget: under $80   Moderate: $80–$120   Deluxe: $120–$200   Ultra-deluxe: over $200

ficiency or studio apartment in the long, low cream-colored stucco building. Typical of many of the area's mom-and-pop motels, this one is quite pleasant. Ask for a unit away from the highway. ~ 95320 Overseas Highway, Key Largo; 305-852-8114. MODERATE.

The innovative seafood dishes at **Sundowner's** won't disappoint. It's a casual but classy place, with friendly waiters who call you by name. The glasswalled dining room faces the bay for splendid sunset gazing. There are steak, pasta and chicken dishes, but best are the nightly fish specials such as crabmeat-stuffed yellowtail with béarnaise sauce, fresh Florida lobster tail and grilled or blackened mahimahi. ~ MM 103.9, Key Largo; 305-451-4502, fax 305-453-9661. MODERATE TO DELUXE.

DINING

Within Marriott's Key Largo Bay Beach Resort, **Gus' Grille** appears as a large, airy space with natural woods, coral-rock walls and a wood-burning pizza oven. Window walls overlook Florida Bay for a spectacular show each evening as the setting sun turns the waters crimson and gold. The food is as gorgeously presented as the view, but, alas, lacks character. But the pizza from the aforementioned traditional oven is outstanding. Outdoors, by the pool, you can sip a piña colada while watching the dive boats come and go. Breakfast, lunch and dinner. ~ MM 103.8, Key Largo; 305-453-0029, fax 305-453-0093; fla-keys.com/keylargo/marriott.htm, e-mail baybeach@reefnet.com. DELUXE.

South of the Border, while purporting to refer to the land of tacos and tequila, really seems to mean the Dade-Monroe county line. The menu is an eclectic mix of the same down-home favorites enjoyed there and just enough Mexican specialities to justify the name (try the fajitas). Catch the game on one of its nine TVs. A breakfast buffet is served on weekends. ~ In the Pink Plaza, MM 103.4, Key Largo; 305-451-3307, fax 305-451-6060. BUDGET TO MODERATE.

The Fish House is a good place for an introduction to typical Keys fare. Conch chowder is "in the red," thick and just spicy enough to suit most palates. Other Keys standards include cracked conch, stone crab in season and the catch-of-the-day prepared at least ten different ways. The tiny lobby features a real fish market; decor includes a ceiling hung with nets and lighted with fish-type Christmas lights. Closed mid-September for two and a half weeks. ~ MM 102.4, Key Largo; 305-451-4665, 888-451-4665, fax 305-451-1727; www.fishhouse.com, e-mail fishhouse@pennekamp.com. MODERATE TO DELUXE.

At the traffic light at MM 99.5, turn toward the ocean and follow side streets until you come to **Calypso's Seafood Grille**. Opened in 1997, this open-air terracotta patio is the domain of Chef Cad, a wiry, witty, chain-smoking vegetarian who knows not only how to cook great food but how to create it. He buys his

◄ *HIDDEN*

seafood every morning from Key Largo Fisheries, located just across the marina, then turns it into dishes like wet black dolphin chargrilled and topped with seared pepperoncinis and feta cheese. Pitchers of sangria are loaded with fresh fruit and dusted with grated cinnamon. His yellowtail Grand Marnier is crispy, light and buttery. Closed Tuesday. ~ 1 Seagate Boulevard, Key Largo; 305-451-0600. MODERATE.

Hidden within a small grove of large coconut palms is the lilac canopy that leads to **Snook's Bayside**, a romantic place with high-backed chairs and displays of family antiques and fine china. This is an intimate spot for fine dining on seafood, Angus beef, veal and chicken inside or out on the patio, complemented by a fine wine selection. A waterfront, all-you-can-eat breakfast brunch buffet rounds out the week on Sunday. ~ MM 99.9, Key Largo; 305-453-3799, fax 305-453-3793; www.snooks.com. MODERATE TO DELUXE.

Sushi Nami is a terrific sushi bar that has a tatami room where you can curl up barefoot on big, satiny cushions. Enjoy traditional fare such as teriyaki, tempura, soba noodles and sashimi. The mounted fish on the walls help you remember you're in the Keys. No lunch served on the weekend. ~ MM 99.5, Key Largo; 305-453-9798. MODERATE.

Cafe Largo serves good Italian food—all the traditional pasta, chicken and veal dishes plus excellent daily specials using yellowtail and dolphin, stone crabs, lobster and other local seafood. The Mediterranean setting is indoors and typical of family-style Italian places. Dinner only. ~ 305-451-4885. On the same property, connected by a walkway, is the **Bayside Grill**. Diners enjoy steak and seafood dishes in the glass-enclosed dining room situated on the waterfront. ~ MM 99.5, Key Largo; 305-451-3380, fax 305-451-4467. MODERATE TO DELUXE.

If you tire of seafood or want a little down-home mainland food, stop at **Mrs. Mac's Kitchen**. This shack-style eatery has about the best chili east of Texas and pita bread concoctions almost too fat to bite down on. The chefs cook up huge breakfasts, broil delicious steaks and feature different theme specials (Italian, meat, fresh local seafood, etc.) for dinner every night. The place is small, with more varieties of beers than seats, so it's noisy and fun. Closed Sunday. ~ MM 99.4, Key Largo; 305-451-3722. BUDGET TO MODERATE.

Ballyhoo's serves the best breakfast in the Upper Keys: mashed potato omelets and Swedish oatmeal pancakes, seafood omelets with hollandaise and good bloody marys and mimosas. The atmosphere is pure Keys: funky tables and chairs, a grumbling wall-unit air conditioner and a view of the highway through windows filmed with coral rock dust. The lunch and dinner menus feature seafood, chicken and steak entrées. ~ MM 98, Key Largo; 305-852-0822. MODERATE TO DELUXE.

Slow down for children and pets as you pass through Mandalay trailer park to reach the historic **Mandalay Restaurant, Marina and Tiki Bar**. This place is so "old Florida Keys"—from the driftwood to the frayed ropes—it could double as a '70s movie set. Nestled on busy Rock Harbor, Mandalay attracts an eclectic mix that includes locals, fishermen, attorneys, writers and adventurous tourists. This arrangement of shack-like structures offers seating at the funky inside bar or at picnic tables on the deck over the water. Featuring seafood straight off the boat, favorite entrées include grouper stuffed with crab meat, seafood alfredo, and Florida lobster. Key lime pie is made on the premises. Don't be surprised if the place is packed: folks will tolerate the tight quarters for the food, which is served until 11 p.m., and nightly entertainment. ~ MM 97.5, 80 East 2nd Street, Key Largo; 305-852-5450. MODERATE TO DELUXE.

◄ HIDDEN

Lauren Bacall and Humphrey Bogart, the stars of the 1948 movie *Key Largo*, apparently never set foot on the island for filming.

Old Tavernier Restaurant grew so popular it had to relocate to a bigger spot just to accommodate the nightly mobs. Now, between the spacious dining room and outdoor veranda along a mangrove canal, there's plenty of room to enjoy what Old Tavernier does best: huge portions of sauce-drenched pastas that arrive bubbling at your table. Nightly specials often depart from pasta with such dishes as rack of lamb, grilled veal chops and fresh fish. Dinner only. ~ MM 90.3, Tavernier; 305-852-6012, fax 305-852-1999. MODERATE.

Key Largo is the main spot for Upper Keys shoppers, so there are shopping centers, groceries and all the functional kinds of stores you might need, as well as tacky souvenir and T-shirt shops.

SHOPPING

There are dive shops all along the highway of Key Largo. One of the premier popular full-service shops is the dockside **Captain Slate's Atlantis Dive Center**. You'll find masks, fins, weight belts, tanks, wet suits and so on for sale and for rent, as well as T-shirts and swimwear. If you want an underwater wedding or would like to meet some dolphins at sea, Atlantis will arrange that, along with their standard assortment of reef trips. ~ 51 Garden Cove, off MM 106.5, Key Largo; 305-451-1325, fax 305-451-9240; www.pennekamp.com/atlantis, e-mail capslate@safari.net.

A sign at the entrance to **Largo Cargo Co.** reads, "Warning, Jimmy Buffett played here." Proceed accordingly—the king Parrothead's music and clothing line cannot be avoided. Expectedly bright and cheery, this store successfully displays tacky novelties alongside tasteful gifts. Pick up lightweight, easy-packing kites

Text continued on page 82.

Kingdoms
Under
the Sea

The unique wonders of the Keys and Everglades do not end at their shorelines. From the shallows of Biscayne Bay to the deeps at the brink of the Gulf Stream lies a vast underwater wilderness unlike any other natural region in the continental United States. Close in are vast carpets of sea grasses, birthplaces and nurseries for shrimp and fish and Florida spiny lobsters, temporary refuges for endangered manatees and sea turtles.

A few miles out lies the coral reef. Here divers can explore a beautiful, silent underwater world of brilliant colors and subdued hues, of curious shapes and vibrant darting creatures. In some places its long spiny fingers almost touch the sun-sparkling surface of the sea. In other regions twisting corridors lead to secret caves at depths almost beyond the reach of life.

The reef is actually a living kingdom made up of billions of little colonies of tiny animals called polyps that snare passing microorganisms with their tentacles. They live in small cups of limestone that they secrete around themselves. The unusual and varied shapes of these cups give them their names: elkhorn and staghorn coral, star coral and brain coral, lettuce, pillar and flower corals.

The coral castles with their exquisite sea gardens host many other sea creatures, such as snails, lobsters, mollusks, crabs, sea cucumbers, starfish, sand dollars and sponges. Around the walls, through the corridors and down the paths swim exotic fish, as many as 300 species of them. The corals grow very slowly, some less than an inch a year, as each new generation builds on the skeleton of its ancestors. Though sturdy in appearance, they are extremely fragile and can be destroyed by changes in water conditions and by careless divers and boaters. In the early Florida tourist days, huge sections of the reef were laid waste by entrepreneurs collecting sea life novelties for eager souvenir shoppers. Coral was harvested with crowbars and cranes; the queen conch population, symbol and food source for early settlers, virtually disappeared.

Many sections of this exotic underwater world are now protected, with tough penalties for even minor assaults on the fragile environment. Mooring buoys for divers and snorkelers have been placed in the most popular areas, to protect the reef from damaging anchors.

The northern end of the reef lies in **Biscayne National Park**. ~ Headquarters at Convoy Point, east of Homestead; 305-230-7275; www.nps.gov/bisc. East of Key Largo, **John Pennekamp Coral Reef State Park**, in combination with the **Key Largo Coral Reef National Marine Sanctuary**, encompasses about 178 nautical square miles of reef and sea grass beds. ~ MM 102.5; 305-451-1202. Southeast of Big Pine Key, the **Florida Keys National Marine Sanctuary** covers a five-square-mile area of spectacular coral formations and exceptionally clear waters. ~ Headquarters at 216 Ann Street, Key West; 305-292-0311. (For more information on the parks, see the area "Beaches & Parks" sections in this chapter.) Reef formations continue down through the ocean to the Dry Tortugas (see "Fort Jefferson" in Chapter Four).

Visitors don't have to be adept scuba divers to explore the wonders and surprises of this underwater world. Even first-time snorkelers reap rich rewards, floating on the surface in the shallowest areas where colors are often brightest and sea life most spectacular. Professional dive shops equip snorkelers and divers and, along with various park headquarters, advise on prime locations, water conditions and transportation options. (It is usually recommended that you avoid charters that transport both snorkelers and scuba divers at the same time.) Underwater visibility averages 40 to 60 feet and may reach 100 feet or more in calm summer weather. Some coral formations rise to within a few feet of the surface.

If you want to catch a glimpse of the reef without getting wet at all, board one of the glass-bottom boats setting out from several locations throughout the Keys, or stop at the living reef exhibit at Pennekamp Park or the Key West Aquarium.

Another underwater attraction is the host of wrecked ships (some claim there are more than 500 of them) that met their fates on the reef in the days before lighthouses marked safe passage through the Florida Straits. Tales of lost treasure and the challenge of archaeological discovery keep hopeful divers returning again and again.

and windsocks or a baseball cap with fake dreadlocks attached. The frog and shark puppets make cute gifts for kids. ~ MM 103.1, Key Largo; 305-451-4242, fax 305-451-3228.

The **Pink Plaza** is one-stop shopping, Keys-style. Among the noteworthy shops are **Fundora Art Gallery** (305-451-2200, fax 305-453-1153; e-mail ThomasFund@aol.com), which specializes in oils, prints and watercolors, as well as Tomas Fundora originals. Closed Saturday and Sunday. The **Island Smoke Shop** (305-453-4014, 800-680-9701, fax 305-453-0448; www.islandsmokeshop.com, e-mail info@islandsmokeshop.com) features cigars rolled by Cuban masters. ~ MM 103.4, Key Largo.

A well-known underwater photographer offers all the necessary equipment—for sale or for rent—for capturing your diving and snorkeling adventures on still or video film at **Stephen Frink Photographic**. He will also process and enlarge your slides. Closed Sunday. ~ MM 102.5, Key Largo; 305-451-3737, fax 305-451-5147; www.stephenfrink.com, e-mail frinkphoto@aol.com.

Too bad **T-Shirt City/Sandal Factory** has such a tacky exterior—neon yellow and blue bubble awnings and giant logos shouting toward the highway—because the merchandise inside reminds of a tropical boutique. The sandal selection for men, women and kids is terrific, and so are the prices. You'll find the latest platform sandals in leather, wood and foam, deck shoes and quality flip-flops, with brands by Mia, Beach Club, Birkenstock and Sebago. There are tasteful T-shirts, linen walking shorts, tropically patterned dresses and shirts, and great straw hats. ~ MM 102, Key Largo; 305-453-9644, fax 305-453-9604; www.sandaloutlet.com, e-mail cliff@reefnet.com.

The **Book Nook** has a large variety of books about the area and Florida in general, as well as maps and charts for divers. They also keep a good selection of classics as well as plenty of recent bestsellers, magazines and newspapers (British and German, too) to keep you busy when you've had too much sun, and "island" music to relax to. ~ MM 100, Waldorf Plaza, Key Largo; 305-451-1468.

Junk is about the last thing you'll find at **Josie's Junk Alley**. Small but unique, this consignment store sells deco, vintage and modern clothing, jewelry and those special "one-of-a-kind" items. ~ MM 99.5, Key Largo; 305-451-1995.

Since 1982, the **Pink Junktique** has specialized in unusual, artsy, funky, high-quality "everything" from the '40s and '50s, from clothing, jewelry and furniture to baskets, books and bowls—all priced to sell. ~ MM 99.5, Key Largo; 305-451-4347.

In a little Quonset hut housing **Island Feet**, you'll step into one of the largest selection of sandals—Birkenstock, Reef Rider, Teva, Rainbow and Kino's—in the Keys. ~ MM 94, Tavernier; 305-852-5691.

The three floors of **Grant Gallery** are stuffed with stylish art and antiques—hand-painted bird cages, clay urns, animal print lamps, washed pine tables, oak and cherry armoires—and flowing, comfortable clothing for women. Clothing prices are exceptionally good, plus you can bargain. ~ MM 92, Tavernier; 305-853-0562.

Several places in the Keys specialize in embossed and hand-painted handbags, some ready-made, many with nautical designs, and others done to suit your own special wishes. You can find them at the **Florida Keys Handbag Factory**, where they also sell T-shirts and "island" clothing. Closed Sunday. ~ MM 91.5, Tavernier; 305-852-8690.

Cover to Cover Books, the only bookstore–coffee house combination in the Keys, is flooded with classical music and the smells of mocha java and almond joy cafés being made. The two former schoolteachers who run it will help you find the right read, from books on Florida and the Keys to gardening, archaeology and mysticism; children's books and games are a specialty. The unusual gifts here include thumb-size tropical watercolors and New Age greeting cards. ~ MM 90, Tavernier; 305-852-1415, fax 305-852-1650; www.cover2cover.com, e-mail c2cbooks@compu source.net.

NIGHTLIFE

Some of the larger hotels and resorts in the area have nightly or weekend entertainment.

If you're willing to experience a raunchy sort of bikers' beach bar in exchange for some possible nostalgia, stop at the **Caribbean Club**. It is claimed that some parts of the movie *Key Largo* were filmed here, and it just may be true. Even if it's not, the sunsets from the deck are terrific. The joint is open from 7 a.m. to 4 a.m. and offers live rock, blues and reggae bands Friday and Saturday nights. ~ MM 104, Key Largo; 305-451-9970.

The twin coral rock and glass gazebos called **Breezers' Tiki Bar** are great for baywatching, especially at sunset, when the canvas shades are drawn up, the tradewinds blow through, and the waitresses serve pricey pastel drinks that match the floor tiles. There's live music Tuesday through Thursday night. Next door, **Gus' After Dark** is Key Largo's only late-night dance club, open Friday and Saturday, complete with live music and revolving strobe lights and a crowd that's mostly mainland Miami. ~ Both located at the Marriott Key Largo Bay Beach Resort, MM 103.5, Key Largo; 305-453-9393, fax 305-453-0093; fla-keys.com/keylargo/marriott. htm, e-mail baybeach@reef.net.

Coconuts is a waterfront spot with live entertainment every night ranging from Top-40 to reggae. Inside, the huge dancefloor has a classy light show; outside, you can enjoy a drink (happy hour is weekdays, 4 to 7 p.m.) on the canopied deck overlooking a canal with boats. Ladies night on Wednesday. ~ MM 100 at Marina del Mar, Key Largo; 305-453-9794.

At **Patrick's Waterfront Bar**, located in Snook's Bayside, the natives gather by car or by boat to watch the sunset and enjoy a friendly drink at the outdoor bar. There is dining seating inside, with live entertainment every evening in the tiki hut. Snook's also has a piano bar inside the restaurant with easy-listening music on the weekends. ~ MM 99.9, Key Largo; 305-453-3799, fax 305-453-3793; www.snooks.com.

Snappers is a restaurant with a great bar alongside a crowded, eventful marina. Every Thursday is "Turtle Club Night," when locals crowd the open-air hut for discounted drinks and SUN-103 Radio broadcasts the daily fishing report. And every April, Snappers stages a reenactment of the Keys' 1982 secession from the United States (a ceremonial secession, in protest to border patrol roadblocks in Florida City, it was followed by a week-long party and a request for U.S. foreign aid). During the reenactment, a miniature bridge to the mainland gets blown up while everyone raises their margaritas to the Conch Republic. ~ MM 94.5, Key Largo; 305-852-5956, fax 305-852-1111; www.theflorida keys.com/snappers.

BEACHES & PARKS

JOHN PENNEKAMP CORAL REEF STATE PARK 🏃 🛶 🚣 🤿 🚤 ⛵ This remarkable place is the first underwater state park in the United States. Together with the adjacent **Key Largo National Marine Sanctuary** (305-852-7717), this park encompasses an area of about 178 nautical square miles, most of which lies out in the Atlantic Ocean north and east of Key Largo. Most visitors come to see the coral formations, seagrass beds and spectacular marine life of the reefs, either by scuba diving, snorkeling or taking a glass-bottom boat tour. Fishing is another popular activity. It's allowed in the mangroves (for mangrove snapper, trout, sheepshead and snook) and in the Atlantic (for gamefish such as kingfish, mackerel and yellowtail). Tropical fish, however, are protected. There are also two small manmade swimming beaches with a replica of a sunken ship offshore. The land section of the park acquaints visitors with mangrove swamps, numerous shore birds and a tropical hardwood hammock with many varieties of indigenous plant life. An excellent visitors center, featuring a replication of a patch reef complete with marine life in a 30,000-gallon aquarium, allows even those who prefer staying on dry land to experience a bit of the underwater world. Other facilities include picnic areas, restrooms, a bathhouse, showers, nature trails, an observation tower, a snack bar, a gift shop, a dive shop, a marina and docks. Day-use fee, $10.75 for a seven-day family vacation pass, plus a $.50 surcharge per person. ~ Entrance at MM

102.5, Key Largo. Much of the park is accessible only by boat; 305-451-1202; www.pennekamppark.com.

▲ There are 47 sites, all with electricity and water, at the state park; $23.69 per night for tent sites, $25.84 per night for hookups.

Private RV and tent campgrounds are nearby. **Key Largo Kampground and Marina** has 38 tent sites and 60 RV sites; $20 to $22 per night for tent sites, $40 to $50 per night for RV sites. ~ MM 101.5, Key Largo; 305-451-1431. **Calusa Camp Resort** has 36 tent sites and 340 RV sites; $25 to $35 per night. The grounds tend to be cramped but offer functional places for divers to stay. ~ MM 101.5, Key Largo; 305-451-0232.

HARRY HARRIS PARK 🏊 🛥 ⛵ 🛶 This county park is one of the few public parks in the area for spending a day beside the ocean. It is spacious, with broad grassy areas and scattered trees. The beach isn't much, but the water is clear and full of fish. Fishing off the pier is not allowed. You can only fish off a boat; the water, however, is shallow. Swimming is also good here. Facilities include picnic areas, restrooms, playgrounds, a basketball court, baseball field and chickee huts. Day-use fee on weekends and holidays, $5 per person. ~ Take Burton Drive at MM 92.5 in Tavernier; it's about a quarter of a mile to the park; 305-852-7161.

The Islamorada area begins at Windley Key (MM 85) and runs through Long Key (below MM 68). The community of Islamorada, on Upper Matecumbe Key, is its center of population. The area's brief ventures have included shipbuilding, tropical fruit and vegetable farming, turtling, sponging and the immensely prosperous business of salvaging shipwrecks. Fishing has always been especially fine in this area, and today tourism is the chief enterprise here.

▼▼▼▼▼▼▼▼▼▼▼
Islamorada Area

The town is a collection of businesses that provide local folk with essentials while inviting visitors to "stay here," "eat here," "party here" and "buy here." Holiday Isle, a gigantic resort and entertainment complex, dominates Windley Key with the latest in youthful party hype.

Laid down about 125,000 years ago, Windley Key is highest in a chain of limestone islands. In the early 1900s, Henry Flagler quarried fill here to build foundations for his Overseas Railroad. One section, **Windley Key Fossil Reef State Geological Site**, has been further cut, revealing fossilized clams, corals, worm holes, and other archaeological treasures from the formerly submerged island. Short, easy-access trails through hardwood hammock lead to the quarry. A visitors center offers explanations and displays. Closed Tuesday and Wednesday. Admission. ~ MM 85.5,

SIGHTS

Windley Key; 305-664-2540, fax 305-664-0713; www.dep.state.
fl.us/parks.

All along Route 1 you'll see signs for boat rentals, diving
cruises and fishing charters. For, as with so much of the Keys,
much of what the area has to offer is out to sea.

This usually calm and beautiful sea was gathered up into a
giant tidal wave on September 2, 1935, that swept away just
about every living thing and manmade object in its wake, including a rescue train full of evacuees. A poignant stone memorial and
the red caboose that houses the **Islamorada Visitors Center** are re-
minders of the storm that also destroyed the remarkable "railroad
that went to the sea." Several other sites, which can be explored
on short boat trips, remind visitors that this Upper Keys region
offers far more than meets the eye. ~ MM 82.5; 305-664-4503,
800-322-5397, fax 305-664-4289; fla-keys.com/islamorada/
index.html, e-mail islacc@ix.netcom.com.

Bud N' Mary's Marina and Dive Center offers occasional boat
cruises that go out to the lighthouse at Alligator Reef, named for
a ship that ran aground here. Along the way you'll have a chance
to do a little snorkeling. ~ MM 79.8, Islamorada, 305-664-2211,
800-344-7352 (dive center); MM 80, 305-664-2461, 800-742-
7945 (marina); www.budnmarys.com.

Stop for a minute at the **Hurricane Monument** to meditate on
the terrible storm of Labor Day 1935. Before the anemometer
blew away, winds were recorded at 200 mph; the barometer fell
to 26.35, one of the lowest pressures ever recorded in the Western
Hemisphere. This moving monument was dedicated in 1937 to the
memory of the 423 people who died in that storm. ~ MM 81.5,
Islamorada.

For a nice, friendly marine show where, if you're lucky, you
might get to hold a hoop for a jumping dolphin or get a kiss from
a seal, stop at **Theater of the Sea**, one of the oldest marine parks
in the world. It may now have fancier, more sophisticated competitors, but this place is still fun and quite personal. There are
myriad sea creatures that can be touched, wild dolphins that join
visitors for a "bottomless" boat trip and beautiful tropical grounds
to explore. Visitors can also swim with dolphins here by reservation (ages 13 and up). Admission. ~ MM 84.5, Islamorada; 305-
664-2431; www.theaterofthesea.com.

Theater of the Sea offers a four-hour scenic cruise and snorkeling trip, **Dolphin Adventure Snorkel Cruise**, aboard the 48-foot
powerboat "Cooter." Its route passes along the shore to Lignumvitae Key, then a short ocean cruise brings guests to historical
Indian Key and Alligator Lighthouse. At Cheeca Rocks, a beautiful shallow reef ideally suited for snorkelers, snorkel equipment
is provided or you can see the reef through the underwater view-

ers. The boat leaves each morning from Snake Creek Bridge (MM 85) but tickets must be purchased at the Theater at least one day prior to sailing.

After a ten-minute boat trip to **Indian Key State Historic Site** ◄ HIDDEN
you'll be presented with the remarkable story of the ten-acre island that was once the prosperous seat of Dade County. Beneath the nearby, usually calm waters of the Atlantic lie the most treacherous reefs off the Florida coast. The reefs were a source of income for Indians and then for Americans, who turned "salvaging" wrecked ships into profitable businesses. At that time the island town was a bustling place and boasted a grand hotel with a large ballroom, a bar and bowling alleys. One famous hotel guest was naturalist John James Audubon, who stayed over on his way to the Lower Keys. He filed one of the first complaints on record—the incessant dancing and partying made it hard for him to concentrate. Today, there is little sign of the merriment that had the bird man grinding his teeth. The town was destroyed in a grisly Indian attack in 1840. Rangers guide visitors on special tours down reconstructed village "streets" among the tall century plants and other tropical growth. Admission. ~ Indian Key; 305-664-2540, fax 305-664-2629.

It's another short boat trip to **Lignumvitae Key State Botanical** ◄ HIDDEN
Site. This key encompasses 280 acres; its virgin sub-tropical forest is a reminder of how all the Keys probably appeared before people came in numbers. One-hour ranger-guided walks through this rare environment introduce such unusual trees as the gumbo-limbo, mastic and poisonwood. The restored **Matheson House**, built in 1919, has survived hurricane and time; it demonstrates how island dwellers managed in the early days of Keys settlement, dependent on wind power, rainwater and food from the sea. Closed

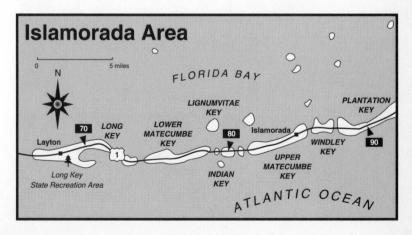

Islamorada Area

0   5 miles
N

FLORIDA BAY

LIGNUMVITAE
KEY

PLANTATION
KEY

LONG
KEY

LOWER
MATECUMBE
KEY

80   Islamorada

70

Layton

WINDLEY
KEY

90

1

Long Key
State Recreation Area

UPPER
MATECUMBE
KEY

INDIAN
KEY

ATLANTIC OCEAN

Tuesday and Wednesday. Admission. ~ Lignumvitae Key; 305-664-2540, fax 305-664-0713; e-mail patwells@terranova.net.

Indian Key and Lignumvitae Key are accessible by private boat only. **Robbie's Boat Rentals** (305-664-9814, 877-664-8498, fax 305-664-9857; www.robbies.com, e-mail robbies@gate.net) runs the shuttle service twice daily for the state park and recreation department. Cost is included in the island admission fee. For Indian Key, boats leave at 9 a.m. and 1 p.m. For Lignumvitae Key, 10 a.m. and 2 p.m. No access to Lignumvitae on Tuesday and Wednesday.

HIDDEN ►

The **Layton Nature Trail** is an almost-hidden loop trail from highway to bay, winding through a dense hammock of carefully marked tropical plants, such as pigeon plum, wild coffee and gumbo-limbo, that are unique to the Keys. For travelers in a hurry, the 20-minute walk provides a good introduction to the flora that once covered most of the Keys. ~ Near MM 66; 305-664-4815.

HIDDEN ►

Located 18 feet below the surface of the Atlantic Ocean, the **San Pedro Underwater Archaeological Preserve** welcomes divers, snorkelers and observers in glass-bottom boats. The *San Pedro* was a 287-ton, Dutch-built galleon in the New Spain fleet that left Havana harbor on Friday, July 13, 1733, and met its doom when hurricane winds drove it onto the reefs. The shipwreck park, dedicated in 1989, features an underwater nature trail where one can view a variety of fish, crustaceans, mollusks and corals. Original anchors, ballast stones, bricks from the ship's galley and concrete cannon replicas enhance the park. ~ Located 1.3 nautical miles south of Indian Key; P.O. Box 1052, Islamorada, FL 33036; 305-664-2540; e-mail patwells@terranova.net.

A **historical marker** west of Layton marks the site of Long Key Fishing Club, established in 1906 by Flagler's East Coast Hotel Company. One aim of the group was to stop the wholesale destruction of gamefish in this mecca for saltwater anglers. The president of the club, which fell victim to the 1935 hurricane, was American author Zane Grey. ~ Near MM 66.

LODGING

The Islamorada business area includes another piece of Route 1 lined with mom-and-pop and various chain motels. If you prefer

THE PURPLE ISLES

Islamorada (pronounced eye-lah-mor-ah-dah) was named by Spanish explorers and means "purple isles," perhaps for the way the land appeared on the horizon, perhaps for the abundant violet snail shells or the brilliant flowering plants found there when the islands were wild.

renting a home, condo or townhouse for a week, or even months, contact **Freewheeler Realty**. ~ 85992 Overseas Highway, Islamorada; 305-664-2075, fax 305-664-2884; freewheeler-realty. com, e-mail freewhel@aol.com.

The most unusual thing about **Plantation Yacht Harbor Resort and Marina** is the open space that surrounds it, a rarity in most developed areas of the Keys. Here the 56 motel-style units are scattered across 48 acres of grassy open land, many with good views of Florida Bay. Units are not new, but they are freshly painted, airy and clean. The resort includes a small, well-kept sandy beach with water clear enough for snorkeling, a freshwater pool, tennis courts, boat trips and rentals. ~ MM 87, Islamorada; 305-852-2381, 800-356-5357, fax 305-853-5357; www.pyh. com, e-mail fun@pyh.com. DELUXE.

Folks who enjoy being where the action is choose to stay at **Holiday Isle Resorts and Marina**, a great complex of lodgings, swimming pools, bars, restaurants and shops strung out along a stretch of Atlantic beach. The six-story main hotel and its three-story neighbor offer oceanfront rooms, efficiencies, apartments and suites with a peach and teal theme. Some are ordinary motel-type rooms; others are luxury apartments with kitchens, bars and wraparound balconies overlooking the ocean. ~ MM 84, Islamorada; 305-664-2321, 800-327-7070, fax 305-664-5171; www. theisle.com. DELUXE TO ULTRA-DELUXE.

If you want the glitz and fervor of Holiday Isle for lower rates, go a mile back up the road to **Harbor Lights** for moderate motel rooms and deluxe-priced oceanfront efficiencies. Owned by Holiday Isle, this place operates a free trolley Friday through Sunday to take guests to the bustling center of things. ~ MM 85, Islamorada; 305-664-3611, 800-327-7070, fax 305-664-5171; www.theisle.com. MODERATE TO DELUXE.

The rooms and villas of **Chesapeake Resort** have lots of cool gray and peach decor, wicker and other appropriate tropical-style furnishings, and access to grills, picnic tables and sunning-lounging areas. There's a small gesture of an ocean beach, a salt lagoon, a jacuzzi and two freshwater pools. The wide expanse of Atlantic for sunrise gazing is a real plus, as are the palms and Australian pines and the friendly white egrets and other seabirds. ~ MM 83.5, Islamorada; 305-664-4662, 800-338-3395, fax 305-664-8595. ULTRA-DELUXE.

At The Islander Motel you can snorkel in the clear ocean water   *resort*
or swim in the freshwater and saltwater pools. The Islander offers pleasant hotel rooms (some with kitchenettes) and fully equipped villas with screened porches. The 24-acre oceanside resort is rich in tropical plants and features shuffleboard. This is a popular place for families. ~ MM 82.1, Islamorada; 305-664-2031, fax 305-664-5503. MODERATE.

Vacationers in search of sheer luxury have been coming to **Cheeca Lodge** for over half a century. Perched on the edge of the Atlantic Ocean, this four-story hotel received a massive facelift in 1989. Much of the original wood remains in the lodge, which has classy lobby areas, spacious rooms, freshwater and saltwater pools, indoor and outdoor dining, children's programs, tennis courts and a nine-hole pitch-and-putt golf course. White-and-blue villas are scattered around grounds shaded by a variety of tropical trees. A fine, long pier invites fishing and serves as a take-off point for scuba divers and snorkelers. ~ MM 82.5, Islamorada; 305-664-4651, 800-327-2888, fax 305-664-2893; www.cheeca. com. ULTRA-DELUXE.

Know those beach scenes in the *Victoria's Secret* and *J.Crew* catalogs? Plenty were taken at **The Moorings**, one of the Keys' most luxurious, least-known lodges. It's adored by the fashion industry, which uses its thousand-foot, porcelain-white beach for photo backdrops (*Vogue, Elle, Glamour*—they all shoot here). But the photo teams keep a low profile, and guests will find The Moorings a place of quiet calm, hidden down a Keys sidestreet on an apron of ocean, its hammock grounds sprinkled with 18 conch cottages. Decor is a mix of tropical and safari chic with lots of wood—cypress, cherry, pine and ash—and splashes of sisal and Mexican tile. There's no room service or maid service (though either can be arranged), no radios or jet skis. But there's probably a gorgeous woman posing for a camera just down the beach. ~ 123 Beach Road, MM 81.5 oceanside, Islamorada; 305-664-4708, fax 305-664-4242; www.mooringsresort.com. ULTRA-DELUXE.

If you are traveling with your boat, you'll like knowing about **Bud N' Mary's Marina and Dive Center**, especially if you enjoy being in the middle of such sea-related activities as snorkeling, fishing and diving charters, party boats, glassbottom boat tours, backcountry fishing trips and sunset and sightseeing tours. They have four motel units (two double beds, small refrigerator, television and telephone) for folks who love quick access to the sea and its offerings. There's also one efficiency above the tackle shop. ~ MM 79.8, Islamorada; 305-664-2461, 800-742-7945, fax 305-664-5592; www.budnmarys.com. MODERATE.

The quiet **Coral Bay Resort** offers motel rooms, efficiency apartments or combinations for families needing suites. The place features tropical plantings, chickee huts, a heated swimming pool and a clear tidal salt pool complete with lobsters and stone crabs in the rocks. It's very popular with families and retired folk who like the quiet and easy access to fishing. ~ MM 75.5, Islamorada; 305-664-5568, fax 305-664-3424; www.the

floridakeys.com/coralbay, e-mail coralbay@terranova.net. MODERATE TO DELUXE.

DINING

The restaurant with the reputation is **Marker 88**, whose Continental cuisine has garnered raves from some of the nation's top culinary magazines. Entrées include fish Martinique topped with tomato concassé and sliced grilled bananas, and rice colonial Bombay—a magic mélange of beef and veal slices, curry, shrimp, scallops, pineapple, banana, pimento and scallions. Nestled beside Florida Bay and shaded by waving palms, Marker 88 is informally elegant and intimate with a rich tropical ambience. The wine list is as impressive as the creative menu. Dinner only. Closed Monday. ~ MM 88, Islamorada; 305-852-9315. DELUXE TO ULTRA-DELUXE.

◄ HIDDEN

Of the many places to eat at Holiday Isle Resort, the classiest is the **Horizon Restaurant** atop the five-story main hotel. You can get fine views of the bay and the ocean while enjoying Keys seafood prepared in a variety of fashions including traditional broiled or fried, and meunière or almondine styles. Cajun-style dolphin-fish fillets and tuna *au poivre* find their way onto the menu. The chef also does a variety of things with Caribbean queen conch, an old-time Keys shellfish now protected locally. Breakfast, lunch and dinner. Closed Wednesday. ~ MM 84, Islamorada; 305-664-2321. DELUXE TO ULTRA-DELUXE.

The shimmering mermaid on the wall of the **Lorelei** may catch your eye, but it's the food that draws locals and tourists alike to this yacht-basin eatery with a nice "early Keys" feel. In fact, it's packed every night, with a friendly fun-loving crowd

---

✔ CHECK THESE OUT—UNIQUE DINING

- *Budget:* Get comfortable on a serape-covered cushion at **Deadhead George's Mexicali Grill**, where you need not be a Grateful Dead fan to enjoy its Mexicali chicken stew. *page 103*
- *Moderate:* Wash down your meal of chargrilled dolphin with a fruity glass of sangria at **Calypso's Seafood Grille**. *page 77*
- *Moderate to deluxe:* Follow the stream of models, fishing guides and business folk to **Morada Bay** and feast on kiwi-stuffed crabcakes, coconut conch chowder and other tropical delights. *page 92*
- *Deluxe to ultra-deluxe:* Start with the stone-crab pie at the Cheeca Lodge's **Atlantic's Edge Restaurant** and see if you can resist the lobster fritters seasoned with Key lime–garlic aioli. *page 92*

Budget: under $10   Moderate: $10–$20   Deluxe: $20–$30   Ultra-deluxe: over $30

that practically worships the stunning view of the Gulf. They do all sorts of things with the catch of the day here—broil, blacken, coconut-fry, grill and meunière. There are traditional conch chowder and fritters, daily blackboard specials and a devastating chocolate-chip Kahlua cheesecake for dessert. Casual outdoor dining with a café-style menu is also available. Don't be surprised if you stay on for the nightly entertainment. ~ MM 82, Islamorada; 305-664-4656, fax 305-664-2410. MODERATE TO DELUXE.

Just before former President George Bush was inaugurated in 1989, he went bonefishing in Islamorada and had dinner at Cheeca Lodge's main dining room, the **Atlantic's Edge Restaurant**. The appetizer was stone-crab pie with scallions and tomatoes, a sublime sample of the excellent gourmet dining available in this elegant restaurant. Pan-seared salmon medallions are prepared with coconut red curry sauce; local mahi is baked in filo; and lobster fritters are seasoned with Key lime–roasted garlic aioli. As if the food weren't enough, there's also a fine wine list. Dinner only. ~ MM 82, Islamorada; 305-664-4651. DELUXE TO ULTRA-DELUXE.

HIDDEN ▶

Set back on the old highway that runs beside the main thoroughfare is a deeply shaded, Easter egg–colored conch-style building. **Grove Park Cafe**, with brightly cushioned and handpainted Bentwood chairs, is a fine-dining restaurant with a wine and espresso bar. The menu features such dishes as chicken Matecumbe (with prosciutto, sage and snow peas in a light cream sauce) and yellowtail tropicale (sautéed snapper in a macadamia-nut crust served over rice with mango-papaya salsa). You can also order box lunches or picnic baskets to go. Lunch features *panini* sandwiches on home-baked *focaccia*. Closed Wednesday. ~ MM 81.7, Islamorada; 305-664-0116. MODERATE TO DELUXE.

Morada Bay opened in 1997 and instantly, the Keys had a fashion model scene. It's not that the models haven't been around—they have for several years, doing photo shoots across Route 1 at the very low-profile Moorings lodge. Morada Bay is the restaurant for The Moorings, though it is not so low profile. The models not only love it here, but so do backcountry fishing guides, the local business elite, the wide-eyed tourists trickling over from neighboring motels to this brisk-white boathouse with shutters the color of hot pink oleanders. There's a brick patio set with artsy wood tables, and a patch of white beach set with white adirondacks, all spread along a wide-open bay. The food is superb, from the tropical tapas (coconut conch chowder and kiwi-stuffed crabcakes) to the charcuterie platter with *saucissons*, olives and hot, crusty French baguette. ~ MM 81.6, Islamorada; 305-664-0604. MODERATE TO DELUXE.

Dino's of Islamorada is in a bland blue building just off the highway, no water in site, but the food is so good none of that matters. Everything's Italian, and not the Anglicized fare so rampant in restaurants, but vigorous antipasti and salads, pungent cheeses flown in weekly from New York, velvety red sauces that have been pressed through a food mill. Dino's is of course Italian-owned, and the family matriarch rules the kitchen, turning out daily specials such as Roma Lasagna (layered with meatballs, ham, sliced boiled egg and béchamel sauce). Her *frittelles* are sweet, puffy fried fingers of dough. If you'd rather go for lighter fare, there's a wood-oven pizzeria here, too. ~ MM 81, Islamorada; 305-664-0727, fax 305-664-9945. MODERATE.

In a weathered old house overlooking Tea Table Relief, **Papa Joe's Landmark Restaurant** really is a landmark, with battered wood floors, pecky cypress walls and ancient air conditioners that chase away the island heat. Papa Joe's does fresh fish seven different ways, including coconut-fried, Oscar and meunière. They will also cook your catch for a slightly lower price. They also serve many steak entrées and have a good early-bird menu. The adjoining waterfront bar is a scenic place to meet local characters. Closed Tuesday. ~ MM 79.7, Islamorada; 305-664-8109. MODERATE.

Little Italy is about as rustic as can be, with shell lamps and wine bottles lining the windows. The food is terrific and plentiful. Bowls come to your table brimming with Sicilian-style seafood like sautéed snapper heaped with fresh tomatoes, black olives, mushrooms, shrimp and scallops in a sherry and lemon butter sauce. There are also many chicken and veal entrées, and traditional favorites such as ravioli and lasagna. Breakfast, lunch and dinner. ~ MM 68.5, Layton; 305-664-4472, fax 305-664-9643. MODERATE.

The Rain Barrel is an artists' village full of top-quality crafts and much more. Many of the craftspeople create their wares right in this tropical setting complete with waterfall. There are stained-glass artisans, jewelers, woodworkers, fine artists and potters, whom you can often see working at their crafts. ~ MM 86.7, Islamorada; 305-852-3084.

A faux castle with a mammoth faux lobster out front, **Treasure Village** is a collection of unique little gift and artisan shops plus one department-sized store. The latter, **Treasure Harbor Trading** (305-852-0511), features fashionable gifts with environmental themes, from clothing to cassettes to massage potions. ~ MM 86.7, Islamorada.

For trendy sporting goods and clothing, as well as fishing tackle that includes handmade rods, gaffs, flies and trolling lures

SHOPPING

and reels, stop at **H. T. Chittum & Co.** ~ MM 82.7, Islamorada; 305-664-4421, fax 305-664-2544; www.htchittum.com, e-mail info@htchittum.com.

If you don't plan to get all the way to Key West, stop at Islamorada's **Key West Aloe** for the complete line of aloe vera cosmetics and fragrances that are produced in the island factory and sold internationally. ~ MM 82.2, Islamorada; 305-664-9269; www.keywestaloe.com, e-mail info@keywestaloe.com.

Island Silver and Spice is the closest thing to a department store in the Keys, with top-quality tropical merchandise ranging from housewares and shoes to jewelry and artwork. ~ MM 82, Islamorada; 305-664-2714, fax 305-664-9026.

Angelika is upscale and boutiquish, a perfumed place of soft linen and flax wear for women, elegant hats and hat boxes, delicate lingerie, tiny purple satchels of corduroy, and silver jewelry beaded with stones. Most merchandise comes from small companies around the country. ~ MM 81.9, Islamorada; phone/fax 305-664-9008.

If you need art for the garden go to **Caribbean Village Shops**. The statuary and fountains, hammocks, and wood and wrought iron furnishings are great pieces. Smaller pieces like painted wood animals and bowls and potted orchids are good gift possibilities. ~ MM 81.9, Islamorada; 305-664-4732.

NIGHTLIFE If the name doesn't scare you away, being surrounded by 22 television screens all showing sporting events might. However, judging from the nightly noisy crowds, **Hog Heaven** is just the sort of jolly spot lots of folks love to wallow in. Occasional live bands. ~ MM 85.3, Islamorada; 305-664-9669.

Nightlife begins in the daytime at **Holiday Isle Resort**, with a host of party areas sporting such names as Jaws Raw Bar, Wreck Bar and the World Famous Tiki Bar. Signs also point you to "Kokomo," a beach bar named after the fact for the Beach Boys' famous song. There's canned and live music to suit a variety of tastes throughout the days and nights. Up in **Horizon**, atop the five-story main hotel, there are fine views of the ocean with quieter live entertainment for listening and dancing. ~ MM 84, Islamorada; 305-664-2321, fax 305-664-5171; www.theisle.com, e-mail info@theisle.com.

The gorgeous ocean view and well-stocked raw bar offset the general chaos at **Whale Harbor Bar and Grill**. This is a busy place where employees and charter-boat crew tend to hang out after their shifts. Live jazz, blues or island music is featured nightly, with gigs beginning in the afternoon during the tourist season. Sit inside or out. ~ MM 83.5, Islamorada; 305-664-9888, fax 305-664-0692.

You can enjoy a quiet drink at a table overlooking the Atlantic in Cheeca Lodge's elegant **Light Tackle Lounge**. There's also deck seating available. ~ MM 82.5, Islamorada; 305-664-4651.

In 1960, Hurricane Donna blew what is now the **Cabaña Bar** out to sea. After it was towed back, the place became a mellow bayside lounge. Live musicians perform reggae and easy-listening "sunset music" nightly. ~ MM 82, Islamorada; 305-664-4338, fax 305-664-2410.

LONG KEY STATE PARK 🏃 🚵 ⛵ 🛶 🚣 🚤 ⛴ Like the key on which it is located, this park is long and narrow—its shoreline of shallow flats and mangrove lagoons all shaped by the usually gentle Atlantic waters. Mahogany, Jamaica dogwood, gumbo-limbo and other tropical trees inhabit the tangled hammocks that, along with the mangrove swamps, can be crossed on boardwalks and viewed from an observation tower. Even though the traffic of Route 1 is closer than you might wish, you can actually camp right next to the ocean, shaded by tall Australian pines. This is a good place for children to wade or swim, and saltwater fishing is excellent adjacent to the park and in deep Gulf Stream waters of the Atlantic. Facilities include picnic areas, restrooms, a nature trail, a canoe trail, showers, an observation tower and canoe rentals; groceries are nearby in Layton. Day-use fee, $3.25 per vehicle, plus $.50 surcharge per person. ~ Located on the ocean side of Route 1 at MM 67.5; 305-664-4815, fax 305-664-2629.

BEACHES & PARKS

▲ There are 60 sites, including 50 with RV hookups; $24 per night, $26 for hookups.

Legend has it that a worker helping to construct the awe-inspiring Seven Mile Bridge was inadvertently responsible for naming Marathon. Overawed by the

▼▼▼▼▼▼▼▼▼▼
Marathon Area

challenge of spanning seven miles of open sea, the man simply called the task a "marathon." The appellation stuck.

Until the Seven Mile Bridge project was actually completed, the railroad line stopped at the outer edge of Vaca Key, said to have been named for the cows that once grazed there. Railroad workers were the major citizens of early Marathon, and the terminal contributed to a thriving local economy. But when the bridge was completed, the port lost its importance and the railroad crews moved on. Marathon quieted down, peopled mainly by fishermen of both the commercial and sport varieties and folk attracted by the laid-back life.

But Marathon is quiet no more. With over 12,000 residents, it is the second largest community in the Keys, topped only by Key West. Tourism and fishing are the chief businesses here;

there is seemingly not a species of southern sea creature that has not been caught in the surrounding waters. Retirement and long-term vacation living are popular, too. A number of small subdivisions have grown up around manmade canals that seemingly give everybody a "waterfront" lot and a place to dock a boat.

The Marathon area actually comprises a collection of islands from Conch Key (below MM 65) to the beginning of the Seven Mile Bridge (MM 47) and includes far more than the bustling, traffic-filled, friendly metropolis and its occasional suburbs and resorts. Just before the outskirts of the city lies the oceanfront community of Key Colony Beach, a designed village where even the smallest houses seem to have their own individual boat docks. And here and there among these islands and from their bridges you'll encounter open spaces and fine views of the ocean and Gulf.

SIGHTS   One of those views hits visitors immediately upon entering the Marathon area via **Long Key Bridge**. If you have not yet been overwhelmed by the realization that when you travel the Keys you're really heading out to sea, get ready. You'll certainly feel the impact after you leave Layton and cross the beautiful bridge over the point where the Atlantic Ocean meets the Gulf of Mexico between Long Key and the first little Conch Key. On most days, this meeting is calm and gentle. The horizon stretches blue on all sides as sea and sky meld. Travelers often stop at the little pull-offs on either end of this bridge—the second longest in the Keys—to take in the vastness of the water and the handsome bridge. Because the shore is sandy here, you will see people wading out in the shallow water or trying out their snorkeling and scuba gear.

After leaving the beautiful scenes at the Long Key Bridge, Route 1 continues through several small Keys, including Duck Key, once site of a salt-making enterprise and now inhabited by showy homes and a large resort, Hawk's Cay. Nearby **Grassy Key** is home of the **Dolphin Research Center**, where you can play and swim with the friendly creatures (30-day advance reservations are required and you must be at least five years old). There are also five daily walking tours. Admission. ~ MM 59; 305-289-1121, 305-289-0002; www.dolphins.org, e-mail drc@dolphins.org.

Continuing on Route 1, you will encounter population pockets and empty spaces, skirt the residential and vacation village of Key Colony Beach, and arrive finally at **Marathon**, the last good-sized town before the famous Seven Mile Bridge. Stop at the **Greater Marathon Chamber of Commerce** for information on this bustling area, which boasts shopping centers, a modern airport, commercial boat yards and lots of facilities for travelers. Closed weekends. ~ MM 53.5, Marathon; 305-743-5417, 800-262-7284, fax 305-289-0183; www.floridakeysmarathon.com, e-mail marathoncc@aol.com.

Hidden from the casual observer, though actually located in the heart of Marathon, is **Crane Point Hammock**, headquarters of Florida Keys Land and Sea Trust. Considered by many to be the most environmentally and historically significant piece of property in the Keys, this bayside 63-acre nature preserve of tropical hardwoods and mangrove wetlands contains many exotic tree specimens, archaeological sites and a historic Bahamian conch-style house. Admission. ~ MM 50, Marathon; 305-743-3900.

◄ HIDDEN

Crane Point Hammock is also home of the **Tropical Crane Point Hammock**, a museum which features a re-created coral reef, displays on pirate life and American Indian and shipwreck artifacts. Admission. ~ Crane Point Hammock; 305-743-9100.

Exhibits at the **Florida Keys Children's Museum**, also in Crane Point Hammock, include a tropical Caribbean lagoon, marine touch tank, hawk habitat, iguana exhibit, historic sailing vessel and an American Indian hut built with palm fronds. Ideal for the entire family. Admission. ~ Crane Point Hammock; 305-743-9100.

If you head toward the ocean at MM 47.5 (11th Street), you will end up around the **commercial fishing docks**, where you can watch the comings and goings of shrimp boats and other craft of the Marathon fleet.

To fully experience the Marathon area, take to the water. As well as the distinctive diving and snorkeling trips to the reef, several sightseeing cruises are offered by local captains to Sombrero Reef and other popular destinations. Contact the Greater Marathon Chamber of Commerce for a list of tour operators. ~ 305-743-5417, 800-262-7284.

Reminiscent of old-time conch cabins, **Conch Key Cottages** are located on their own tiny island accessible by a short causeway. This handful of rustic wooden cottages, boasting Dade County pine–

LODGING

◄ HIDDEN

vaulted ceilings, paddle fans, tile floors and kitchens, comes in a variety of sizes; some have jacuzzis and screened porches and all are within easy access of a pleasant little beach. There's a heated swimming pool and dock for all guests to use. Best of all, the cottages and apartments are away from busy Route 1 (though you may still hear the buzz from the motorway). ~ 62250 Overseas Highway, Walker's Island; 305-289-1377, 800-330-1577, fax 305-743-8207; www.floridakeys.net/conchkeycottages, e-mail river@safari.net. DELUXE TO ULTRA-DELUXE.

If you like a resort where everything is at your fingertips, the 60-acre **Hawk's Cay Resort and Marina** will fulfill your dreams. Here you can sleep in a spacious room decorated in salmon and teal and furnished with wickerwork rattan, dine in several very fine restaurants, bask beside the pool or on a pleasant manmade beach, play tennis and golf, or make arrangements with the concierge for charter fishing, diving or just about anything the Keys have to offer. The entire huge property is elegant but casual. Two-bedroom villas are also available. ~ 61 Hawk's Cay Boulevard, Duck Key; 305-743-7000, 800-432-2242, fax 305-743-0641; www.hawkscay.com. ULTRA-DELUXE.

Many motels and small hotels line the narrow but pretty Atlantic Beach at Key Colony Beach. The **Key Colony Beach Motel** offers 38 small, carpeted, functional rooms, and you can dive into the large heated pool on those rare days when the ocean is too cold. ~ 441 East Ocean Drive, Key Colony Beach; 305-289-0411; members.aol.com/kcbmotel, e-mail kcbmotel@aol.com. MODERATE.

The **Ocean Beach Club** is a three-story coral affair with cool blue decor that suits its oceanside setting. Besides the deluxe-priced rooms, there are ultra-deluxe-priced apartments with fully furnished kitchens, a small freshwater pool, a jacuzzi and lots of beach chairs for sunbathing on the rare (for the Keys) strip of sand. Guests can watch the waves or fish from the pier. ~ 351 East Ocean Drive, Key Colony Beach; 305-289-0525, 800-321-7213, fax 305-289-9703; www.fl-web.com/oceanbeach. DELUXE TO ULTRA-DELUXE.

At roadside, it looks like the front of an ordinary motel. But don't be fooled by the plain exterior. Follow the lane that leads to the bay, and you'll find yourself in a shady oasis. This is **Banana Bay Resort**, ten secluded acres that will make you totally forget the endless stream of cars buzzing by at the doorstep on Route 1. The 61 guest rooms are decorated in Caribbean plantation–style, and most have private verandas. The resort offers an exercise room, a large freshwater pool with restaurant and lounge, tennis courts, boat and watersport rentals and charters for fishing, sailing and diving. There's a poolside continental breakfast buffet included in the rate. ~ MM 49.5, Vaca Key; 305-743-3500, 800-226-2621, fax 305-743-2670; www.bananabay.com. DELUXE TO ULTRA-DELUXE.

Route 1 on both sides of Marathon is lined with motels, hotels and "botels," the latter being places where you can tie up your boat just outside your lodging door. And you'll find that "resorts" can be anything from a small collection of cottages to a grand mul-tiacre, full-service facility with a whole range of entertainments right on the grounds.

You can have a basic motel room or a fully equipped effi-ciency at the **Valhalla Beach Resort Motel** and feel as if you are on a private island with a quiet Atlantic inlet and waving palms. The nine units are strictly basic, but the tiny beach, little boat docks and considerable distance from traffic make this a quiet and special place. ~ MM 56.5, Marathon; 305-289-0616. MOD-ERATE.

◀ *HIDDEN*

The clean and functional rooms and efficiencies at **Bonefish Bay Motel** offer a cozy base of operations. Located just north of Vaca Cut, the '50s-style motel has a pool and access to the beach and a dock. The owners host a weekly cookout at the outdoor bar-becue. ~ MM 53.5, 1265 Overseas Highway, Marathon Shores; 305-289-0565, 800-336-0565. MODERATE.

Sombrero Resort and Lighthouse Marina offers bright, com-fortable garden and waterfront efficiencies that have kitchen-ettes, as well as one-bedroom condos. Everything about the place is appropriately light and airily tropical, from the sparkling pool to the cheerful tiki bar. There are four tennis courts along with a pro shop, fitness center, sauna and 79-slip marina. Children are encouraged, making it a good family lodging. ~ 19 Sombrero Boulevard, Marathon; 305-743-2250, 800-433-8660, fax 305-743-2998; www.sombreroresort.com, e-mail sombreroresort@ juno.com. DELUXE TO ULTRA-DELUXE.

If you're looking for a bed and breakfast—and they are scarce in the Keys—try the **Hopp-Inn Guest House**, situated in an ocean-side home. There are five rooms for rent, each with private bath and entrance, air conditioning, views of the ocean, good breezes and a continental breakfast. They also offer several apartments, without breakfasts but with full kitchens, at deluxe to ultra-deluxe rates. Papayas, bananas and figs grow right outside the door. ~ 500 Sombrero Beach Road, Marathon; 305-743-4118. MODERATE TO ULTRA-DELUXE.

◀ *HIDDEN*

If you're in search of unique lodging, you might consider the double-decker houseboats at **Faro Blanco Marina Resort**. Securely moored, the boats are accessible from little private docks in a sheltered basin. These sedate blue-grey craft provide handsome quarters furnished formally enough for any ship's captain, and you can throw open the French doors to enjoy the comings and

Text continued on page 102.

Days of the Dolphins

As far back as the shadowy times of prehistory, man has been fascinated by dolphins. In Greek mythology, Apollo once took the form of a dolphin to lead a boat to Delphi. Various coastal communities around the world have greeted the dolphin as a bearer of good fortune, guider of lost ships, saver of human lives. Though scientists cannot interpret the actions of dolphins in terms of human emotions, it is easy to see why these lovely marine mammals have captivated the imagination for so many centuries. Stand on a Florida beach and watch a pod of dolphins surface and dive, or leap gracefully above the waves. The show almost seems designed for your benefit. Or sail into the Gulf of Mexico, accompanied by dolphins who dart in and out of your path, seemingly playing with you as you tack and turn. Though much of the dolphin's life remains a mystery, there is no question that they are highly intelligent.

Dolphins, like whales, are cetaceans. The greatest confusion, perhaps, comes from distinguishing dolphin from porpoise. To the casual observer, the most obvious physical difference is that most dolphins have a pronounced beak and a dorsal fin with a curvature toward the tail, while none of the porpoises has a discernible beak, and all but one have a triangular dorsal fin. Also, dolphins have cone-shaped teeth, while porpoise teeth are spade-shaped.

Another misconception that needs to be cleared up relates to seafood menus. Don't panic when you read "dolphin" among the special dinner entrées. This refers to a popular tropical game fish, not to the gentle mammal. It would make things easier if only restaurants would agree, once and for all, to stick to its other name, mahimahi.

Dolphins live a complex social life, often traveling in large herds broken down into family units called pods. Mothers keep an eye on their calves for up to five years, displaying deep affection throughout infancy. Researchers report that dolphins forced to live alone display unhappiness. Adolescents isolate themselves into groups of their own sex, not returning to socialize with the whole group until they become mature adults. No wonder we are tempted to think of them in human terms!

Yet however much we might like to identify with dolphins, and though their brains are similar in size to ours, dolphins possess many abilities that man can only envy. Most impressive is *echolocation*, use of a wonderful biological sonar that allows dolphins to locate food and interpret other objects, no matter how dark or murky the water, by sending out and echoing back their curious clicks and squeals and whistles. And unlike us, they can dive to great depths for long periods of time without developing painful, life-threatening bends. Located on the tops of their heads are the nostrils, remarkable blowholes with two internal passages, one for each lung.

Though fewer dolphins ply the waters surrounding South Florida than once swam here, sharp-eyed visitors can still reap their share of sightings in the wild. Besides, the Florida Keys have long been one of the centers for the study and training of these sea mammals. At the **Theater of the Sea**, the oldest marine-mammal facility in the world (established in 1946), you can learn about the Atlantic bottlenose dolphins, California sea lions, sea turtles and other marine creatures that inhabit the 17-acre park's three-acre natural saltwater lagoon. Admission. ~ MM 84.5, Islamorada; 305-664-2431, fax 305-664-8162. Several motels and resorts boast their own private dolphin pets who put on shows for or swim with their guests.

Swim with a dolphin? Yes, it is possible (for a handsome fee), and it can be a rewarding and, some say, almost mystical experience well worth the price. At the **Dolphin Research Center**, the income from your swim helps support an extensive program of therapy, teaching and research. Admission. ~ MM 59, Grassy Key; 305-289-1121; www.dolphins.org, e-mail drc@dolphins.org. You also can make a swim appointment at **Dolphins Plus**, an education and research center. It also hosts Island Dolphin Care, a non-profit organization that works on dolphin-assisted therapy for disabled children. Admission. ~ MM 100, Key Largo; 305-451-1993, fax 305-451-3710; e-mail info@dolphinsplus.com.

As interest in dolphins increases, critics of human-dolphin encounters express concern about possible harmful effects on these sensitive animals in the wild; the federal government has launched an education campaign that encourages people to admire from a distance (it is illegal to feed wild dolphins). The research centers will be delighted to share information on these subjects with you.

MM
48.5

goings in the harbor. Cottages on the bay are also available. Guests have access to an Olympic-size swimming pool, four restaurants and two full-service marinas. Even more unusual are the two apartments in a four-story lighthouse dominating the marina. The interiors have a cozy, timeworn feel, with scads of old wood, creaking stairs and odd-shaped cubbyholes and cabinets. ~ 1996 Overseas Highway, Marathon; 305-743-9018, 800-759-3276, fax 305-743-2918. MODERATE TO ULTRA-DELUXE.

HIDDEN ►

Most unusual for Marathon, being both arty and avant garde, **Seascape** sits squarely on the ocean, a rambling 1950s house that's been transformed by a New York artist and Boston photographer. The facade is '50s funky faux brick, but inside the lobby and nine guest rooms are airy spaces with crisp yellow walls and the couple's island-inspired accents: headboards painted with fish, a tropically tiled table. There's jazz and the *New York Times* in the lobby, daily breakfasts of fresh-squeezed juice and pastries, and afternoon wine and cheese. And there's a swimming pool set into a grassy point on the Atlantic. ~ 1075 75th Street (just south of Marathon Airport, turn toward the ocean at 76th Street), Marathon; 305-743-6455, 800-332-7327, fax 305-743-8469; floridakeys.net/seascape. DELUXE TO ULTRA-DELUXE.

Hidden Harbor Motel, typical of the dozens of moderately priced motels that line Route 1, has an added attraction—a large aquarium on the grounds devoted to an ongoing environmental project. Here you can observe large tropical fish and endangered turtles. A small marina and some rooms with kitchenettes also enhance the place, along with a freshwater pool for people, picnic facilities and some pretty coconut palms. ~ MM 48.5, Marathon; 305-743-5376, 800-362-3495, fax 305-743-2552; www.thefloridakeys.com/hiddenharbor. MODERATE.

HIDDEN ►

Knights Key Inn is a two-story unit of older vacation apartments, almost hidden alongside a neighboring campground, where you can dock your boat for free. You have a great view of the Seven Mile Bridge. Rooms are old-fashioned with a slightly nautical decor. There is a small picnic area with bougainvillea and palm trees. ~ 40 Kyle Way West, MM 47, Marathon; 305-289-0289, 800-743-4786. MODERATE.

DINING

They call the **Porto Cayo at Hawk's Cay Resort** a formal dining room, which makes it a Keys rarity, but it's not so formal that you and your family can't relax and enjoy it. The waiters and waitresses wear khaki shorts and white polo shirts, and there's live piano music as well as linen cloths and potted plants, creating a nice ambience for enjoying the gourmet menu. Dinner entrées include baked fettuccine asiago, linguine al pomodoro and nightly seafood specials. Closed for special events. ~ MM 61, Duck Key; 305-743-7000. MODERATE TO DELUXE.

As its name suggests, this large nautical-themed restaurant is at the **Water's Edge**. It's on an inlet, rather than the open ocean, and overlooks an informal marina area. However, the setting is attractive, and the activity surrounding the boats moored just outside the windows is endlessly entertaining. The restaurant is actually part of Hawk's Cay Resort, but is several blocks away— far enough to allow hotel guests to feel they've "gone out" to dinner. The American menu is varied and interesting, with an emphasis on fresh seafood. There's also a children's menu and an all-you-can-eat soup and salad bar. Dinner only. ~ 61 Hawk's Cay Boulevard, Duck Key; 305-743-7000. MODERATE TO DELUXE.

A teeny roadside stop with filmy jalousy windows and a handful of vinyl-topped tables, **Gallagher's** seems an unlikely candidate for gourmet food. But gourmet it is, from the filet mignon *au poivre* to the lobster chunks sautéed in escargot butter with garlic and shallots. For those who desire simpler dishes, there is broiled yellowtail and sometimes chicken and dumplings, and always a homebaked pie. Little extras like a relish tray and homemade rolls with honey only add to this unusual dining experience. Dinner hours are limited and reservations are recommended, so call ahead. Closed Tuesday and Wednesday. ~ MM 57.5, Marathon; 305-289-0454. MODERATE TO DELUXE.

Don Pedro demonstrates a creative use of a strip shopping center unit. Cuban cuisine is the feature of this sparkling blue-and-grey eatery located on an insignificant corner. All the entrées, such as *lechón asado* (roast pork), *churrasco* (Argentine steak), *boliche asado* (pot roast), and *picadillo* (a tasty hamburger dish), come with yellow rice, black beans, fried bananas and crispy Cuban bread. The very filling meals may be accompanied by steamy, thick Cuban coffee or homemade sangria and topped off with a dessert of flan, a traditional baked custard. Closed Sunday. ~ MM 53, Marathon; 305-743-5247, fax 305-743-0518; www.keysdirectory.com/donpedro/index.html, e-mail oremar@marathonkey.com. BUDGET TO MODERATE.

Grateful Dead fans will immediately recognize the skeletons painted outside **Deadhead George's Mexicali Grill**. Cult association aside, this is a fun, lively restaurant run by tie dye–wearing employees who serve up really good food. Plant yourself on a serape-covered cushion and indulge in a monstrous steak burrito (served "wet") with rice and beans, or a bowl of creamy Mexicali chicken stew with sweet red onions, olives and cilantro. ~ MM 52, 6950 Overseas Highway, Marathon; 305-743-5556; www.deadheadgeorge.com. BUDGET.

The art deco menu plus the comical cartoons of fictional chefs beaming at you from the walls hint that **Chef's** is probably a fun place to eat. The small but well-balanced menu offers such items as rack of lamb, lobster sombrero and lobster sautéed with artichokes and mushrooms and served on pasta in a garlic and wine sauce. The fish du jour is prepared five different ways including blackened and baked with a pecan-butter topping. There is an open grill and a glassed-in dining area alongside the tennis courts. Closed Sunday. ~ Sombrero Resort, 19 Sombrero Boulevard, Marathon; 305-743-4108. MODERATE TO DELUXE.

The best food in Marathon is at **Barracuda Grill**. The dining room is small and minimalist, mostly white, with low-lit art parked on the walls and a sleek bar in the back. Sizzling offerings include "Voodoo Stew" with fish, calamari and shrimp. Other great plates: crunchy fried catfish, cracked conch, spicy Caribbean quesadilla and shrimp scampi with lobster butter and Key lime juice. There's a good selection of wines. ~ MM 49.5, Marathon; 305-743-3314. DELUXE.

You'd better like seafood if you stop at **The Cracked Conch**, which claims to have been "cracked up and conched out since 1979." Concessions are made for landlubbers, however, in the steak and chicken entrées. The main thing, of course, is the mollusk that comes out of the pretty pink shell—chowdered, frittered, cracked, burgered and sautéed. This is an unpretentious little place that is Keys to the core—that is, it sports a spacious bar and is not air-conditioned. But it's wide open to whatever breezes can be captured, and there's open-air seating out back under the branches of a great mahogany tree. ~ MM 49.5, Marathon; 305-743-2233. MODERATE TO DELUXE.

HIDDEN ► Located in Banana Bay Resort and Marina, the **Banana Cabana Restaurant** retains an old Florida Keys charm. The waitstaff and the dining room's somewhat mismatched but immaculate decor strike a comfortable chord with locals and visitors alike. The terrific Continental cuisine prepared with a Caribbean flair includes Snapper Banana Cabana, with crab meat, avocado and imperial sauce. Or try coconut-encrusted chicken breast, topped with orange-rosemary sauce. Outside, tables by the lit, aquamarine pool encourage a leisurely meal, finished off with tropical mango cake. There's also an impressive wine list. ~ MM 49.5, 4590 Overseas Highway, Marathon; 305-289-1232, 800-565-4880; www.bananabay.com. MODERATE TO DELUXE.

The lighthouse that distinguishes Faro Blanco Resort is authentic, and so is the fine dining at the resort's restaurant, **Kelsey's**. Along with creative treatments of local seafood, this sedately casual place prepares rack of lamb, roast Long Island duckling and grouper sautéed with mushrooms, roasted almonds and artichokes. The restaurant is lush with greenery, and its windows overlook the marina. Dinner only. Closed Monday during the summer. ~ 1996 Overseas Highway, Marathon; 305-743-9018. MODERATE TO DELUXE.

If you wind down 15th Street past where you think it ends, you'll come to **Castaway**, a no-nonsense eatery on the working wharf where locals have been coming for several decades. There is a basic seafood menu with chicken and steak for the misguided, but the big come-on here is shrimp "steamed in beer—seconds on the house." They ply you with luscious hot buns dripping with honey even before you begin. There's a varied selection of wine and beer. Dinner only. Closed Sunday and from September through mid-October. ~ Turn toward the ocean just below MM 48, Marathon; 305-743-6247. MODERATE.

◄ *HIDDEN*

Don't miss **The Quay Shops**, a little cluster of weathered-grey boutiques that includes **Bayshore Clothing** for tropical fashions and **It's a Small World** (305-743-8430, fax 305-743-0619; e-mail joan@bayshoreclothing.com) for out-of-the-ordinary children's togs and toys. **Marine Jewelry** (305-289-0628) offers gold and coral jewelry with nautical and sea-related themes (gold-capped shark teeth and gold Florida lobsters). Closed Sunday. **Enchanted Elephant** (305-289-0646) has eco-friendly gifts and an elephant "museum." ~ MM 54, Marathon.

SHOPPING

◄ *HIDDEN*

The **Bougainvillea House Gallery** is a local-art buyer's paradise. Featuring fine art and jewelry, the artists' cooperative exhibits the work of 14 artists. Oils, watercolors, ceramics, photography and blown glass are among the mediums represented. Most of the subject matter relates to the Keys. Closed Monday. ~ MM 53.5, 12420 Overseas Highway, Marathon; 305-743-0808.

If you are looking for classy cosmetics and upscale women's and men's clothing with name brands such as Calvin Klein, Rialto, ETC. and Esprit, you'll find them at **The Sandpiper**. ~ K-Mart Shopping Plaza, MM 50, Marathon; 305-743-3205.

Being the largest populated area in the Middle Keys, Marathon has several shopping plazas and all the basic stores needed for daily living, as well as the usual souvenir dens. For originally designed, handpainted Florida Keys handbags and tropical clothes, stop at the **Brown Pelican Store**. ~ K-Mart Shopping Plaza, MM 50, Marathon; 305-743-3849.

Anthony's features a vast array of women's swimsuits, as well as trendy name brand sportswear, lingerie and sleepwear. ~ 5800 Overseas Highway, Suite 25, MM 50, Marathon; 305-743-5855.

If you forgot your diving gear, don't fret, head for **Fantasea Divers**. This shop sells everything you need for underwater living including masks, snorkels, fins and regulators. You can also pick up after-dive necessities like sunglasses, hats, souvenir T-shirts, sandals, shoes and, just in case, a spear gun. Rentals are also available. ~ 4650 Overseas Highway, MM 49.5, Marathon; 305-743-5422.

If you are doing your own cooking, or you'd just like to peruse the catches-of-the-day, explore the collection of **seafood markets** along the wharves at the end of 11th or 15th Street. These are outlets for some of the area's serious commercial fishing. ~ On the oceanside near MM 48.

NIGHTLIFE   The **Water's Edge** overlooks the water beside the showy marina at Hawk's Cay. There's a casual mood and live music on Friday and Saturday nights. ~ MM 61, Duck Key; 305-743-7000.

Lots of locals drop in at **Ocean's Landing** to hear the live music and enjoy a planter's punch or a Goombay smash. Usually there's a singer and a guitar with a little comedy thrown in. Families eat here during earlier hours; it's that kind of friendly waterside spot. ~ On the causeway to Key Colony Beach, near MM 54; 305-289-0141.

For Force 5 blues try the **Hurricane Bar**. Every night but Monday decent bands take the stage, belting out Cajun, rock and traditional Delta blues. ~ MM 49.5, 4650 Overseas Highway, Marathon; 305-743-2220.

Happy hour offers live entertainment and hors d'oeuvres at **The Tiki Bar**. ~ Holiday Inn, MM 54, Marathon; 305-289-0222.

The Quay is so popular that it has clones in Key Largo and Key West. You can enjoy the sunsets, full seafood meals and tropical drinks at this wicker-furnished, brightly decorated Gulfside spot. ~ MM 54, Marathon; 305-289-1810.

Chef's Lounge, at the Sombrero Resort, is a tiki bar where your drink will be delivered to you poolside. ~ 19 Sombrero Boulevard, Marathon; 305-743-4108.

You can dance or play darts as local and imported bands play soft rock and other music every night at **Angler's Lounge** at Faro Blanco Resort. This second-story nightspot has windows all around and a wonderful view of the harbor and bay. ~ MM 48.5, Marathon; 305-743-9018.

Several arts organizations are active in the Marathon area, sponsoring or producing concerts and plays year-round. For information on what may be going on during your stay, contact the **Marathon Community Theatre**. ~ P.O. Box 500124, Marathon, FL 33050; 305-743-0994, fax 305-743-0408.

BEACHES & PARKS

HIDDEN ►

SOMBRERO BEACH PARK   This community park is mostly a generous windswept area with a few palm trees and a long, narrow spit of sand along the ocean, offering one of the few public beaches around. Though not spectacular, it is a good place for some sun and relaxation and an ideal romping spot for children. Swimming is pleasant in usually clear, calm ocean water. There are picnic areas, barbecues, restrooms and a playground. ~

Located on Sombrero Beach Road at MM 50 in Marathon; 305-743-5417, fax 305-289-0183; e-mail marathoncc@aol.com.

▼▼▼▼▼▼▼▼▼▼▼▼
Lower Keys Area

The Lower Keys, which begin at MM 40 just below the Seven Mile Bridge and extend to around MM 5, are *different*. They are different in geological make-up, in flora and fauna and even in ambience and pace from the rest of the Keys. Geologically, their fossil coral base is layered with a limestone that's called oolite (for its egg-shaped granules). Some of the islands of the Lower Keys are forested with sturdy pine trees, others with tall tropical hardwoods where orchids and bromeliads thrive. A number of endangered species, including the unique Key deer, struggle for survival on these low-lying islands.

Big Pine Key is the largest of the islands and second in area only to Key Largo in the entire Keys. Wildlife refuges and shopping centers share this island, the former protecting much of the unique plant and animal life, the latter offering necessary services for the people who choose to live in what seems a quieter, lonelier region than those on either side.

The Lower Keys boast the best public beach south of the mainland and access to a fine protected section of coral reef offshore in the Atlantic. Though there are pockets of development, from collections of little frame houses to assorted elegant residences, frenetic modernization seems to have been held at bay. With some unassuming screened-in eateries, scattered modest lodgings and significant protected wild areas, this region offers more chances to experience the "old Keys" than any other.

SIGHTS

Perhaps the most impressive sight in the Lower Keys is its initial access, the magnificent **Seven Mile Bridge**, spanning the sea between Marathon and Sunshine Key. The bridge that carries the Overseas Highway today is the "new" bridge, built in 1982 to replace the terrifyingly narrow but equally impressive structure that parallels it on the Gulf side. The old bridge, referred to as "the longest fishing pier in the world," crosses **Pigeon Key**. From the new bridge the key appears something very desirable, palmy and perfect, with handsome yellow and white conch houses sparkling in sunlight. There is water everywhere, the green of the gulf merging with blues of ocean. One assumes that many a motorist, bound for Key West, has looked over at Pigeon Key with astonishment.

It's unlikely that Henry Flagler's crew felt the same way about Pigeon—nearly 400 holed up here in camps while they toiled on the railroad from 1908 to 1935. The camps were hot and muggy and swarming with mosquitoes much of the year, and people went crazy. There is the story of the bridge foreman's wife, who had an affair with the camp cook. When the pair was discovered, the wife took a rope to the second floor of her house, looped it around a ridge beam, and hung herself.

In recent years ghost experts have been brought in and some say they can feel the spirit of the departed wife, especially in the second-floor attic of the 1912 **Bridge Tender's House**. This is what the docent will tell you if you take the guided tour of Pigeon Key, offered Tuesdays in summer and more often the rest of the year, depending on when volunteer guides are available. All other days, visitors can board a vintage trolley train over to Pigeon Key, watch a film on the island's history, then explore the seven buildings that date from 1912.

Start in the 1912 **Assistant Bridge Tender's House**, renovated to look as it did in 1912: painted deep yellow and propped on cone-shaped pilings. There's a museum inside with a model of the old seven mile bridge and photographs of those early times and residents, including Priscilla Coe Pyfoam, who lived here from 1938–41 when Pigeon Key was a fish camp. Now over 100 and living in Florida's Panhandle, Pyfoam came down to celebrate the museum opening in 1997. Admission. ~ Visitors Center is at MM 48, at the west end of Marathon and across from Pigeon Key; 305-743-5999, 305-289-0025; www.pigeonkey.org, e-mail pigeonkey@aol.com.

Unlike the upper and middle Keys, most of the Lower Keys seem to lie at right angles to the highway. Their geology, and hence their vegetation and wildlife, differ in many respects from that of their neighbors to the northeast. **Bahia Honda Key**, for example, features some white sand beaches; many unusual species of plants and birds are found throughout the Lower Keys. ~ MM 36.7.

As you look across to the southern peninsula of Bahia Honda Key, you will see a magnificent section of the old **Flagler Bridge**, with the railroad trestle on one level and the automobile highway arching above it, a masterpiece of engineering for its day.

At MM 33 you arrive at **Big Pine Key**. Stop at the **Lower Keys Chamber of Commerce** for information about this area. Big Pine Key is second only to Key Largo in size, but its character is quite different. Here there are blooming subdivisions, pine trees, good-sized shopping centers and freshwater holes formed in the oolitic rock foundation of the island. The contest between development and the wild is apparent. Closed Sunday. ~ MM 31; 305-872-2411, 800-872-3722; www.lowerkeyschamber.com.

Living in uneasy relationship with the ever-growing population of Big Pine Key are the Key deer, a miniature subspecies of white-tailed deer that grow to be only about three feet tall at the shoulder. In the 1940s, the population almost disappeared, inspiring the establishment of the 8500-acre **National Key Deer Refuge**.

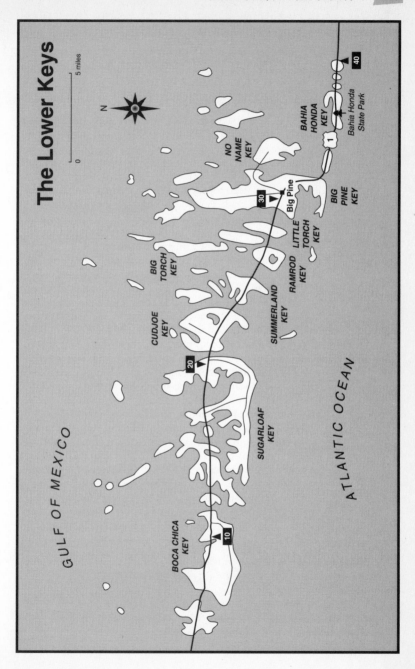

The Lower Keys

GULF OF MEXICO

ATLANTIC OCEAN

BOCA CHICA KEY

SUGARLOAF KEY

CUDJOE KEY

BIG TORCH KEY

SUMMERLAND KEY

RAMROD KEY

LITTLE TORCH KEY

NO NAME KEY

Big Pine

BIG PINE KEY

BAHIA HONDA KEY

Bahia Honda State Park

N

5 miles

0

Occasionally you can spot America's tiniest deer in the wilderness areas of the refuge, especially in the early morning or late afternoon, but be warned that there are heavy fines for feeding or harming these endangered, fragile animals. Closed weekends. ~ Headquarters at Big Pine Key Plaza on Key Deer Boulevard, one-quarter mile north of Route 1, MM 30.5; 305-872-2239, fax 305-872-3675; e-mail r4rw_fl.nkd@fws.gov.

Not far from the town of Big Pine lies a good-sized freshwater rock quarry pond called **Blue Hole**, the only one of its kind in the entire Keys. It is inhabited by several alligators, who often lie near the shore, as well as turtles and various wading birds and fish. ~ Key Deer Boulevard, two and a quarter miles north of Route 1. The nearby **Jack C. Watson Nature Trail** meanders through a typical Big Pine Key habitat of palms and slash pine and skirts a unique hardwood hammock.

HIDDEN ► Only reachable by boat, **Looe Key** has been absorbed into the large **Florida Keys National Marine Sanctuary** but is still an exceedingly popular diving site. The spectacular coral formations of this five-square-mile area and the crystal-clear waters make it delightful even for novice snorkelers. Several wrecked ships also lie within the sanctuary, including the 1744 British frigate HMS *Looe*. ~ Located 6.7 nautical miles southeast of Big Pine Key; headquarters at 216 Ann Street, Key West; 305-292-0311. Call the Chamber of Commerce for snorkeling and diving information.

HIDDEN ► Enjoy a sea kayaking adventure in the Great White Heron National Wildlife Refuge by calling **Reflection Nature Tours**. Their wildlife and educational trips give you a chance to see coral and sponges in the shallow water of the red mangroves. ~ Tours depart from Montes Restaurant, MM 25, Summerland Key; 305-872-2896; www.mindspring.com/~paddler.

By now you have probably noticed that some of the telephone poles along the Overseas Highway seem to be topped with great untidy piles of sticks and twigs. These are **osprey nests**. If you look closely, you will occasionally see a bird with its young. Ospreys are regular residents of the Keys; some seem uninhibited by the cars and 18-wheelers that constantly whiz beneath them.

HEY, HEY, HEY—IT'S FAT ALBERT!

If you survey the sky on the Gulf side, you'll catch a glimpse of **Fat Albert** floating high above the water. A large, white, blimp-shaped radar balloon, he's diligently on the lookout for illegal drug traffickers and other inappropriate interlopers. To keep him from being *too* diligent, he is moored to a missile tracking station on Cudjoe Key.

If you take a detour toward the Gulf on lower Sugarloaf Key, you'll get a glance at the **Perky Bat Tower**. This Dade County pine curiosity was built in 1929 as the brainchild of Richter C. Perky, who hoped to get the menacing mosquito population under control by importing a population of insect-devouring bats to take up residence in this louvered bat condo. Some say the bats never arrived, others claim that they came and, not satisfied with their carefully designed accommodations, took off for preferable climes. At any rate, the novel structure still stands and is on the National Register of Historic Places. ~ Off Route 1 at MM 17.

◄ *HIDDEN*

Heading toward Key West, you will see increasingly less development and more mangroves. Here and there you'll spot folks fishing off the old bridges. The densest residential area surrounds the Naval Air Base on Boca Chica Key. When you reach Stock Island, you have arrived in the suburbs of Key West.

Generic motels and small resorts appear here and there in the Lower Keys; rates are often lower than in nearby Key West. If you look hard, you'll also discover that some of the very best lodgings in this area are the hidden ones. Be aware, however, that Monroe County's efforts to maintain enough affordable housing for locals reduces the availability of certain types of vacation rentals. This primarily affects your ability to rent a home or apartment for less than 28 days. The pool of vacation properties in Big Pine Key, which has relatively few hotel/motel rooms, has dropped dramatically. Your best bet here is to make arrangements well in advance.

LODGING

There are three handsome duplex cabins on the Gulf side of **Bahia Honda State Park**. Though the cabins are not really hidden because you can see them from the highway, many visitors are unaware that the six grey frame units on stilts are available for rental. The fully equipped lodgings with spacious decks can accommodate up to six people. Make reservations by phone or in person, up to a year ahead. ~ MM 36.7, Bahia Honda Key; 305-872-2353. DELUXE.

If you'd like to rent a vacation home away from the highway, contact **Big Pine Vacation Rentals**. All the homes are on the waterfront, either on open water or canals, all with boat dockage and fishing. Three-night minimum stay required. ~ MM 29.5, Big Pine Key; 305-872-9863, 800-654-9560; e-mail bpvacation@ aol.com. DELUXE.

The motto of **Barnacle Bed and Breakfast**, "barefoot oceanfront living with panache," says it all. The owners built their elegant home in the shape of a six-pointed star, creating a collection of interestingly designed, distinctive rooms around a central atrium where gourmet breakfasts are served. Guests stay in ei-

◄ *HIDDEN*

ther of two rooms with private baths in the main house or in the efficiency in the many-angled annex. Kayaks and bicycles are available for guests free of charge. ~ 1557 Long Beach Drive, one and a half miles from MM 33, Big Pine Key; 305-872-3298, 800-465-9100, fax 305-872-3863; cust.iamerica.net/barnacle, e-mail barnacle@iamerica.net. DELUXE.

HIDDEN ▶ **Casa Grande**, a Spanish hacienda–style home, offers three handsomely furnished large rooms with private baths. A little shaded pavilion sits beside a small beach, hot tub, grill and picnic table. The varied gourmet breakfasts are served on a lovely screened patio. ~ Long Beach Drive, one and a half miles from MM 33, Big Pine Key; phone/fax 305-872-2878. DELUXE.

Deer Run Bed and Breakfast offers three rooms with separate entrances and private baths in a very attractive Florida-style house with high ceilings, Bahama fans and good views of the ocean. A 52-foot veranda overlooks the sea and the natural grounds where Key deer roam. The owner has cleverly decorated the outdoor area with driftwood and other jetsam deposited by the Atlantic currents onto the beach. Guests enjoy an outdoor hot tub and full breakfasts. Outdoor hammocks, chaise lounges and a barbecue grill help you feel at home. Adults only. Guests have free access to bicycles and a canoe. Two-night minimum stay. ~ Long Beach Drive, two miles from MM 33, Big Pine Key; 305-872-2015, fax 305-872-2842; e-mail deerrunbb@aol.com. MODERATE TO DELUXE.

HIDDEN ▶ The windswept, old-time one- and two-bedroom cottages at the **Old Wooden Bridge Fishing Camp** are especially popular with anglers and divers who don't need a lot of amenities other than a comfortable, plain cabin, a full kitchen and access to the water. Rental boats are available, or you can stroll on over to the Bogie Channel Bridge for some great fishing. ~ Punta Risa at Bogie Channel; take Wilder Road at MM 30 and follow signs to No Name Key; 305-872-2241. MODERATE.

The family that owns **Parmer's Place** has been adding more and more units to this attractive quiet collection of rooms, apartments and efficiency suites for more than two decades. The result is an assortment of older and newer individually designed units, each named for an indigenous bird or fish. Tropical landscaping and a pool enhance the locale. For a treat, request "Sail Fish," a large efficiency with a pretty porch right beside Pine Channel. ~ At end of Barry Avenue, a half mile off Route 1 toward the bay at MM 28.5, Little Torch Key; 305-872-2157, fax 305-872-2014; parmersplace.com, e-mail ltresort@aol.com. MODERATE TO DELUXE.

HIDDEN ▶ "Tropical paradise" is a worn-out phrase, but it really fits **Little Palm Island**. This five-acre island of waving palms and green lawns features 14 luxurious two-suite bungalows, each one facing the water. You'll enjoy generous thatched-roof quarters with abundant windows, British Colonial decor, a private sundeck and outdoor bamboo shower, meals in the excellent restaurant, boat transportation from Little Torch Key and enough quiet to calm the most jangled nerves. If you want to go fishing, touring nature preserves, diving or sightseeing, Little Palm will make the arrangements; but if you want to stay around, you can sail, windsurf, browse in the gift shop, get a massage or just luxuriate on the island once enjoyed by Harry Truman and other notables. ~ Offshore at MM 28.5, Little Torch Key; 305-872-2524, 800-343-8567, fax 305-872-4843; www.littlepalmisland. com, e-mail getlost@littlepalmisland.com. ULTRA-DELUXE.

There's nothing special about the motel rooms at **Looe Key Reef Resort**, but it is very popular with divers, having a dive shop, boat ramps and dive trips to Looe Key Sanctuary available for guests. There is also a restaurant, lounge and swimming pool. ~ MM 27.5, Ramrod Key; 305-872-2215, 800-942-5397, fax 305-872-3786. DELUXE.

The ultimate bed-and-breakfast getaway is aboard the **Witt's End**, a 51-foot luxury sailing yacht featured in *Gourmet* magazine. Captained by an experienced husband-and-wife team, B.J. and Greg Witt, the ship has all the comforts of home and an accomplished chef to boot. A stay includes breakfast, served on deck, and dinner. ~ MM 25, Summerland Key; 305-744-0022, fax 305-745-1476; e-mail captwitts@aol.com. ULTRA-DELUXE.

Sugar Loaf Lodge is one of the "full service" resorts with average but pleasant motel rooms and efficiencies facing the water. Full service here means a pool, restaurant and lounge, a marina, mini-golf, tennis and fishing charters. It's also very convenient to Key West. ~ MM 17, Sugarloaf Key; 305-745-3211, 800-553-6097, fax 305-745-3389. DELUXE TO ULTRA-DELUXE.

DINING

Island Reef is an ambitious little place that serves paella, *picadillo* and *palomella* steak (served with rice, beans and plantains) right alongside comfort foods like Yankee pot roast and chicken pot pie. There's also plenty of seafood, including baked dolphin and coconut shrimp with honey mustard sauce. No matter what you order, you'll find the cuisine exceptional. Dine inside the pine-walled café or outside on a shaded patio. ~ MM 31.3, Big Pine Key; 305-872-2170. MODERATE.

The cedar walls and floors—offset by a whole stuffed deer—create a rustic atmosphere at **Key Deer Bar & Grill**, a down-home eatery serving up steak, seafood and pizzas. Friday and Saturday nights feature prime rib. ~ MM 31, Big Pine Key; 305-872-1014, fax 305-872-1015. BUDGET TO MODERATE.

Open for breakfast, lunch and dinner, the **Dip 'N Deli** is a nice place whose name tells all. There are fresh salads, 22 kinds of

sandwiches, soups and lots of ice cream treats, including old-fashioned sodas and milkshakes. On the dinner menu are barbecue,
chicken and steak entrées. There's also lots of local chatter going
on, as well as the refreshing break from the ever-present seafood.
~ MM 31, Big Pine Key; 305-872-3030. BUDGET TO MODERATE.

Restaurants don't get more Keys-y than **K.D.'s Steak and Seafood**. It's plastered on the outside with pastel-colored seashells,
while inside are wood ceilings strung with tattered fishnets, dusty
fish parked on the walls, and an endless shellacked bar favored
by local charter captains. There are lobster and stone crab in season, as well as fresh fish dishes, steaks, chicken and baby back
ribs. ~ MM 30.5, Big Pine Key; 305-872-2314, fax 305-872-0125.
MODERATE TO DELUXE.

The most Jamaican things about **Montego Bay** are its name
and a few spicy dishes that emulate that island's fiery "jerk" sea-
soning. This MoBay is two large, pleasant rooms, one of which
is a lounge. Both are dark-walled with bamboo accents, and
there is a small rock garden and fish pond beyond sliding glass
doors off the dining room. The menu is mostly American in character, with fresh local seafood, hand-cut steaks, veal and pasta.
Red Stripe beer does show up, however. ~ MM 30, Big Pine Key;
305-872-3009. MODERATE.

HIDDEN ▶

To get away from it all in style, plan to dine at the restaurant
on **Little Palm Island**. You have to call ahead for a reservation;
they will tell you when the boat will pick you up to take you to
the lovely, luxurious island resort. If you're wise, you'll go in time
to watch the sunset while sipping a cocktail beside the sandy
beach or partaking of the fish of the day, pan-seared Gulf shrimp,
breast of chicken or any of the other Continental entrées. ~ Offshore from Little Torch Key, MM 28.5; 305-872-2551, fax 305-
872-4843; www.littlepalmisland.com, e-mail getlost@littlepalm
island.com. ULTRA-DELUXE.

Montes Restaurant & Fish Market is a bare-bones place with
plastic-covered round picnic tables and good old-fashioned fried
seafood platters and baskets with french fries, cole slaw and
sauce. Sit on the porch beside the canal and enjoy what you're
supposed to eat in the Keys—conch chowder, conch salad, conch
fritters, stone crabs and steamed shrimp. ~ MM 25, Summerland
Key; 305-745-3731. MODERATE.

Mangrove Mama's is such a wildly decorated, side-of-the-
road, banana tree–surrounded eating establishment that you
probably wouldn't stop unless someone recommended it—and
plenty of Lower Keys folks do just that, with great enthusiasm.
The floor is concrete, tablecloths are minimal, the chairs don't
match and resident cats look longingly at your dinners. But the
menu, though brief and to the point, is somewhat fancier than
you'd expect, with such treats as baked stuffed shrimp and chicken

and scallop Caribbean, sautéed with bacon and served in a creamy dijon sauce. The Key lime pie is superb and the herb teas and homemade rolls are as pleasant a surprise as the handsome brick fireplace, used on very rare chilly nights. Mama's has live music on weekends. ~ MM 20, Sugarloaf Key; 305-745-3030. MODERATE TO DELUXE.

SHOPPING

For all the basic necessities, the main place for shopping in the Lower Keys is the **Big Pine Key Shopping Plaza.** ~ On Key Deer Boulevard just off Route 1 at MM 30, Big Pine Key.

Edie's Hallmark Shop is far more than its name implies. Here you'll find gifts, party goods and a book section with top-notch vacation reading, as well as a good supply of Florida and Keys books and guides. Closed Sunday in summer. ~ Big Pine Key Shopping Plaza, Big Pine Key; 305-872-3933.

At **Blue Moon Trader**, the New Age is alive and well. Standing high on stilts, the pretty pink "earth-friendly" building welcomes visitors with the sound of wind chimes and houses several levels of gifts and services for "conscious living"—jewelry, pottery, crystals and lots of other things. Bring your kids to play, receive a tarot card reading or get a massage for yourself. ~ MM 29.7, Big Pine Key; 305-872-8864.

NIGHTLIFE

Locals frequent the lounge at **Key Deer Bar-B-Q**, where there's occasional live rock and blues, as well as a pool table. ~ MM 31, Big Pine Key; 305-872-1014, fax 305-872-1015.

◄ *HIDDEN*

For an evening with the locals, drop in at the **No Name Pub**, a funky, run-down eating and drinking establishment with a carved-up wooden bar, over 20 kinds of beer and a jukebox. There's occasionally a pig roast and always the "best pizza in the known universe." This is a fun place that just about anybody can direct you to. ~ North Watson Boulevard, Big Pine Key; 305-872-9115.

At **Coconut's Lounge** there's live weekend entertainment including pop, rock and country-and-western bands. ~ MM 30.5, Big Pine Key; 305-872-3795.

Three nights a week there's live rock-and-roll performed by local bands at **Looe Key Reef Resort.** ~ MM 27.5, Ramrod Key; 305-872-2215.

Pirate's Lounge is a typical resort-motel nightspot. This one has weekend entertainment and dancing, and boasts oversized piña coladas and strawberry daiquiris. ~ Sugar Loaf Lodge, MM 17, Sugarloaf Key; 305-745-3211.

BEACHES & PARKS

LITTLE DUCK KEY PARK 🐾 🐟 This little park on the ocean provides a place for a roadside rest and a swim just after you cross the Seven Mile Bridge, heading down the Keys. It's only a tiny strip of shallow beach with a few windblown trees, but the beach is sandy, the swimming better than many places and the water usually clear enough for snorkeling. There are restrooms and a picnic area. ~ Located on the ocean side of Route 1 at MM 40.

BAHIA HONDA STATE PARK   This state park offers what many consider the best swimming beaches in the Keys— wider and leading into deeper water than most. Remnants of the undeveloped Keys remain in this beautiful park—silver palms, satinwood, dwarf morning glories and a number of rare birds such as the roseate spoonbill and white-crowned pigeon. You may camp in the wide open spaces (best choice during mosquito season) in view of a handsome segment of Henry Flagler's original old bridge, or in the shady hardwood hammock at Sandspur Beach. Fishing is excellent, both in the bay and the ocean; guides are available during tarpon season. Swimming is also excellent, both in the Atlantic Ocean and Gulf of Mexico. Facilities include picnic areas, restrooms, vacation cabin rentals, a bathhouse, nature trail, concession stand, marina, snorkel shop and limited groceries. Day-use fee, $4 per vehicle, plus $.50 surcharge per person. ~ Entrance on ocean side of Route 1 at MM 36.7; 305-872-2353.

▲ There are 80 tent sites (48 with water and electricity); $24 per night ($2 more for hookups).

Outdoor Adventures

SPORT-FISHING

You can fish on a pricey, custom-designed charter or by joining one of the numerous party boats on a scheduled trip.

Charters and guides for light tackle fishing in the creeks and deeper ocean waters out of Key Largo can be had from **Back Country Adventures**. Captain Harry Grigsby will take groups out after barracuda, grouper and tarpon. ~ 59 North Blackwater Lane near MM 105, Key Largo; phone/fax 305-451-1247. Among many other charter services, **The Sailor's Choice** is a good choice for families or first-time fishers. They take large groups out daily for deep-sea fishing, in search of yellowtail, grouper and dolphinfish. ~ MM 100 at the Holiday Inn; 305-451-1802.

In Islamorada, there are also dozens of sportfishing outfits to choose from, including the partyboat **Gulf Lady** for full-day, offshore dolphin fishing. ~ MM 79.8 at Bud N' Mary's Marina; 305-664-2461, 800-742-7945. **Holiday Isle Resorts & Marina** will make arrangements for both backcountry and offshore fishing trips and charters for yellowtail, marlin, tuna and sailfin. Groups of up to six only. ~ MM 84.5; 305-664-8986 ext. 642.

In Marathon, charter booking services are offered by **The World Class Angler** for flats, bridge or reef fishing. ~ 5050 Overseas Highway; 305-743-6139, fax 305-743-0392; www.world

classangler.com. **Marathon Lady Party Boats** offers day and night fishing trips in and around the Florida Keys for local reef-bottom fishing. ~ MM 53 at Vaca Cut; 305-743-5580. For flats fishing, join Captain Barry Meyer on the **Magic**. He'll trailer his boat to meet you anywhere in the Keys for fly- or spin-casting for tarpon or light-tackle bonefishing. ~ MM 50; 305-743-3278.

In the Lower Keys, you can go tarpon fishing out of Bahia Honda State Park with **Captain Dave Wiley**. They also take shallow-water trips to Great White Heron Wildlife Refuge for shark, barracuda and bonefish. ~ MM 27.5, Ramrod Key; 305-872-4680, fax 305-872-4536; www.keywestflats.com, e-mail outcast 97@aol.com. **Charter Boat Kismet** has offshore and reef fishing. ~ MM 28.5, Little Torch Key; 305-872-3223, fax 305-872-1967; e-mail captmacb@aol.com. Try backcountry fishing with the **Outcast** at Sugarloaf Marina. They specialize in tarpon and bonefishing. ~ MM 17, Sugarloaf Key; 305-745-3135.

DIVING

On any calm and beautiful day the sea to the east of Florida's Upper Keys is dotted with boats. They belong to the scuba divers and snorkelers who are captivated by the beauty of the continental United States' only living reef. Others search the remains of ships wrecked on that same lovely reef. Many communities in the Keys have dozens of scuba shops and dive centers designed to meet the needs of both novice snorkeler and sophisticated diver.

Route 1 in the Key Largo area seems like one continuous dive shop. To meet your diving needs, the **Coral Reef Park Company, Inc.** offers dives geared toward novices; instruction ranges from resort to open-water to review courses. ~ John Pennekamp Coral Reef State Park, MM 102.5; 305-451-1621, fax 305-451-1427.

✔ **CHECK THESE OUT—UNIQUE OUTDOOR ADVENTURES**

- Board the Dolphin Adventure Snorkel Cruise for a scenic trip to Cheeca Rocks, passing by Indian Key and Alligator Lighthouse along the way. *page 86*
- Join wrecked ships and colorful marine life when you dive at Looe Key, a five-square-mile site featuring amazing coral and crystal-clear waters. *page 110*
- Follow that old "when in Rome" advice—the Keys are *the* place to go sportfishing, but be careful you don't cross lines with one of your many fellow anglers! *page 116*
- Kayak through a maze of mangrove-locked backwaters or out into the Great White Heron National Wildlife Refuge. *page 119*

American Diving Headquarters is another choice for a range of chartered dives within Pennekamp Coral Reef State Park. ~ MM 105.5; 305-451-0037, 877-451-0037, fax 305-451-9291. In Tavernier, try the **Florida Keys Dive Center**. ~ MM 90.5; 305-852-4599.

Diving courses, gear and trips are available in Islamorada through **Lady Cyana Divers**. The Davis ledge dive features fish so dense you sometimes can't take pictures of the coral. ~ MM 85.9; 305-664-8717, 800-221-8717; www.ladycyana.com, e-mail ladycyana@ladycyana.com. **Holiday Isle Resorts & Marina** has two daily dives, one for beginners and one for intermediate and advanced divers. The more difficult dive visits the wreck of the *Eagle*, a 287-foot freighter. ~ MM 84; 305-664-2321.

MARATHON AREA   For trips, lessons and equipment contact **The Diving Site**. The morning dive usually takes you out to a wreck for exploration; the afternoon might end up in Samantha's reef or Coffin's Patch for shark feeding or some of the most magnificent coral you've ever seen. ~ MM 53.5, Marathon; 305-289-1021. Choose between 50 different sites for shallow diving or excellent snorkeling with **Fantasea Divers**. Dives usually last four hours and consist of two different sites. Sobrero's reef is popular with divers, where coral shoots grow up to 15 feet from the sand. ~ 4650 Overseas Highway, Marathon; 305-743-5422.

LOWER KEYS AREA   **Looe Key Reef Resort and Dive Center** is a full-service dive center that offers a five-hour, three-location trip to the Looe Key Sanctuary reef. For beginners, there's expert instruction. ~ MM 27.5, Ramrod Key; 305-872-2215, 800-942-5397, fax 305-872-3786; www.diveflakeys.com. Another full-service center is **Cudjoe Gardens Marina and Dive Shop**. Up to six people can get on board their operations to Looe Key's protected finger reefs. Basic open-water courses are taught. ~ MM 21, Cudjoe Key; 305-745-2357. **Inner Space Dive Shop** has excellent four-five PADI and Navy certification courses. For advanced divers and snorkelers, the main attraction is the Looe Key reefs, which are strictly no-touch sanctuaries. ~ MM 29.5; 305-872-2319.

SNUBA is the latest thing in underwater exploration. This is a shallow-dive system where the air supply (read tank) follows on the surface, allowing you to dive down to 25 feet. SNUBA Tours can arrange this; lessons are also available. ~ MM 97 at the Westin Beach Resort; 305-451-6391, fax 305-451-0720; e-mail snubajef@terranova.net.

BOATING   In Key Largo the best prices for boat rentals are at John Pennekamp Coral Reef State Park's **Coral Reef Park Company**. Snorkeling and glass-bottom boat tours are also available. ~ MM 102.5; 305-451-1621, fax 305-451-1427. You can also rent fully equipped motorboats for open fishing at **Italian Fisherman Marina**. ~ MM 104; 305-451-3726.

In Islamorada, try **Holiday Isle Resorts & Marina** for catamarans and motorboats for snorkeling and fishing expeditions. ~ MM 84; 305-664-2321. There are also motorboats at **Robbie's Boat Rentals**, which rents on an hourly, half- or full-day basis. ~ MM 77.5; 305-664-9814, fax 305-664-9857; e-mail robbies@ gate.net. Or try **Bud N' Mary's Marina and Dive Center** for motorboat rentals, glass-bottom boat tours, snorkeling and guided boat trips. ~ MM 79.8; 305-664-2461. **Bayview Inn** rents powerboats and Sea Doos (waverunners). ~ MM 63, Conch Key; 305-289-1525, 800-289-2055, fax 305-289-1382; www.bayviewinn. com, e-mail info@bayviewinn.com.

Between Islamorada and Marathon, you can rent recreational watercraft at **Pier 68 Boat Rentals**. ~ MM 68.2, Layton; 305-664-9393, fax 305-517-2761; e-mail pier68@bellsouth.net.

In Marathon you can rent powerboats from **Fish 'n Fun Boat Rentals**. ~ MM 53.5; 305-743-2275. **Rick's Watercraft Rentals** has waverunners and outboard motorboats. ~ MM 49.5; 305-743-2450, 800-694-6848.

In the Lower Keys, you can rent offshore powerboats at **Dolphin Marina**. They also run snorkel and dive trips out to **Looe Key**. ~ MM 28.5, Little Torch Key; 305-872-2685. Or try **Cudjoe Gardens Marina**, which rents powerboats and waverunners. ~ MM 21, Cudjoe Key; 305-745-2357.

CANOEING & KAYAKING

The **Coral Reef Park Company** offers canoes and kayaks for exploring the park. ~ MM 102.5, John Pennekamp Coral Reef State Park, Key Largo; 305-451-1621, fax 305-451-1427.

In Marathon, you can rent kayaks at **Ocean Paddler South**, which also has outlets in Summerland Key and Islamorada. ~ MM 48.5; 305-743-0131. On Big Pine Key, **Reflections Nature Tours** takes novice and experienced paddlers into the Great White Heron National Wildlife Refuge to see tropical wildlife in its native habitat. They also offer trips to Key Deer Refuge. You may also board his skiff for half- and full-day non-paddling excursions. ~ P.O. Box 430861, Big Pine Key, FL 33043; 305-872-2896, 305-304-6785; www.mindspring.com/~paddler. Also in Big Pine Key, **Lost World Expeditions** offers three- to four-hour kayaking trips into the wild, with an emphasis on nature identification and the role of ecosystems. ~ P.O. Box 431311, Big Pine Key; 305-872-8950; www.keys-kayak-canoe-tours.com.

SAILING

In the Key Largo area you can rent sailboats from **Coral Reef Park Company, Inc.** ~ MM 102.5, John Pennekamp Coral Reef State Park; 305-451-1621, fax 305-451-1427. **Caribbean Water-**

sports offers two-hour enviro-tours into Everglades National Park or Indian Key State Park aboard either Zodiac inflatables or Hobie Cat sailboats. Other recreational sports (kayaking, snorkeling, fishing) can be arranged. ~ MM 97 bayside at the Westin Beach Resort, 305-852-4707, 800-223-6728, fax 305-852-5160; MM 82 oceanside, at the Cheeca Lodge Resort, Islamorada, 305-664-9598, 888-732-7333; www.caribbeanwatersports.com, e-mail cws @caribbeanwatersports.com.

In Islamorada, book sailing cruises through **Holiday Isle Resorts and Marina**. ~ MM 84; 305-664-2321.

Go sailing bare boat or with a tour guide out of Marathon with **Sailing Adventures**. ~ MM 48.3, Faro Blanco Marina Resort; 305-743-9018, 800-759-3276. Or sail aboard **Amantha**. ~ MM 48.3, Faro Blanco Marina Resort; 305-743-9020. Cruises for as many as six people on a 56-foot private yacht are available from **Latigo Charters**. Choose from a sunset dinner cruise, a bed-and-breakfast cruise, extended vacation cruises and two types of wedding cruises. ~ 1021 11th Street, Marathon; 305-289-1066, 800-897-4886; www.latigo.net, e-mail latigo@gate.net. **Hootmon Sailing Charters** is available for snorkeling trips and a sunset champagne cruise every evening. You can even take some learn-to-sail classes with licensed captains Ann and Dan Malone. ~ MM 49.5 at the Banana Bay Resort, Marathon; 305-289-1433.

Enjoy an unforgettable five-hour tour aboard the *Emerald See*, **Strike Zone Charters'** 40-foot catamaran. Snorkel over the reef, visit the "back country" and relish a fish cookout on a private island. ~ MM 29.5, Big Pine Key; 305-872-9863, 800-654-9560, fax 305-872-0520; www.strikezonecharter.com, e-mail strikezone@aol.com.

Keys visitors are increasingly interested in exploring the fragile ecosystems that surround the islands and Florida mainland. **Easy Adventures** explores Indian Key and Lignum Vitae Key from a comfortable canopied motorboat. Ecotours, fishing and snorkeling cruises are available and are geared toward families. The captain and guide is Anne Baxter, a former Everglades National Park ranger. ~ MM 81.5 bayside at the World Wide Sportsman Marina; 305-852-4553; e-mail keysboat@aol.com.

WIND-SURFING

Windsurfers can find boards and lessons at **Caribbean Watersports**, which has two locations: MM 97 bayside, at the Westin Beach Resort, Key Largo, 305-852-4707, 800-223-6728; and the Cheeca Lodge Resort, MM 82 oceanside, Islamorada, 305-664-9598, 888-732-7333; www.caribbeanwatersports.com, e-mail cws@caribbeanwatersports.com.

HOUSE-BOATING

One of the best ways to capture the essence of the Keys is to just laze away a few days aboard a slow-moving, pontoon houseboat. Just such a craft can be rented from **Houseboat Vacations of the Florida Keys**, with houseboats available for three nights to a week. ~ MM 85.9, Islamorada; 305-664-4009.

Many Keys resorts provide tennis for their guests. Tennis and racquetball courts are available to nonmembers at the **Sugarloaf Sports and Leisure Club**. Neat but relaxed, the club also offers a heated swimming pool, a jacuzzi, a bar and a restaurant. Fee. ~ MM 19.5, 19269 Bad George Road, Sugarloaf Key; 305-745-3577. The **Islamorada Tennis Club** is open to the public with both clay and hard courts and night lighting. ~ MM 76.8; 305-664-5340.

TENNIS

◄ *HIDDEN*

Bikeways parallel Route 1 intermittently down through the Keys. **Reflection Nature Tours** offers guided bike-trail rides. ~ P.O. Box 430861, Big Pine Key, FL 33043; 305-872-2896, 305-304-6785; www.mindspring.com/~paddler.

BIKING

Bike Rentals   You can rent beach cruisers, children's bikes and mountain bikes at the **Equipment Locker Sport & Bicycle**. Locks are included with rentals. ~ MM 53, Marathon; 305-289-1670.

Residential development and the lack of sandy beaches limit hiking possibilities in the Keys.

HIKING

KEY LARGO AREA   A hiking/biking path runs from MM 106 in upper Key Largo for about 20 miles. This is a walking route parallel to Route 1. It ties in with a short nature trail, passes the John Pennekamp Coral Reef State Park, follows an old road to a county park and leads to some historic sites.

Route 1 from Miami and the slightly more northerly scenic **Card Sound Road**, which veers off from Route 1 at Florida City, lead to Key Largo, where Route 1 becomes the **Overseas Highway**, continuing on through the Keys all the way to Key West.

▼▼▼▼▼▼▼▼▼▼
Transportation

CAR

Note: Mile markers, often called mile posts, can be seen each mile along Route 1 in the Keys. They appear on the right shoulder of the road as small green signs with white numbers, beginning with Mile Marker (MM) 126 just south of Florida City and ending at MM 0 in Key West. When asking for directions in the Keys, your answer will likely refer to a mile marker number. We use them throughout the Keys, except for in Key West, where street addresses are mostly used.

Many visitors to the Keys choose to fly to Miami (see Chapter Two for more information). However, there are two small airports in the Keys located in Marathon and Key West. The **Marathon Airport** is Florida's most attractive little airport, with a green

AIR

tin roof and parade of palm trees. A clay-tiled lobby is cooled by ceiling fans with canvas sailboat mast-style blades. Check in at the coral rock counters of USAir Express or American Eagle.

Servicing the Upper Keys, **The Airporter** provides regularly scheduled shuttle service from Miami International Airport to Key Largo, Homestead, Islamorada and other areas. ~ 305-852-3413, 800-830-3413. **Upper Keys Transportation, Inc.** provides limousine service to Miami International Airport 24 hours a day with personally scheduled reservations. ~ 305-852-9533, 800-749-5397.

BUS

Greyhound Bus Lines (800-231-2222) services a few Keys locations. They are in Key Largo at MM 102, 305-296-9072; in Big Pine Key at MM 27.5; and in Marathon at 12222 Overseas Highway, 305-296-9073.

CAR RENTALS

Avis Rent A Car (800-331-1212) and **Budget Rent A Car** (800-527-0700) are located at the Marathon Airport. **Value Rent A Car** (800-468-2583) at the Winn Dixie Shopping Center and **Enterprise Rent A Car** (800-325-8007) will arrange airport pickup. In Key Largo, call **Enterprise Rent A Car** (800-325-8007).

TAXIS

In Marathon, call **Action Express Taxi**. ~ 305-743-6800, fax 305-289-3111.

AERIAL TOURS

A most unusual way to see the Keys—unless you're a pelican—is to skim along close to the water. And now you can try it yourself, in an ultralight aircraft. Introductory 20-minute rides are offered, and flight instruction is available through **Ultralight Rides**. ~ 163 Barry Avenue, MM 28.5, Little Torch Key; 305-872-0555.

Sight sharks and stingrays—from a safe distance. Wildlife excursions in the air are offered at **Fantasy Dan's Airplane Rides**. Sunset and champagne flight are available by reservation. ~ MM 17, Sugarloaf Key Airport; 305-745-2217.

Ecologically based flight tours of the Keys are the specialty of **Air Tours of South Florida**. Their eight-passenger Piper Chieftain airplane will fly a path that you help select—they'll even go all the way out to Key West. ~ 879 Northwest 10th Street, Homestead; 305-248-1100, 800-628-3610.

FOUR

Key West

The Spanish called it *Cayo Hueso*, Island of the Bones. That's what the amazed explorers found when they first landed here—human bones scattered about—but no one ever discovered where they came from. Were they Indian bones? The remains of some grisly massacre? No witness ever came forward to tell the tale. Be that as it may, the word *hueso* was eventually anglicized to "west," and the name "Key West" has stuck through the town's curious and colorful history.

Though not quite in the tropics, Key West is to all appearances a tropical island. Lying low on a shimmering sea, it boasts backyards lush with hibiscus, oleanders, frangipani and kapok and mango trees. Its generous harbors are filled with hybrid fleets of battered fishing craft, glass-bottom boats and handsome yachts. Date and coconut palms rustle like dry paper in the usually gentle and dependable breezes that come in off the sea. Heat pervades, but even in midsummer it's seldom unbearable. Key West is a small-town sort of place where narrow streets are lined with picket fences and lovely old frame houses. At the same time, it's a traveler's haven with classy hotels and happy hours. The cul-de-sac of the Overseas Highway, it's unlike any other city in the United States.

Four miles long from east to west and two miles in width, Key West provides more contrasts than one could dream up for any town, especially one located on a little island over a hundred miles out to sea from mainland Florida. Once the wealthiest city per capita in the country, it was at a later date also the poorest. Men have made fortunes here and have lost them, too, leaving legacies of fine, ornate houses along with quaint, weathered shanties. The military presence has waxed and waned repeatedly as the needs of war have demanded, each time leaving its mark on the architecture and society of the island as well as on the archaeology beneath the sands. Tourists have descended in hordes, then gone away, depending on the economic status of the nation.

During its trauma-filled history, the city has nearly been destroyed several times—by hurricane, by fire, by economic crises. But Key West has always risen phoenix-like from the ashes of defeats that would have flattened a less determined population. Closer to Havana than to Miami, its residents are descendants of the English, Cuban, Bahamian, African and myriad other folk who have found this tiny place to be an appealing home.

Some of the first residents, after the American Indians, were the English Bahamians who came to make their fortunes salvaging the ships that met their doom on the Atlantic reefs. These folks were called "conchs" after the large shells they used for food, decoration and musical instruments. Later came the sponge fishermen who, for a while, provided 90 percent of all sponges sold in the United States. Cigar makers from Cuba numbered as many as 6000, producing millions of hand-rolled cheroots in the late 19th century. Hordes of workers came to continue Henry Flagler's railroad past the Seven Mile Bridge out to Key West about 30 miles away.

Numerous well-known artists and writers, most notably Ernest Hemingway, Tennessee Williams and Elizabeth Bishop, have found Key West a place of inspiration. For half a century, Pulitzer Prize winners have come and gone, including poet Wallace Stevens, who wrote that Key West "looked like something in a dream."

Tennessee Williams was one who found not only creative inspiration but social tolerance. One of Key West's first gay literary figures, he was lured by its feverish ambience and beautiful young sailors. Since his arrival in the 1940s, Key West has been a playground for homosexuals. Today, gays account for 20 percent of the city's population, serve on the city council and are largely responsible for the island's wonderful flamboyancy. Each year, more than 400,000 gay men and women visit the island. And though AIDS has recently tempered what has been called "the wildest tropical port on the gay sexual tour," the gay scene still swings on the 700–800 block of Duval Street.

Many other groups also have woven color and contrast into the rich island tapestry. Jazz performers, county-and-western singers and classical musicians have contributed to the sounds of the town. Loafers have discovered Key West to be a comfortable spot for idling away the hospitably hot days. Fortune-tellers and spiritualists, magicians and tattoo artists offer their shows and services around the island. Street performers come in every level of talent and weirdness, including one who hoists a grocery cart with his teeth.

Indeed, travelers will find that Key West has much to tantalize the senses. Today's Key West is foremost a tourist town, one of the nation's chief travel destinations. Whatever your interest, you will soon discover something to your liking, whether it be tours, nightlife, souvenir shops, art events, festivals, a nightly sunset celebration or courtyard cafés drenched in tropical foliage. Lately, young Europeans have been lured by those cafés, and by the island's bohemian lifestyle, heeding the billboards that beckon travelers to "go all the way" to this tip of the Florida boot.

▼▼▼▼▼▼▼▼▼▼

Key West

While it's easy to stay busy as a tourist here, it's just as easy to miss some of Key West's most enchanting features. For Key West has held on to many of its contrasts. While you might want to do all the routine visitor activities, you would also be wise to allow yourself enough time to stroll among the old houses, to admire the tropical trees, to taste some *bollitos* at a

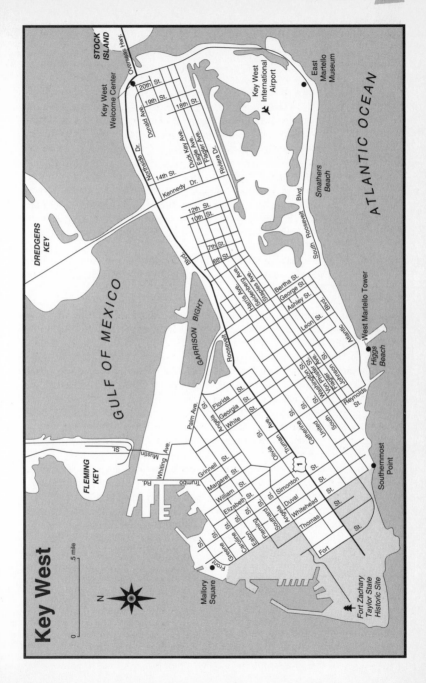

Key West

0 ___ .5 mile

N

STOCK ISLAND
Overseas HWY.
Key West Welcome Center
20th St.
19th St.
18th St.
Donald Ave.
Northside Dr.
Duck Key Ave.
Eagle Ave.
Flagler Ave.
Riviera Dr.
Key West International Airport
East Martello Museum
ATLANTIC OCEAN
14th St.
Kennedy Dr.
12th St.
10th St.
South Roosevelt Blvd.
Smathers Beach
DREDGERS KEY
GULF OF MEXICO
7th St.
6th St.
Seidenberg Ave. (Staples Ave.)
Harris Ave. (Staples Ave.)
Bertha St.
George St.
Ashley St.
Bird
Leon St.
West Martello Tower
Higgs Beach
GARRISON BIGHT
Roosevelt Blvd.
Atlantic
Washington St.
Johnson St.
Flagler Ave.
Reynolds St.
South St.
United St.
Palm Ave.
Florida St.
Georgia St.
White St.
Arela
Catherine St.
Olivia Ave.
Truman Ave.
Southernmost Point
FLEMING KEY
St.
Mustin Ave.
Whiting Ave.
Trumbo Rd.
Grinnell St.
Margaret St.
William St.
Elizabeth St.
Simonton St.
Duval St.
Angela St.
Whitehead St.
Thomas St.
Fort St.
Greene St.
Caroline St.
Eaton St.
Fleming St.
Southard St.
Front St.
Mallory Square
Fort Zachary Taylor State Historic Site

neighborhood grocery, to fire the imagination with retold tales of pirates and preparation for wars. Plan to tour the cemetery, watch for birds, meet the fishing fleet, explore the fort, talk to folks who live here, and you will begin to get a feel for this most unusual and varied town.

Key West is basically divided into two sections—Old Town, the place where tourists spend most of their time—and the "new town," where residents live and shop and carry out their daily lives.

The initial impression of Old Town is usually one of narrow streets, big old houses crowded together, highrise hotels that block the view, too many T-shirt shops and tourists and plenty of confusion. But don't be dismayed. Key West is easy to get to know, and there are all sorts of tours and printed guides and maps to help you. Once you are oriented, you'll have time to enjoy the salt air, to catch a bit of history, to appreciate the brilliant tropical trees whose blossoms gather in a carpet beneath your feet.

Unless you were born here, you will never get to be a genuine "conch," but it will probably not take you long to find plenty to your liking in the great variety of this island city that has never had a frost.

SIGHTS   It's easy to get around Key West. The Overseas Highway (Route 1) carries you through the newer section into Old Town via Roosevelt Boulevard. You may go either to the right, along the Gulf of Mexico past the yacht club and marinas, or to the left, along the Atlantic shore. If you take the former route, plan to stop in at the **Key West Welcome Center** for maps and an introduction to the area. This is near MM 4, but from here on you can stop counting mile markers and return to familiar street numbers. ~ 3840 North Roosevelt Boulevard; 305-296-4444.

By following Route 1 you will arrive in **Old Town**, the historic and main tourist area of Key West, just about where North Roosevelt Boulevard becomes Truman Avenue. This is a helter-skelter sort of place, with grand old Victorian houses, inviting alleys, junky souvenir shops, rocking-and-rolling bars, classy hotels, intimate guest houses, crowded marinas, street hawkers and incredible sunsets all tossed together into a colorful, noisy, artsy collage.

Away from Old Town, the remainder of the island includes settled residential areas, predictable shopping and a number of interesting sights that should pull you away from the tourist trappings. Here you are likely to run into those descendants of old Key West and the lower Keys who proudly refer to themselves as "conchs." The original settlers were named after the giant shells that were so much a part of their sea-oriented lives.

Although Old Town is small enough for pleasant walking, and the whole island for biking, it helps to get oriented on one of several available tours. Besides, you'll pick up some very interesting history of this unique island city. The trackless **Conch Tour Train** has been orienting visitors for over 30 years with narrated 14-mile island tours, leaving at regular intervals daily. Fee. ~ Two depots, one near the Welcome Center at 3850 North Roosevelt Boulevard and one at 303 Front Street; 305-294-5161, 800-868-7482; www.historictours.com, e-mail keyott@historictours.com.

The **Old Town Trolley Tour** meanders through the historic old streets and has the added advantage of unlimited drop-offs and pick-ups on your ticket, so when you see something of particular interest, you can stop and explore, then hop back on the next trolley that comes by. The trolley leaves every 30 minutes from the Welcome Center and most major hotels. Fee. ~ 305-296-6688, fax 305-292-8939; www.historictours.com.

For a more indigenous excursion, join the **Key West Nature Bike Tour**. It is hosted by Lloyd Mager, an environmentalist who, during his 20 years in Key West, has never owned a car or a motorbike. The casual 90-minute ride meanders down hidden side streets, visits little-known oddities (including several local people) and explores the island's luxurious foliage. A passionate guide, Mager started his tours because he "couldn't stand that someone would leave here never smelling a gardenia or tasting a mango or feeling the thrill of Key West by bike." ~ 305-294-1882.

◀ HIDDEN

If you'd rather get oriented on your own, stop at the **Key West Chamber of Commerce** and pick up a *Pelican Path* walking guide or *Solares Hill Guide to Old Key West*. The latter, definitely the best local guide to Old Town, is named for the island's highest point, which rises a whole 16 feet above sea level. In the old days, the Solares guide was witty and weird, but along with some of Key West, it has turned decidedly proper. Still, there are many historical and hidden gems and a few strange stops, including the old Busy Bee Bakery and a lane called Love and Grunt Bone Alley, where grits and grunts were once eaten. ~ 402 Wall Street; 305-294-2587, 800-527-8539; www.fla-keys.com.

✔ CHECK THESE OUT

- Enjoy Key West by bike on a **Key West Nature Bike Tour**, visiting not only sights but people as well. *page 127*
- Join the throngs of sun-worshippers who gather at **Mallory Square** each sunset to bid farewell to Old Sol for the night. *page 133*
- Peruse the tombstones at the **Key West Cemetery** for "grave" and sometimes amusing epitaphs. *page 133*
- Treat yourself to live music and West Indian fare at **Blue Heaven**, once a popular bordello and Hemingway's personal boxing ring. *page 147*

The factory that was parent to the **Key West Cigar Factory** dates back to the mid-19th century. Though smaller than the original establishments, this shop is the place to watch cigars being hand-rolled the way they've always been. ~ 3 Pirates Alley at 306 Front Street; 305-294-3470, 888-670-3470, fax 305-294-8703; www.keywestcigars.com. Cigars are also rolled and sold at **Rodriguez Cigar Factory**. Closed Sunday. ~ 113 Kino Plaza; 305-296-0167.

The Richard Peacon House was built in the late 1800s by the owner of Key West's largest grocery store. It has distinctive octagon-shaped verandas and, some say, a ghost. ~ 712 Eaton Street.

A wonderful example of bureaucratic snafus is the **U.S. Customs House and Post Office**, an imposing three-and-a-half-story red brick Romanesque revival structure, which, according to local tour guides, was built to specifications dictated by Washington in 1891. It has four full-size fireplaces and a steeply pitched roof designed to shed snow. (Well, it worked.) ~ Front and Greene streets.

History buffs will enjoy searching for the gun turret from the **Battleship USS Maine**. Not exactly hidden, but somewhat hard to find, this is a little monument dedicated to the memory of the Union Soldiers who fought during the Civil War. ~ In the park in front of the Customs House, Front and Greene streets.

The impressive **Key West United Methodist Church** has two-foot-thick walls that were made from solid limestone quarried right beside the sanctuary. Built between 1877 and 1892, the handsome church has a native mahogany ceiling and a teakwood chancel. Currently not open to the public. ~ Eaton Street at Simonton Street; 305-296-2392, fax 305-296-4702.

The most notable feature of Old Town is the architecture. Many of the beautiful old houses you see were built of wood by ships' carpenters in a blend of styles that came to be known as **conch-style houses**. Influenced by the varied backgrounds of their owners and the demands of the hurricane-prone climate, the result is an eclectic architectural heritage unique to this island city.

For an introductory sampling of these conch houses, start at the corner of Eaton and William streets, where two **Bahama Houses** stand side by side. These dwellings are the only ones known to have been shipped in their entirety to Key West from the Bahamas. Built in the mid-1800s by master shipbuilders, they bear unusual beaded siding, mahogany window sashes and broad verandas. ~ 730 Eaton Street and 408 William Street.

Next door, the **Samuel Filer House**, built around 1885, is a study in black and white contrasted with an etched cranberry glass transom and double-screen door. ~ 724 Eaton Street.

Only the front of the **Bartlum/Forgarty House** was floated over from the Bahamas on a schooner. The mid-19th-century dwelling is constructed with wooden pegs. ~ 718 Eaton Street.

No gimmicks, only immaculately preserved history awaits at the **Donkey Milk House**. The 1866 Classic Revival house is named for the donkey-drawn carts that once gathered in the courtyard to collect milk for their local deliveries. The home's original owner was Peter Williams, a U.S. marshal who saved his neighbor's house from Key West's devastating 1886 fire by dynamiting Eaton Street. In 1890, after his wife bore their second set of twins, he purchased another house, wheeled it across the island and attached it to the back of this one. Where the two houses meet, it's impossible to tell. There are, however, many gems here, including the 1890 Spanish tile floor and the black walnut staircase, the hand-decorated ceilings and the turn-of-the-century leather mirror and wooden thermometer in one of the bathrooms. The light fixtures—both gas and electric—tell the story of how modern conveniences came late to Key West. By appointment only. Admission. ~ 613 Eaton Street; 305-296-1866, fax 305-296-0922.

With delicate double balustrades, beveled glass and fan windows, ornate trim and 22 rooms, the Queen Anne–style **Curry Mansion** presents a three-story display of millionaire life at the turn of the century. Only the Bahama-style hinged shutters are common to other, less opulent homes of early Key West. The showcase house is open for tours daily, showing off the luxurious appointments and fine 19th-century furnishings. Admission. ~ 511 Caroline Street; 305-294-5349, fax 305-294-4093; www. currymansion.com, e-mail frontdesk@currymansion.com.

Although Key West's first lighthouse was built in 1825, a hurricane swept it away some 20 years later. A new structure was built inland in 1847 and guided ships through the water until 1969. Today, along with the adjacent lighthouse keeper's house, it contains the **Lighthouse Museum** operated by the Key West Art and Historical Society. For a panoramic view of this flat little island, climb the 88 steps to the top. See the huge Fresnel lens that cost $1 million back in the mid-19th century, vintage photographs and nautical charts, ship models and memorabilia from area lighthouses. Admission. ~ 938 Whitehead Street; 305-294-0012, fax 305-296-6266.

Though many famous authors have spent time in Key West, none has left as strong a mark as Ernest Hemingway. He and his wife Pauline bought a fine old coral-rock house in which they lived from 1931 until the end of their marriage in 1940. Today, the **Ernest Hemingway Home and Museum** is a tribute to "Papa's" life and work, for it was here that he created such masterpieces as *To Have and Have Not* and *For Whom the Bell Tolls*. Tours are given daily, reflecting on Hemingway's works and his rigorous lifestyle. Through the marvelous house and luxuriant grounds roam sleek six-toed cats, said to be descendants of Hemingway's own; they lie irreverently on his works, snooze on his Spanish furniture and stalk the rooms that still reflect the writer's colorful personality. An on-site bookstore sells Hemingway's works, as well as prints inspired by the literature and the house itself. Admission. ~ 907 Whitehead Street; 305-294-1136, fax 305-294-2755; www.hem ingwayhome.com, e-mail info@hemingwayhome.com.

You may have to wait in line to have your picture taken at the spot marking the **Southernmost Point**. "Ninety miles to Cuba," reads the sign beneath the kitschy-looking striped buoy surrounded by folks with cameras. ~ Ocean end of Whitehead Street.

The **Audubon House & Tropical Gardens** is a fine sample of early Key West architecture; its restoration inspired a city-wide interest in preserving other historic structures. Furnished with fine antiques of the 18th and 19th centuries, the three-story frame house is held together entirely by wooden pegs and is an excellent example of the shipbuilders' craft. It now serves as a museum housing an extensive collection of works by John James Audubon, the famous painter and naturalist. A lush one-acre tropical garden surrounds the house. The gift shop offers museum-quality prints, art objects, jewelry and posters. Admission. ~ 205 Whitehead Street; 305-294-2116.

At the **Key West Municipal Aquarium** you can touch a starfish or watch a shark being fed. Opened in 1934, the aquarium was the first visitors' attraction built in the Keys. Today the exhibits include a turtle pool, shark tanks, live coral and many other samples of Atlantic and Gulf underwater life. The "Atlantic Shores" exhibit is a red mangrove ecosystem complete with wildlife. Guided tours and feedings take place four times a day. Admission. ~ 1 Whitehead Street; 305-296-2051, fax 305-293-7094; www.historictours.com, e-mail keyaqu@historictours.com.

If you've ever wondered how much a gold bar weighs or if rubies still sparkle after centuries on the bottom of the sea, visit **Mel Fisher Maritime Heritage Society Museum**. The place literally dazzles with gold chains, jewel-studded crosses and flagons, and great piles of gleaming coins—all treasures gathered by Fisher and his crew of divers from the sunken ships *Atocha* and *Margarita*. You really are allowed to lift the gold bar, though you can't take it with you. Admission. ~ 200 Greene Street; 305-294-2633; www. melfisher.org, e-mail info@melfisher.org.

Duval Street is the main street of Old Town, though it cannot be compared to any other Main Street in America. It begins on the gulf and ends at the ocean, yet walking it one has little sense of the water. Instead Duval seems one long masquerade of old and new architecture, thin white porches and lavish gingerbread, flowering trees of outlandish proportions, store windows with strange and fabulous displays, metal blenders groaning from smoothie stands, guitar players hoping for a dollar, hucksters whispering toward restaurants and stores. Near dusk the snake handler strolls Duval with his albino boa. And the sun-weathered cookie lady prowls on her three-wheel bike, calling "Cooookkkkieees!"

Key West is at its best and worst on Duval Street, though some locals would say mostly worst. It is not uncommon to hear Conches say they "haven't ventured on Duval in years," though one should be skeptical of such talk, Key West being such a small island. Truth is the two ends of Duval couldn't be more different. "Upper Duval," on the southeast end, is quieter and classier, with its string of galleries and cafés and bistros, pretty inns and their lush gardens, and a wine bar where one can sip a glass of gewürztraminer beneath the Christmas palms.

"Lower Duval," to the northwest, is tumultuous and tacky. T-shirt shops seem to mutate here every few months, and there are many bars and lots of gaseous cars cruising with their bass at full bore. Some blame Lower Duval's demise on the cruise ships that dock down here several times a week, disgorging passengers

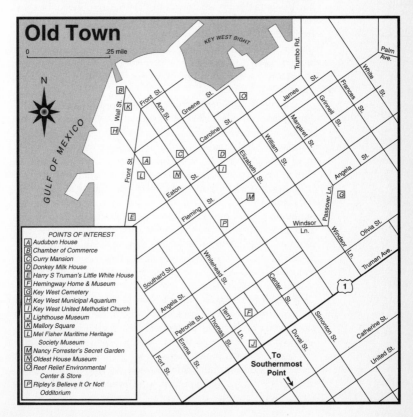

Old Town

0   .25 mile

N

GULF OF MEXICO

KEY WEST BIGHT

POINTS OF INTEREST
A Audubon House
B Chamber of Commerce
C Curry Mansion
D Donkey Milk House
E Harry S Truman's Little White House
F Hemingway Home & Museum
G Key West Cemetery
H Key West Municipal Aquarium
I Key West United Methodist Church
J Lighthouse Museum
K Mallory Square
L Mel Fisher Maritime Heritage
     Society Museum
M Nancy Forrester's Secret Garden
N Oldest House Museum
O Reef Relief Environmental
     Center & Store
P Ripley's Believe It Or Not!
     Odditorium

To
Southernmost
Point

in search only of a beer and a T-shirt. They find both at Planet Hollywood and Hard Rock Cafe, among the new chain entrants to Lower Duval (others include Taco Bell, Ben & Jerry's and Coffee Beanery).

Duval does have its high points, including the **Oldest House Museum**. This nine-room pine home was built in 1826 by a ship's carpenter for Capt. Francis and Emeline Watlington and their nine daughters. Learn about life on this salt-marsh, mosquito-infested island at a time when the treatment for yellow fever was a mustard poultice and provisions arrived via schooner. A professional wrecker, Watlington saved lives and salvaged cargo from ships wrecked on the reef. The museum documents this fascinating trade, which attracted honest men as well as unscrupulous opportunists. Admission. ~ 322 Duval Street; 305-294-9502.

The oldest church in Key West was established in 1832. It was prophetically dedicated to St. Paul, the quintessential shipwreck victim. Two later churches on the site were swept away by hurricanes (a third burnt down). In 1919 a magnificent white masonry structure went up, and that one, **St. Paul's Episcopal Church**, lasted. Embellished with noteworthy stained-glass windows and sporting an 8000-pound, 2000-pipe organ, today's church is a peaceful place to spend a quiet moment away from the antics of Duval Street. ~ Duval and Eaton streets; 305-296-5142, fax 305-294-6687.

Enrico Caruso once sang at the **San Carlos Institute**, and Cuban patriot José Martí delivered many rousing speeches from the balcony of the auditorium. This is actually the fourth San Carlos Institute, others having succumbed to fire and hurricane. Founded in 1871 to teach Cuban immigrants the language and customs of their adopted country, to preserve the history and heritage of the land they had left behind, and to plan the campaign that would free Cuba from Spain's domination, the institute now houses a museum and a library as well as hosting special events and theatrical performances. The pale yellow building, with its turrets and columns and gingerbread and its 16-foot-high doors of Cuban cedar, had deteriorated badly, but was recently restored, and is now open for tours. Closed Monday. Admission. ~ 516 Duval Street; phone/fax 305-294-3887.

Ripley's Believe It Or Not! Odditorium resides in The Strand, the gloriously ornate 1930s movie house. It definitely is an odd place, with a pricey admission fee and 10,000 square feet of believable and unbelievable gimmicks. There's a "hurricane hallway" where you're nearly blown away and a "tropical rainforest" with drums, daggers and "authentic" shrunken heads. On the positive side, kids will love it. Admission. ~ 527 Duval Street; 305-293-9694.

Every visitor to Key West inevitably witnesses a sunset at **Mallory Square**, a Key West institution that will make you feel like you're part of a Mayan ritual. You'll find bagpipers, jugglers, fire-eaters and people who think it's fun to stand on one foot for half an hour. As the great moment nears, a cheer rises from the crowd, reaching fever pitch as the sun hits the horizon. ~ Northwest end of Duval Street.

Mad Max meets sustainability at **Reworx**, a futuristic museum where industrial scrap metal is transformed into fine art. Sculptor Cynthia Wynn's fascination with industrial-size gears and mechanical hardware led her to recycle the scrap into mammoth home furnishings—picture a bed frame constructed from giant chain, I-beams and a bulldozer sprocket. Artist Valerie Hoh conceived the heavy-metal museum environment, taking cues from recycling-art-crazed customers at Pandemonium, her art/furnishings shop, located next door. Admission. ~ 825 Duval Street; 305-292-3273.

The city of Key West grows many of its landscaping plants at the **Charles "Sonny" McCoy Indigenous Park**, a showplace for trees and plants native to the region. You may wander inside the gates of the park during the daytime and learn to recognize the lignum vitae, silver palm and a number of tropical trees found only in the Keys. There is a fish pond hidden away in the back. Closed weekends. ~ Atlantic Boulevard at White Street; 305-292-8157.

Also on the grounds is the **Wildlife Rescue of Florida Keys**, where injured birds are rehabilitated and then released back into the wild. From an observation platform that offers a view of the island's salt pond, you can see heron, ibis, gallinule and migratory birds that gather here. ~ McCoy Indigenous Park, White Street and Atlantic Boulevard; 305-294-1441.

The historic **West Martello Tower** is the enchanting home of Key West Garden Club's **Joe Allen Garden Center**. The remains of the once-upon-a-time fort, with its crumbling brick walls and arches and its massive banyan trees and old palms, create a pleasant, restful environment for numerous bromeliads and other tropical flora usually confined to greenhouses, and spectacular seasonal displays. Closed Sunday and Monday. ~ Atlantic Boulevard and White Street; 305-294-3210.

"I Told You I Was Sick," reads the straightforward message immortalized on a gravestone in the **Key West Cemetery**. Due to the rocky geology of the island, many of the stone-encased caskets rest above ground, often carrying curious and, what seem now, humorous messages such as the one placed by a grieving widow: "At Least I Know Where He's Sleeping Tonight." History abounds in this enchanting and poignant spot, too, as in the special memorial to those who died at the sinking of the U.S. Battleship *Maine* in Havana harbor in 1898. You may stroll the cemetery until 6 p.m.; tours are given on Tuesday and Thursday. ~ Angela and Margaret streets; 305-292-8177.

St. Mary Star of the Sea is the second-oldest Catholic church in Florida. Built at the turn of the century of Miami oolite quarried in the Keys, the interesting building features pressed-tin arches and metal columns. On the grounds stands a small **grotto** in honor of the Lady of Lourdes, built many years ago by a nun, who prayed it would provide protection from hurricanes. So far, the grotto seems to have served the purpose she planned, receiving credit from many believers for the absence of any killer storms since the sister's dedicated work was undertaken. ~ 1010 Windsor Lane; 305-294-1018.

From the top of the citadel of the **East Martello Museum** you can get a magnificent view of the island and the Atlantic, just as the Union Army builders of this 1862 Civil War brick fortress planned. Today the historic structure houses 11 rooms and a large collection of Key West artifacts and serves as both a museum of Key West history and a gallery displaying the work of Keys artists. The fort's tower alone, with vaulted ceilings and spiral staircase, is worth a visit and, at the top, it affords you a view of the Gulf and the Atlantic. Admission. ~ 3501 South Roosevelt Boulevard; 305-296-3913.

Few developments have caused so much controversy on this tiny island as the **Truman Annex**. Owned for decades by the Navy, the quiet, shady 103-acre parcel was the last big piece of undeveloped land on Key West when it was auctioned in 1986 to a wealthy Sikh from Maine. Since then, expensive condominiums, a complex of Victorian-style houses, marinas and luxury hotels have been built. But the public is still welcome to tour the grounds and historic buildings, which include the surgeon's quarters, the old weather station and the marine hospital. ~ Main entrance at Thomas and Southard streets; 305-296-5601.

Today you can drive through the annex's wrought-iron gates, past the Bahama-style police with white pith helmets, and watch

RELIEF FOR REEFS

Before you visit the coral reef, stop by the **Reef Relief Environmental Center and Store**. The tiny place is packed with exhibits and information on the fragile coral reef ecosystem—the reef, mangrove forests and seagrass beds—and how to protect it. It's run by the nonprofit Reef Relief, one of Florida's most powerful environmental organizations. ~ 201 William Street; 305-294-3100, fax 305-293-9515; www.reefrelief.org, e-mail reef@bellsouth.net.

the new conch houses go up while the old ones tumble down. Here also is **Harry S Truman's Little White House**, where presidents Truman, Eisenhower, Kennedy and Carter vacationed. The handsome white clapboard building, built in 1890, has two facades and spacious porches enclosed with wooden louvers. Admission. ~ 111 Front Street; 305-294-9911, fax 305-294-9988.

Drive through the Truman Annex and you will find the **Fort Zachary Taylor State Historic Site**, a treasure trove of Civil War weaponry and memorabilia. The excavations of the 1845 fort have revealed beautiful mid-19th-century arched brickwork, parade grounds and the largest collection of Civil War cannons in the U.S. The park itself has an excellent swimming beach. Admission. ~ Southwestern point of island, off Southard Street; 305-292-6713, fax 305-292-6881.

◄ *HIDDEN*

The Botanical Garden Society maintains a small but nicely laid-out and well-marked **Botanical Garden** where you can get acquainted with many of the trees and other indigenous flora that grow in this distinctive region. There are two freshwater ponds, and if you look hard enough, you may catch sight of a rare butterfly. ~ College Road and Aguero Circle, Stock Island.

◄ *HIDDEN*

You won't find signs for **Nancy Forrester's Secret Garden**, a well-hidden spot of interest to environmentalists and plant fanciers. More than 25 years ago, Nancy began to create an informal rainforest for herself, and later opened it to the public. Narrow paths wind through the property, leading to small glades where benches and tables invite you to relax and enjoy the sounds of silence. Traipse down the lane that looks like a private drive beside a real estate company and you'll find the small white gate. You're welcome to bring your own lunch. Admission. ~ One Free School Lane, which leads off Simonton Street in the 500 block; 305-294-0015.

For picture-window views of the coral reef in the Atlantic Ocean, as well as late afternoon sunset cruises, climb aboard the glass-bottom sightseeing boat **Fireball** or **Pride of Key West**. Admission. ~ World-Famous Glassbottom Boats, north end of Duval Street; 305-296-6293, fax 305-294-8704; e-mail glassbottom boat@sprynet.com.

As you might expect, in Key West you can find countless accommodations—from bare-basics motels to outrageously expensive resorts. Unfortunately, bare basics often carry a moderate price tag in Key West, now that the island is wildly popular year-round. Some of the best values can be found at the island's varied guesthouses, many with whimsical architecture splashed with tropical colors and surrounding exquisite little courtyards. A number of the guesthouses cater to gays only, so be sure to ask about the house policy. If you want help finding a place to stay, contact the **Key**

LODGING

West Reservation Service. ~ 628 Fleming Street; 800-327-4831, fax 305-296-6291.

The **Hilton Key West Resort and Marina** posts some of Key West's highest rates, for which you get a bayfront locale and sprawling marina, shops and eateries and fine dining, and rooms that are modern and minimal, with eggshell walls and wall-to-wall teal carpets. There is, alas, too much carpet, and some rooms are musty. You can board a little boat over to Sunset Key, where there are gingerbread homes for rent through the Hilton's **Sunset Key Guest Cottages**. Or you can simply lie in a chair on the beach at Sunset, order a cocktail from the tiki bar, and watch the men and their monstrous machines construct million-dollar homes where once there was Navy munitions. ~ 245 Front Street; 305-294-4000, 800-221-2424, fax 305-294-4086; www.hilton.com. ULTRA-DELUXE.

Quietly dominating the edge of Old Town, the soft pink, metal-roofed **Hyatt Key West** is a maze of well-lit stairs and balconies from which you can observe Key West's famous sunsets without the folderol of Mallory Square. The cool pastel decor suits the location beside a small private beach and marina. A pool, jacuzzi, exercise room, fine restaurants, an indoor/outdoor lounge and numerous watersport rentals and tours make this one of the choicest lodgings—and one of the most convenient for Key West sightseeing. ~ 601 Front Street; 305-296-9900, 800-233-1234, fax 305-292-1038; www.hyatt.com. ULTRA-DELUXE.

Pier House has long been one of Key West's most popular hotels. It sprawls along the Gulf with rambling tin-roofed villas and acres of docks. Here you get all the goodies of an elaborate resort—superb restaurants, lively nightspots, a therapeutic spa—with that classic laid-back Keys mood. A small beach is soft and picturesque, the swimming pool expansive, and the grounds jungly. Old Town shops and sights are a short stroll away. ~ 1 Duval Street; 305-296-4600, 800-327-8340, fax 305-296-9085; www. pierhouse.com, e-mail info@pierhouse.com. ULTRA-DELUXE.

The Historic Florida Keys Preservation Board honored the **Cuban Club Suites** its "Five Star Award of Excellence," a fitting honor for this restoration of one of Key West's most important historical structures. The second-floor balcony affords views of Duval Street similar to those seen by the island's first Cuban émigrés, whose primary social/political club operated from this building in the 1900s. Today the suites are furnished in a tropical Victorian style, with cathedral ceilings; amenities include fully equipped kitchens and lavish bathrooms. Suitable for up to six people, units run larger than many Old Town residences. ~ 1102 Duval Street; 305-296-0465, 800-432-4849, fax 305-293-7669; www.keywest cubanclub.com, e-mail info@keywestcubanclub.com. DELUXE TO ULTRA-DELUXE.

The lushest place on the island is surely **The Gardens Hotel**. Now a small, luxurious European-style hotel, it was once the Peggy Mills Botanical Garden. The late Mills, known around town as Miss Peggy, searched the world for rare species, importing orchids from Hawaii and Japan, and palms and canopy trees from Latin America. She also brought in 87,000 bricks to create the footpaths that now curl through the garden. Five handsome buildings of crisp white, including Mill's original 1870s house, offer elegant rooms with French doors, wood floors, marble baths and porches. Continental breakfast can be taken in the glass sunroom or on the veranda. There's a pool and jacuzzi. ~ 526 Angela Street; 305-294-2661, 800-526-2664, fax 305-292-1007; www.gardens hotel.com. ULTRA-DELUXE.

Constructed just after the Great Fire of 1886, **Eaton Lodge**, a two-and-a-half-story Greek Revival Victorian mansion that's been featured in every major publication from *National Geographic* to the *New York Times*, sports a distinctive diamond-patterned balustrade along the balcony and veranda. The non-smoking rooms and suites are furnished in authentic period pieces with colorful comforters on the beds—maybe carved mahogany or wrought-iron four-posters—all have refrigerators and private baths. Each opens onto a wonderful garden that was created by Genevieve Warren, one of the home's earliest owners. Its winding pathways lead past a fish pond, around a pool and whirlpool spa to the side of the old cookhouse and onto a brick-paved terrace, where morning breakfast, which includes home-made tropical fruit bread is served. It's hard to believe that the quiet of this lush and peaceful oasis is just steps away from the hustle and bustle of Duval Street. ~ 511 Eaton Street; 305-292-2170, 800-294-2170, fax 305-292-4018; www.eatonlodge.com. DELUXE TO ULTRA-DELUXE.

Built in 1890 and featuring a handsome metal-roofed turret on one corner, **The Artist House** is one of many conch houses turned hostelry. Guests may have one of six rooms with private bath, refrigerator and antique or period reproduction furnishings, including four-poster or genuine brass beds. A jacuzzi and sundeck are set among lush tropical plantings in the garden; breakfasts are continental. Rich period wallpapers and superb restoration make this an elegant lodging. ~ 534 Eaton Street; 305-296-3977, 800-593-7898, fax 305-296-3210; www.artist housekeywest.com, e-mail ahkw@bellsouth.net. DELUXE TO ULTRA-DELUXE.

With its vast jungle garden and unusual assortment of lovely rooms, **Island City House** is unquestionably one of the best guesthouses in Key West. Choose from the 1880s Arch House with its studio suites and gingerbread trim; the 1880s Island City House mansion with its creaky wood floors and homey antiques; or the 1980s Cigar House with its spacious modern suites overlooking the pool and jacuzzi. All rooms have kitchens, though a cart loaded with fresh fruit and pastries beckons poolside every morning. ~ 411 William Street; 305-294-5702, 800-634-8230, fax 305-294-1289; www.islandcityhouse.com, e-mail islcity@flakey sol.com. DELUXE TO ULTRA-DELUXE.

Westwinds is a historic bed and breakfast with 22 guest rooms scattered among four peach-colored conch houses (two units share a bath). In the rooms, you'll find wicker furnishings, a ceiling fan, air conditioning and a phone; only one of the buildings has rooms with TVs. Except for two units in the main conch house, all have private baths. Guests enjoy lounging around the exotically landscaped pool area. It is here that the continental breakfast is served in the morning. No children under 12 are allowed. ~ 914 Eaton Street; 305-296-4440, 800-788-4150, fax 305-293-0931. MODERATE TO ULTRA-DELUXE.

A Cuban cigar factory in the 1880s, **Simonton Court** is now a gardeny compound spread across two acres of bougainvillea and hibiscus, lattice and brick lanes. There are 26 rooms in ten cottages and buildings, including the two-story inn with floors of Dade County pine; the luxurious mansion with period antiques, spacious verandas and marble baths; and cottages of pink clapboard and coral stucco. All the rooms are immaculately restored and have refrigerators, TVs and VCRs; many have kitchenettes. Plunge pools and swimming pools are set among the trees, and it is very quiet here. No children allowed. Popular with gay and straight travelers alike. ~ 320 Simonton Street; 305-294-6386, 800-944-2687, fax 305-293-8446. ULTRA-DELUXE.

Locals like Fleming Street. It has the library, a bike lane, many canopy trees and the famous Fausto's Food Palace. It also has the pink-washed **Ambrosia House**, with seven comfortable rooms, all variously themed. The Safari Room, for instance, has wall-to-wall Dade County pine, a poster bed draped in silky netting, and animal print bedspreads and cushions. Mini-fridges and coffee-makers come with every room, and there's a rambling wood deck out back with a pool, hot tub and fishtail palms. ~ 615 Fleming Street; 305-296-9838, 800-535-9838, fax 305-294-2463. DELUXE TO ULTRA-DELUXE.

Enjoying a similarly ideal spot, **Fleming Street Inn** also backs up to Nancy Forrester's Secret Garden, a lush green space of quietude. Eight extra large rooms go minimalist with blond platform beds, lattice-style headboards and crisp white comforters. There are also three lovely, bi-level suites in an 1880s house of tall ceilings, white pickled wood and staircases spiraling up to bedrooms with skylights. The suites have their own pool, and a second pool

rests among a brick courtyard with a wall of leggy bamboo palms.
~ 618 Fleming Street; 305-294-5181, 800-820-5397, fax 305-296-
2425. ULTRA-DELUXE.

After a major renovation of this 1880s-era classic revival compound of four buildings, the Marquesa Hotel has landed securely
on the National Register of Historic Places. Each of the 27 rooms
is luxurious and formal, with antique appointments, pastel walls,
gleaming white woodwork and distinctive fabrics. Every corner
is a masterpiece of workmanship. The property includes an award-
winning restaurant and two sparkling pools in a tropical garden.
~ 600 Fleming Street; 305-292-1919, 800-869-4631, fax 305-294-
2121; www.marquesa.com. ULTRA-DELUXE.

There's a funky, European air about Eden House that recalls
a time when Key West was laid-back, diverse and loaded with
characters. Think clean and comfortable, with patchwork hints of
resort luxury. With 40 units, the place meanders through the better part of a block, and includes a pool, jacuzzi, waterfalls, porch
swings and thick foliage. The staff is fun and friendly. ~ 1015
Fleming Street; 305-296-6868, 800-533-5397, fax 305-294-1221;
www.edenhouse.com, e-mail mike@edenhouse.com. MODERATE
TO ULTRA-DELUXE.

The charming main house, with it cozy library and comfortable furniture gives Merlinn Inn a warm, centralized feel even
though doors to most rooms line up motel-style, facing a well-trav-
eled street. The lush tropical garden extends the compound's living area and provides intimate out-of-doors nooks and crannies.
Enjoy extreme privacy as well as a sense of community with the
owners and other guests. ~ 811 Simonton Street; 305-296-3336,
800-773-1894, fax 305-296-3524; www.merlinnkeywest.com,
e-mail merlinnc@aol.com. MODERATE TO DELUXE.

One of the island's lushly planted resorts, Paradise Inn is full
of light and space—its winding limestone and brick footpaths,
bubbling whirlpool and kidney of a pool open to sunshine. There
is much floral exotica: pink tabebuias and night-blooming jas-
mine, purple-flowered sky vines trailing along gingerbread piazzas,
and ylang-ylang trees whose heady blossoms smell like Chanel
No. 5. Families like it here; the rooms are spacious suites or cottages with one or two bedrooms and baths of marble. Continental breakfast included. There's plenty of on-site parking,
too—a rare and welcome feature in Key West. ~ 819 Simonton
Street; 305-293-8007, 800-888-9648, fax 305-293-0807; www.
theparadiseinn.com, e-mail paradise@keysdigital.com. ULTRA-
DELUXE.

Ethereal peach buildings trimmed in white gingerbread stand
along a pretty beach at Marriott's Casa Marina and Reach Resort.
This balmy address has lovely terraced suites with Mexican tile

floors, ceiling fans, wet bars, commanding views of the ocean, a swimming pool and a health club. ~ 1435 Simonton Street; 305-296-5000, 800-874-4118, fax 305-296-3008; www.keywest.com/reach. ULTRA-DELUXE.

The **Curry Mansion Inn** provides 28 guest rooms with private baths. Most are in the beautiful backyard annex that surrounds the pretty deck and pool, eight are in the Victorian home across the street and four are in the fine old historic mansion itself. Furnishings are mostly fine wicker, and every bed is covered with a handmade quilt. Rooms in the annex are all pastel and white, creating a cool, fresh feel even on the hottest summer day. Rates include complimentary happy hour and a European breakfast with various freshly baked breads. ~ 511 and 512 Caroline Street; 305-294-5349, 800-253-3466, fax 305-294-4093; www.currymansion.com, e-mail frontdesk@currymansion.com. ULTRA-DELUXE.

The owners of **La Te Da** have exquisitely restored every inch of every building, including 16 spacious and plush guest rooms tucked within a helter-skelter maze of porches, balconies and sundecks. There are two bars and a fancy restaurant that starts indoors beneath twinkling chandeliers and continues around a sparkling pool. Still remaining is the balcony where José Martí campaigned in 1890 for funds to support the Cuban revolution. Gay-friendly. ~ 1125 Duval Street; 305-296-6706, 800-528-3320, fax 305-296-0438; e-mail lateda-kw@aol.com. DELUXE TO ULTRA-DELUXE.

Unless you're up for sleeping on a seawall or pier, you can't spend a night any closer to Cuba than at the **Southernmost Motel in the USA**—it really is what it says. Accommodations are ordinary but gleaming, and the large motel has pseudo-gingerbread trim, two heated pools and a tropical deck with a tiki bar and a pool bar, all contributing to its being a comfortable lodging handy to Key West tourist sights. ~ 1319 Duval Street; 305-296-6577, 800-354-4455, fax 305-294-8272; www.oldtownresorts.com. DELUXE TO ULTRA-DELUXE.

Key West has but two bed and breakfasts by the sea, **Dewey House** and **La Mer**, Queen Anne confections right next to each other and sharing the same owners and same sense of civility. Every morning breakfasts of mango, papaya and puffy croissants are set on the terracotta terrace overlooking tiny, palmy South Beach, where locals perform their sunrise yoga. Every afternoon there are cheese and wafers and long, tall glasses of iced tea. Both houses are handsome, though Dewey House is more luxurious with its rooms of deep green and honey, high ceilings and wrought-iron poster beds, big baths with round whirlpool tubs behind glass doors, and French doors opening to wood-deck balconies.

Room 404 at La Mer is extra big and has a veranda on the ocean. La Mer serves a continental breakfast and high tea daily. ~ 1319 Duval Street and 506 South Street, respectively; 305-296-5611, 800-354-4455, fax 305-294-8272; www.oldtownresorts.com. ULTRA-DELUXE.

Coconut Beach Resort is a timeshare, but not in the sense that springs to mind, with bleak, child-battered rooms and salesmen staring hungrily at you from a lobby corner. Coconut Beach is run as a hotel, a savvy, seabreezy place of whitewashed and gabled houses running along the ocean, its vast sundeck framing a swimming pool and waterfall, its raised trellised walkways ambling around rare and exotic flora. Rooms range from studios to two-bedroom suites, all decorated in contemporary styles of tiled floors and blond rattan furniture, and most looking out across ocean. ~ 1500 Alberta Street; 305-294-0057, 800-835-0055, fax 305-294-5066; www.coconutbeachresort.com, e-mail cbrkw@flakey sol.com. ULTRA-DELUXE.

> The Wyndham Casa Marina Resort was created as the final resort along Henry Flagler's railroad in 1921.

A member of the international Youth Hostel Association, the **Key West International Youth Hostel and Seashell Motel** has dorm rooms for males, females and mixed couples in a quiet residential neighborhood; motel rooms are moderate to deluxe. All ages are welcome, but nonmembers must have a valid picture ID. There are full kitchen facilities and lockers and bicycles to rent. ~ 718 South Street; 305-296-5719, fax 305-296-0672. BUDGET TO MODERATE.

Even if you don't choose to stay at the **Wyndham Casa Marina Resort & Beach House**, you should drop in and indulge in the Sunday brunch or at least explore the lobby of this 1921 historic landmark. This handsome Spanish-style hotel radiates historic elegance. The pine floors gleam like glass. The French doors leading to a spacious loggia and the restaurant's restored mahogany coffered ceiling pay tribute to Flagler's dreams for the Keys. A beachfront restaurant, two pools, a jacuzzi, a health club, lighted tennis courts, a water sports center and an airport shuttle add modern luxury. ~ 1500 Reynolds Street on the ocean; 305-296-3535, 800-626-0777, fax 305-296-3008; www.casamarinakey west.com. ULTRA-DELUXE.

Looking more like it should be in Disney World than Key West, the **Sheraton Suites** sports a cluster of faux Bahamas-style buildings coated in radiant peach and purple. In the lobby, teal benches and purple chairs look cartoonish; at the meandering pool, water cascades from fake boulders; and in the rooms, blue waves dance on the pastel bedside stands. All 180 rooms are 508-square-foot suites offering living rooms with sofa beds, wet bars with micro-

Text continued on page 144.

Fort Jefferson

Like a scattering of tiny emerald beads, a cluster of coral reef islands dot the Gulf of Mexico 68 miles west of Key West. Ponce de León named them "Tortugas" for the turtles he found there, sailors called them "Dry" because they hold no fresh water. But the Dry Tortugas do hold a national park centered around a magnificent 19th-century fort.

To see **Fort Jefferson** from the air, surrounded by azure sea, walled moat and white sand, is like conjuring up a fairy tale, enriched with popular legends of pirate treasure. Walking through the open sally port and arched hallways, one steps into a vast area whose silence is broken only by seagull cries and the calls of migratory birds. ~ For information, contact the park at 305-242-7700, fax 305-242-7711; www.nps.gov/drto, e-mail drto_information@nps.gov.

Fort Jefferson, from its perch on Garden Key, appears much as it did in its brief 19th-century heyday. German and Irish craftsmen, with the assistance of slaves, created the spectacular brick- and stone-work from millions of bricks brought by sailing ships from Pensacola and Virginia, and granite and slate brought from New England. The eight-foot-thick walls stand 50 feet high and feature handsome arches and wide views of sea approaches. Fort Jefferson's half-mile hexagonal perimeter made it the largest link in the chain of coastal fortifications built from Maine to Texas in the first half of the 19th century. It encompasses almost all the land of its tiny key, creating the illusion that it floats on the glistening tropical sea.

Though at first glance the fort seems complete, it was never actually finished. Begun in 1846, work continued for 30 years, but Fort Jefferson's importance came to an end with the invention of the rifled cannon. When federal troops occupied the fort throughout the Civil War, they discovered its foundations were not built on solid coral reef as was originally thought, but on sand and coral boulders. The walls began to show cracks as foundations settled with the shifting of the sea floor.

Fort Jefferson's most inglorious claim to fame came in 1865. To this lonely and inescapable reef were sent the "Lincoln Conspirators," four men convicted of complicity in the assassination of President Abraham Lincoln. Most noted of these was Dr. Samuel Mudd, the physician who had innocently set the broken leg of John Wilkes Booth following the shooting of the president. Sentenced to life imprisonment at Fort Jefferson, Mudd was eventually pardoned following his gallant efforts at treating the almost 300 garrisoned men who were struck with yellow fever at the fort during the 1867 epidemic. Today visitors can explore Mudd's cell and envision the bleakness of his fate.

The Army formally abandoned Fort Jefferson in 1874, following more yellow fever and a serious hurricane; it never saw any military action. And many military men may have felt grateful, for duty at Fort Jefferson, where water was scarce, mosquitoes thick and hurricane winds ferocious, was not coveted. But fortunately for historians and travelers, President Franklin D. Roosevelt proclaimed Fort Jefferson a national monument in 1935, thus preserving its unique heritage and its spectacular architecture.

To visit Dry Tortugas National Park and Fort Jefferson, you can go by ferry boat (one and a half to two hours) or seaplane (35 minutes) from Key West. Contact the park (305-242-7700) or the Key West Chamber of Commerce (305-294-2587, 800-527-8539; www.fla-keys.com) for further information.

Seaplanes of Key West provides service to the Dry Tortugas. ~ 305-294-0709, 800-950-2359, fax 305-296-4141; www.seaplanesofkeywest.com, e-mail info@seaplanesofkeywest.com.

Yankee Fleet offers daily runs between Key West and Dry Tortugas National Park. ~ Oceanside Marina, Stock Island; 800-942-5464; www.yankee-fleet.com, e-mail carol@yankee-fleet.com.

You can spread a picnic, pitch a tent in the shade of tropical trees or sunbathe on the tiny, pristine beach, but you must bring every-thing with you, for only restrooms are available on the island. An excellent self-guiding tour, introduced by an explanatory slide show, orients visitors to the wonderful wild fort that you may roam to your heart's content. Snorkelers need only wade out waist-deep from the little beach to behold the colorful array of marine creatures that dart among the patches of living coral in the crystal-clear Gulf water.

wave ovens and refrigerators, louvered doors and two televisions. Many have jacuzzi tubs and some have balconies. The public beach is just across the street and there's a day-and-night shuttle to Duval Street. ~ 2001 South Roosevelt Boulevard; 305-292-9800, 800-452-3224, fax 305-294-6009; www.sheratonkeywest. com, e-mail info@sheratonkeywest.com. ULTRA-DELUXE.

DINING

Marvelous Gulf views, candlelit tables and soothing piano music are reasons for reveling in the **Pier House Restaurant**, the only four-diamond restaurant in Key West. As an added treat, the cuisine is consistently outstanding, relying heavily on innovative treatments of local seafood, fruits and vegetables. Musts here are the conch bisque and the jumbo shrimp wrapped in apple-smoked bacon and topped with bleu cheese. A heady chocolate decadence dessert comes crowned with a fragrant red rosebud. Dinner only. ~ 1 Duval Street; 305-296-4600; e-mail info@pierhouse.com. DELUXE.

A rowdy, noisy, casual atmosphere is usual at the **Half Shell Raw Bar**, and, like as not, you'll find someone's faithful pooch tethered to the large anchor outside. There's no air conditioning, but open windows and the waterfront location coax in the ocean air. Under a wall collage of license plates and currency, patrons gobble up the freshest seafood and down huge quaffs of cold beverages. ~ Land's End Village, 231 Margaret Street; 305-294-7496. MODERATE.

HIDDEN ▶

The marriage of German cuisine and island ingredients is surprisingly successful. The menu at **Martin's** offers traditional *sauerbraten* with *spatzle* and red cabbage alongside innovative dishes such as fresh sautéed grouper topped with a dijon crust and served with champagne kraut and rosemary potatoes. Nestled on an artsy lane, this spot has a tiny romantic dining room, canopied garden tables and a darling outdoor bar stocked with delicious dark biers. Martin's is known for fabulous Sunday brunch and homemade desserts. ~ 416 Appelrouth Lane; 305-296-1183. MODERATE.

Completed in 1998, the city's Harbor Walk curves around Key West Historic Seaport, past a section of newish eateries. The **A & B Lobster House** has had a vantage over this portion of the bight since the 1950s. Thanks to a classy restoration that revitalized the restaurant's swanky appeal, the A & B offers elegant dining and a harbor view that Key Westers have held dear for half a century. On an island where chefs lean toward Caribbean cuisine, Chef Konrad Jochum presents refreshingly simple, traditional fare (à la some New England fishhouse); his plump oysters Rockefeller and seafood cream-sherry pan roasts are exquisite. Fresh ingredients, including aged Black Angus steaks and Maine lob-

ster, are flown in. ~ 700 Front Street, upstairs; 305-294-5880.
ULTRA-DELUXE.

Pepe's Café and Steakhouse is like a wonderful old boathouse,   ◄ *HIDDEN*
outfitted in battered wood walls, tiller-top tables and rumpled fishing snapshots. Opened in 1909 by a Cuban fisherman, it moved
from prominent Duval Street to a lonesome byroad. All the better:
except for locals, few know of the eatery's great burgers and baked
oysters. There are also pork chops, steak, seafood and creamed
chip beef on toast for breakfast. A vine-covered patio offers outdoor dining. ~ 806 Caroline Street; 305-294-7192. MODERATE.

B.O.'s Fish Wagon looks like a heap of flotsam washed up on   ◄ *HIDDEN*
a street corner—and it is, nets and buoys and license plates all
huddling beneath a thatched roof of questionable integrity. But
it's well known as the place for a great Key West lunch, or at least
an entertaining one, the many culinary options including a "square
grouper" sandwich. There are also shrimp and softshell crab sandwiches, oyster po'boys, chili, barbecues and *picadillo*. Sometimes
there are specials such as fried zucchini with mustard and toasted
garlic sauce. Lunch daily, dinner on Friday. ~ 801 Caroline Street,
at William Street; 305-294-9272. BUDGET TO MODERATE.

Finnegan's Wake is a piece of the Ould Sod transported directly
across the water complete with a huge, dark-wood, mirrored bar
that surely was stolen from some Irish pub. There's a great selection of beers that includes Guinness and Harp Ale, and a rosy-
cheeked bartender who can drop into a brogue as thick as Irish
stew. Before you can say "Faith and begorrah," he'll have you with
an ale in your hand joining in the sing-along that happens most
nights. The menu is more Irish than Paddy's pig; try potato leek
soup, Dublin pot pie or County Cork corned beef and cabbage.
In spite of all the boisterous fun that goes on in the bar area, the
dining room is comfortable and spacious, and there's a shaded
outdoor eating area. ~ 320 Grinnell Street; 305-293-0222, fax
305-293-8593. BUDGET TO MODERATE.

In a tiny white building near the cemetery, **Seven Fish** offers   ◄ *HIDDEN*
bistro fare and "ambient music by DJ Trance Porter." Prices are
good, maybe the best value in Key West, and the menu is eclectic,
with meatloaf and mashed potatoes listed alongside tuna sushi.
There are Chinese noodles with pork or chicken, turkey burgers
with vegetable macaroni and cheese, and nightly specials such as
angel hair pasta with lobster, shrimp and fish sauce. Decor is Deco
minimalist, with exposed wood rafters and a gleaming little bar.
Tables are tightly arranged, so go early or late if elbow room is important to you. ~ 632 Olivia Street, at Elizabeth Street; 305-296-
2777. MODERATE.

Often when celebrities attach their name to a place it ensures
mediocrity. Not so with **Kelly's Caribbean Bar, Grill & Brewery**,

owned by actress Kelly McGillis and husband Fred Tillman. Their island fare is colorful, zesty and inventive, their home-brewed beer truly tasty, and their courtyard setting spacious and well-liked by locals. Some of our favorite dishes: jumbo coconut shrimp with a pineapple dipping sauce, whole yellowtail snapper with a raspberry vinaigrette and Jamaican jerk chicken with tamarind sweet-and-sour sauce. ~ 301 Whitehead Street; 305-293-8484, fax 305-293-9405. MODERATE TO DELUXE.

Antonia's is in a big, handsome, open room with a high ceiling of polished wood and a long, glittery bar attended by pretty people. Much pasta and wine is consumed at Antonia's, and many business deals consummated. There is no lunch, but there is a man in the window all day, his floured hands kneading and rolling and cutting pasta. You can have a half or full order of pasta, but otherwise things are elaborate and pricier: grilled rack of lamb chops with mustard and rosemary, beef tenderloin and veal medallions. ~ 615 Duval Street; 305-294-6565, fax 305-294-2743; www.antoniaskeywest.com. MODERATE TO DELUXE.

Duval is tourist territory, but that doesn't stop the locals from crowding into **Camille's** for breakfast every morning—or evening, depending on your lifestyle. You can go light with fruit, yogurt and fresh-baked muffins, or sumptuous with egg combinations, waffles or french toast, an omelette or a bagel and smoked salmon. Sandwiches are available, too, but definitely take a back seat to the breakfast goodies. The decor is sort of fun and funky—movie posters and publicity stills, masks, stained glass, a trophy-type elephant head (gray plush) on the wall. Sit at the counter and you'll have a great view of lots of cooks tripping over each other in a kitchen smaller than the one in your last yacht. No dinner Sunday and Monday ~ 703½ Duval Street; 305-296-4811. MODERATE.

When you pick up a menu and see words like *mesclun*, *ancho* and *risotto*, you know you're in for an inventive evening, foodwise. **Cafe Marquesa** doesn't disappoint. With dishes such as barbecued Key West prawns with white bean mash, oven-roasted plum tomatoes and grilled corn relish, you can see that this is no café, this is fine dining at its best. You and I know that *haricot vert* is just a green bean, but it tastes better in French and when served up with seared dolphin with papaya-cucumber salsa and black-bean flan. The tiny but toney Marquesa's ambience, with its smoke-free air, its elegant tables and trompe l'oeil wall, is as entrancing as its imaginative menu, and the service is knowledgeable and discreet. ~ 600 Fleming Street; 305-292-1244, fax 305-294-2121; www.marquesa.com. DELUXE TO ULTRA-DELUXE.

HIDDEN ▶

If it weren't for the intoxicating aroma of garlic and olive oil and herb-spiked sauces, you might drive right by **Mangia Mangia**, hidden as it is in a quiet neighborhood. But find it you should, because the pasta is the freshest around. The rigatoni with jumbo shrimp is topped with a salad of radicchio, arugula and Belgian endive. The *bolito misto de mare* is a combination of seafood and *pappardello* pasta in a clam broth with white wine and herbs. It's served on marble-topped tables inside or in a courtyard of many palm trees, with oil lamps flickering on your table. Dinner only. ~ 900 Southard Street; 305-294-2469. MODERATE.

The boisterous burgers-and-ribs joint that was Compass Rose has been reinvented as **Michaels**, calm and candlelit, a balmy patio beneath pink frangipani and coconut palm, with a little water garden and fountain. Steak is the star at Michaels, USDA Prime beef that's grilled to order and accompanied by garlicky mashed potatoes. Everything else is very good, too, from the seared duck to the veal chop stuffed with basil, mozzarella and prosciutto. Go for Sunday brunch and order the pound cake french toast. ~ 532 Margaret Street, at Southard Street; 305-295-1300. DELUXE.

◄ HIDDEN

"You don't have to die to get here," says the sign at the door to **Blue Heaven**. Located in Bahama Village, the two-story 1880 building was long ago a popular bordello, and Hemingway later came here to spar with his boxing mates in the yard. There's a small dining room, but true lovers of the Caribbean will prefer to sit at hand-painted picnic tables in the deeply shaded courtyard, where roosters reign over small harems secure in the knowledge that they will never be anyone's dinner. The menu offers well-prepared West Indian–style and vegetarian entrées such as Jamaican jerk chicken and Caribbean barbecued shrimp. Breakfast is hot and hearty or light and tasty daily until noon, and there's live music every night—perhaps a jazz guitar, harp or dulcimer. ~ 729 Thomas Street; 305-296-8666, fax 305-296-9052. MODERATE.

The Key West Kite Company was the first kite store in Florida.

Café des Artistes is so small and unspectacular on the outside, it's impossible to imagine that inside awaits the most elegant of spaces, with arches, crisp white linens and twinkling crystal lamps, offering rich, tropical cuisine of the most sensational order. From the roast half duckling with fresh raspberry sauce to the lobster tango mango (flambéed in cognac with saffron butter), every inspired dish tastes as luscious as it looks. Dinner only. ~ 1007 Simonton Street; 305-294-7100, fax 305-296-5504. ULTRA-DELUXE.

When you crave something hot and heady and Mediterranean, go to **Cafe Blue**. The garlic soup and chopped salad with cumin vinaigrette are invigorating, the grilled lamb burger and shrimp scorpio will make your lips tingle. Formerly Full Moon Saloon, a dark, smoky Key West institution, the cafe is bright and a little swanky, with tabletops washed in blue, tropical and animal print pillows scattered against cushioned benches, and *cha-cha-cha* music on the CD player. There's patio dining but it faces a busy street. Oh, and there are $1 mimosas at lunch—very nice. ~ 1202 Simonton Street; 305-296-7500. MODERATE.

HIDDEN ▶

Key West supports at least five sushi restaurants. For less expensive but excellent sushi and Japanese food, **Origami** is relatively informal and offers tropical courtyard seating. ~ 1075 Duval Street; 305-294-0092. MODERATE TO DELUXE.

HIDDEN ▶

For a filling and tasty meal, try **El Siboney**, a Cuban restaurant where they serve generous portions of *ropa vieja* (it means "old clothes," but it's really a beef dish), stuffed shrimp and crab and some fine pork dishes—all with black beans and rice. Other side dishes include *plátanos* and *casava*, a sometimes tasteless starchy yucca dish, but here well seasoned and worth a try because it's good for you. White lace cloths add a touch of class to this plain family place. ~ 900 Catherine Street; 305-296-4184. BUDGET TO MODERATE.

HIDDEN ▶

Welcome to neighborhood café dining at its finest. With just seven tables and a tiny bar, **Mo's** is a whirlwind of kitchen clatter, great smells and the sounds of people having fun. Owned by a French-Canadian brother/sister team, Mo's is famous for appetizers, such as country patés and baked cheddar. Entrées include fresh spinach salad with Mo's dijon dressing, vegetarian casseroles, seafood lasagna and sumptuous roast lamb. Rena's apple pie is to die for. The place gets decked out in terrific decorations at Christmas and Halloween. Dinner only. Closed Sunday and Monday and from June to September. ~ 1202 White Street; 305-296-8955. BUDGET TO MODERATE.

The first thing you notice at **Martha's** is the lovely and clever decor. Slender vertical lighted fish tanks seem magically suspended in midair. Each dining level is raised slightly above the one in front of it, affording everyone a view of the Atlantic that lies beyond the broad glass expanse. In this land of the sea and its harvests, however, Martha's is noted for its prime rib and other beef dishes, though there are plenty of seafood entrées. There's an impressive wine list, and piano music nightly. Dinner only. ~ 3591 South Roosevelt Boulevard; 305-294-3466, fax 305-294-2950. MODERATE TO DELUXE.

HIDDEN ▶

Relax in **Ambrosia's** traditional Japanese atmosphere and pace yourself for indulgence. From the first bite of *hijiki* to the last spoon of green tea creme brulée, Ambrosia sushi and sashimi satisfies the senses. Chef Masa's rolls of exotic seafood, rice and caviar, and precision-sliced local tuna are tasty works of art. The cooked dishes, such as beef tataki and various tempuras, are equally exquisite. Dinner only. Closed Tuesday. ~ 1100 Packer Street; 305-293-0304. DELUXE.

HIDDEN ▶

The Rusty Anchor is run by a local family who have turned a one-time leaky-floored shrimpers' bar into a favored eating spot for locals from Key West and elsewhere. Charter boat captains send their customers here because, as one said, "It's just the best," a good example of the word-of-mouth publicity that keeps folks coming. The location is unlikely, proving that the reputation of good seafood, well-prepared conch fritters and, surprisingly, barbecued baby-back ribs, are all it takes to make an open-air eatery a success. Closed Sunday. ~ On the corner of Old Shrimp Road across from the dog track, Stock Island; 305-294-5369. MODERATE.

SHOPPING

Key West is the place to spend your money. The Old Town streets in the waterfront area are a mass of shops and boutiques offering everything from imported flamingos to artful fabrics. Visitors do most of their shopping in the dozens of glitzy and funky shops in Old Town; practical shopping is available in several centers in the newer areas.

◀ *HIDDEN*

The **Restaurant Store** is hidden down a sidestreet in a quiet part of Old Town and caters mostly to commercial kitchens. Home chefs, however, will go crazy over all the great gadgetry and great prices. Closed Sunday. ~ 313 Margaret Street; 305-294-7994, 800-469-7510; www.keywestchef.com, e-mail therestaurant store@prodigy.net.

Not quite all the sponge fishermen are gone from Key West, as explained on a continuous video at the **Sponge Market**. "Sponge King" C. B. McHugh demonstrates the harvesting and treating of sponges and tells their history on the film; the store has bins of these marvelous nonpolyfoam wonders and other gifts. ~ 1 Whitehead Street; 305-294-2555.

Proximity to the cruise ship docks means Clinton Square Market Mall shops lean toward touristy. One exception is **Wild Side Gallery**, whose unusual, nature-inspired art comes in many mediums, from ceramics and wood and glass to jewelry and oils, and by many artists across the country. There are wall masks of raku and gourd, burnished earthenware jars, copper and wire sculpture—all brilliant, delicate, exceptional. ~ 291 Front Street; 305-296-7800.

Peppers of Key West can raise beads of sweat on even the coolest cucumbers. This hot-sauce boutique carries over 400 brands of the fiery condiment and specializes in Caribbean sauces. Customers are encouraged to test the products at the tasting bar. Related books, kitchen gadgets and local pepper art are also sold here. ~ Clinton Square Market Mall, 291 Front Street; 305-295-9333; www.peppersofkeywest.com.

Located in a historic old one-time waterfront grocery, the **Key West Art Center** is a cooperative for local artists. Works for sale include paintings and drawings of seascapes, sunsets and Key West street scenes, as well as sculpture and other art. ~ 301 Front Street; 305-294-1241.

HIDDEN ▶ Vintage-fabric connoisseurs and pillow freaks take note: the **Seam Shoppe**, a working upholstery shop, stocks bolts of stunning, ultra-cool textiles, as well as tassels, braid and piping—and will create custom pillows from any of them. Owner Cindy Meyer collects mint-condition original fabrics and replicas; classic designs include giant tropical flora and animal-pattern motifs. Just window shopping is a trip down memory lane. ~ 1114 Truman Avenue; 305-296-9830.

Brightly colored silkscreened fabrics and clothing are for sale at **Key West Hand Print Fabric and Fashion**. ~ 201 Simonton Street; 305-294-9535, fax 305-292-8965; www.keywestfashion.com.

For exotic kites, colorful nylon windsocks and just about any toy that flies, visit the **Key West Kite Company**. They also carry a wide variety of flags and banners. ~ 409 Greene Street; 305-296-2535.

The Cat House is a full-service gift shop for all cats and cat lovers. You'll find T-shirts, cards, toys and other purr-fect gifts. ~ 411 Greene Street; 305-294-4779; e-mail cathousekw@aol.com.

If **Kino Sandals** doesn't have a perfect pair of their uncomplicated footwear to fit you, they can make you some on the spot. They've been making sandals for men, women and children for almost as long as anyone can remember. Closed Sunday. ~ 107 Fitzpatrick Street; 305-294-5044.

At the **Key West Aloe Fragrance & Cosmetic Factory** you can see them make cosmetics from aloe vera, try samples and purchase the popular suntan, skincare and hair products for men and women. ~ 540 Greene Street; 305-294-5592. **Key West Aloe** also carries all the aloe vera cosmetics, as well as many other gift items. ~ 524 Front Street; 305-294-5592, 800-445-2563; www.keywestaloe.com.

HIDDEN ▶ If the **Sea Store** isn't open when you go by, it's probably because the owners are out dealing with important ecological matters, which makes them expert advisors on local wildlife and natural habitats. If it is closed, come back later and browse among shipwreck treasures such as old bottles, ballast stones and pieces-of-eight from galleons. The store also carries fine handcrafted tropical wood and driftwood pieces designed and made by the owner. ~ 614 Greene Street; 305-294-3438.

Though he's usually on the road performing and recording, Jimmy Buffett and his eclectic blend of Caribbean and cowboy music have become a trademark of Key West, where the singer got his start. Now Buffett fans can pop into his local **Margaritaville Store** for all kinds of memorabilia from tapes to T-shirts. ~ 500 Duval Street; 305-296-3070, 800-262-6835, fax 305-296-1084; e-mail info@margaritaville.com.

Fast Buck Freddie's is a wonderful hodgepodge of a department store left over from the days before malls. Browse through racks of trendy tropical clothing, funny posters, fine candies, swimwear, home furnishings and gift items. ~ 500 Duval Street; 305-294-2007.

It's impossible to miss the **Environmental Circus**, parked as it is on the middle of Key West's main drag, sending billows of incense smoke into the street, beckoning with windows full of water pipes and counterculture patches. Inside this vintage establishment, one of Florida's biggest and oldest head shops, are postcards albums, and books on growing pot. ~ 518 Duval Street; 305-294-6055.

A portion of the profits from the Margaritaville Store and its monthly newsletter/catalog, *Coconut Telegraph*, go to the "Save the Manatee Fund," one of Jimmy Buffett's numerous environmental projects.

The **China Clipper** is a direct importer of fine-quality Chinese antiques, furniture, artwork, porcelain and bronze. ~ 333 Simonton Street; 305-294-2136; www.chinaclipper.com.

Haitian Art Co. imports metal and wood sculptures, carvings, papier-mâché and brilliantly colored paintings in handcrafted frames by Haitian artists. ~ 600 Frances Street; 305-296-8932; e-mail info@haitian-art-co.com.

Key West Island Books carries a large collection of natural history books, books about Key West and books by authors who have lived here. They have new, used and rare volumes, and have book signings and readings throughout the year. ~ 513 Fleming Street; 305-294-2904.

It may not be the first thing you'd think of to buy in a vacation paradise, but why not? **Island Needlework** specializes in supplies and preprinted designs for wallhangings, belts, pillows, and so on. Mostly needlepoint, but some counted cross stitch also. ~ 527 Fleming Street; 305-296-6091.

Lucky Street Gallery is a marvelous cache of paintings, glassworks, pottery, jewelry, metal sculptures and other zany pieces for the avant garde. Closed Sunday and Monday. ~ 1120 White Street; 305-294-3973; e-mail luckystg@aol.com.

Even for Key West, the **Lazy Way Shops** are strange. Tucked ◄*HIDDEN* inside a makeshift building is a helter-skelter maze of hammocks, crystals, wood pelicans and other tourist items, including "Conch Republic" silver coins. ~ In the alley just east of the intersection of Elizabeth and Greene streets; 305-294-3003.

The sign out front says **Perkins & Sons–Marine Exchange**. In ◄*HIDDEN* back of that is another sign saying, "We're Open—Unless Not." The window, too, is somewhat confusing, being a three-foot-deep jumble of nautical "stuff" that boggles the mind with its variety. But if there's a sailor on your gift list and you like to rummage for treasures, this erstwhile sponge warehouse might be the place to find one. ~ 901 Fleming Street; 305-294-7635.

Because it's away from the bustling commercial area, you might miss **Whitehead Street Pottery**, located in what was once ◄*HIDDEN* a Cuban grocery. Every piece here is one-of-a-kind, including many beautiful and durable copper-red and raku art pieces glazed with metallic oxides. ~ 1011 Whitehead Street; 305-294-5067.

HIDDEN ►

It's hard to know whether **Five Brothers Grocery** should be classified as a shop or a restaurant, but I'll choose the former because there are no chairs or tables, just some cramped shelves of basic groceries and some favorite items for local Spanish cooking. The main reason for stopping here, though, is the counter food; locals maintain the Cuban sandwiches and *bollitos* are the best anywhere. You can also take out espresso, *café con leche*, *papa rellena* and a can of papaya for dessert. This is not a tourist place but a tiny neighborhood grocery. In fact, a sign warns, "This isn't Burger King. You do it My Way!" ~ 930 Southard Street; 305-296-5205.

NIGHTLIFE   If you wondered where the nighttime action was as you traveled down the Keys, you'll discover it's almost all here in Key West. Entertainment begins long before sunset and goes on far into the early morning hours. A number of nightclubs seem to spill right out through their open windows and doors onto the street.

Sunset in Key West is an *event*, so don't miss it. Join the crowds of visitors, performers and hawkers of wares who gather each late afternoon at **Mallory Square**. To bagpipes and drums and cheers from the crowd, the sun dependably disappears into the sea every night (unless it's overcast, which is rare), providing Key West's most spectacular and least costly evening's entertainment. ~ Northwest end of Duval Street.

There's often entertainment at the **Turtle Kraals Bar**, including live blues bands and turtle races. Once a turtle cannery, it's now an old-style Key West eating and drinking spot. You can see turtles and other sea creatures here while you relax and have a drink. ~ 2 Land's End Village, end of Margaret Street; 305-294-2640.

You should at least stick your head into **Sloppy Joe's** because it has hooked onto the Papa Hemingway legend in as many ways as it can. Papa and Sloppy Joe were drinking buddies, apparently, and it's said that some of the tales that showed up in literature were founded on stories they shared in the backroom here. Just follow your ears and you should find it most anytime of the day or night. There's live rock: softer music in the afternoon, rhythm-and-blues and a rockin' band until 4 a.m. ~ 201 Duval Street; 305-294-5717, fax 305-294-4085; www.sloppyjoes.com.

Capt. Tony's Saloon, "where everybody is a star," is the location of the *real* Sloppy Joe's, where Ernest Hemingway wrote *To Have and Have Not*, among other titles. Anyway, the real star here is Cap'n Tony, a wiry white-haired codger who has polished his role as local character until it shines. Rowdy and fun, with all sorts of live musicians from country to blues, it's a Key West institution dating back to 1851—the oldest bar in all of Florida. Come and see memorabilia of all the famous people who have had a drink here, or play pool. ~ 428 Greene Street; 305-294-1838.

For those who must have predictable surroundings, **Hard Rock Cafe** and **Planet Hollywood** await on Duval Street. In 1996 Hard Rock moved into the elaborate old Queen Anne building occupied by the Elks Club most of this century, and now it is strange to see hostesses antennaed with headsets, hovering about the gingerbread. Within a few months Planet Hollywood had sprung up just two blocks down, drawing people from the Key West sunshine into its blue-and-orange, neonish atmosphere. The Planet is but yards from the cruise ship docks, and passengers can't seem to get enough. ~ Hard Rock: 313 Duval Street, 305-293-0230; Planet Hollywood: 108 Duval Street, 305-295-0003, fax 305-295-9339.

The Top has the best view of any night spot in Key West, from the top of the 1925 La Concha hotel. Listen to relaxing music while you sip your drink and watch the sunset. ~ 430 Duval Street; 305-296-2991.

You'll find a bar, live rock-and-roll nightly and, of course, plenty of Jimmy Buffett music at the **Margaritaville Café**, where Jimmy, no longer "wastin' away," makes occasional impromptu appearances. You can enjoy the music and the American-Caribbean food until closing time. Occasional cover. ~ 500 Duval Street; 305-292-1435, 800-262-6835, fax 305-296-1084; e-mail info@ margaritaville.com.

While not a club proper, **Mangoes** attracts an eclectic late-night mix of locals, visitors and bar-hoppers. People-watchers love the view from the open patio bar/restaurant. Located on a busy downtown block, Mangoes' patrons are practically guaranteed a cultural "show" as the post-midnight parade rambles along Duval Street. Enjoy the impromptu scene over a mango colada or another exotic drink. ~ 700 Duval Street; 305-292-4606.

Some would say you haven't really done Key West until you've played pool at the Parrot, and that would be the **Green Parrot**. The bar seems ancient, and it is in fact a long-time haunt of the island's more peculiar and dubious characters, who hold forth at the bar beneath a circus sailcloth and old ceiling fans set at top speed, and who take turns at the pool tables and jukebox. The floors are coming up and the walls are covered with strange signage (including a cockeyed sign that says simply, "Balance"). Here you can find cold drafts, Jello shooters, and Key West's best margaritas on the rocks. During Fantasy Fest, the Parrot hosts great costume contests, like "Amazon Women and Their Men." ~ 601 Whitehead Street; 305-294-6133.

Drop in at **Flagler's Lounge**, where you can enjoy jazz, country or salsa music in a glamorous, brass-and-glass, 150-seat nightclub surrounded by history. ~ Marriott Casa Marina, 1500 Reynolds Street on the ocean; 305-296-3535.

Should the mood strike for a really good glass (or three) of wine, drop by **Grand Vin**. The wine bar in this old white, Bahamian-style house offers numerous possibilities by the glass, including "flights" of three half-glass tastings. Sit out on the porch and people-watch, or inside at the bar, where the owner will keep opening bottle after bottle after bottle. . . . ~ 1107 Duval Street; 305-296-1020, fax 305-292-2220.

Two Friends Patio Restaurant features live calypso, blues and Broadway tunes nightly in the winter season in its big, popular open-air lounge. The festivities sometimes spill out onto the street. There is a patio restaurant attached and a raw bar for late-night eating. ~ 512 Front Street; 305-296-9212.

On the sunset deck of second-story **Havana Docks Bar** you can get an eyeful of the Gulf and an earful of live tropical island sounds entertaining the crowd. Dancing and revelry goes on late into the night. ~ Pier House, 1 Duval Street; 305-296-4600.

Schooner Wharf Bar, once strictly local, has been "found" by at least part of the masses, though it's still big fun. Pick a plastic chair in the pearock or beneath a wood shake awning, with painted buoys and fishnets everywhere, dogs roaming (lots and lots of dogs!), the Key West Bight swollen with boats. Bands play most of the time, and when they're not, the "bar magician" will show you his tricks. ~ 202 William Street; 305-292-9520, fax 305-292-1727; e-mail schoonerwb@aol.com.

HIDDEN ►

On Friday nights, the best place to see Key West's power elite isn't a posh hotel bar by the sea but an inland street corner filled with flotsam. **B.O.'s Fish Wagon**, camped out on the corner parking lot at Caroline and William streets, is where old-monied families come to drink long-neck beer, catch up on island gossip, and listen to live country and blues music. Fridays only. ~ 801 Caroline Street; 305-294-9272.

THEATER, SYMPHONY AND DANCE   The arts are alive in Key West, too. A variety of popular and classical concerts, plays and dance programs are presented at the **Tennessee Williams Fine Arts Center**. ~ Florida Keys Community College, 5901 West Junior College Road; 305-296-1520.

The **Waterfront Playhouse**, operated by the Key West Players, Inc., presents an assortment of plays, films, reviews and musical comedies throughout the year. ~ Mallory Square; 305-294-5015 box office, 305-296-8269 information, fax 305-296-0174. The **Red Barn Theatre** is a professional company presenting several productions from December through June. ~ 319 Duval Street; 305-296-9911, fax 305-293-3035; www.redbarntheatre.com.

It's a surprise to many visitors that Key West has very few beaches, and those it does have are far from sensational. On the south side of the island, along the Atlantic Ocean, you can dip into the water or lie in the sun at one of several narrow public beaches that tend to get very crowded.

BEACHES & PARKS

SMATHERS BEACH This city-owned beach is where locals lie in the sun in the daytime and take walks at night. There's nice water for swimming but a rocky bottom. Facilities include restrooms, picnic areas, bathhouses, water-sport rentals and concession stands. ~ Off South Roosevelt Boulevard west of the airport.

HIGGS BEACH This beach area is popular with families, as swimming is possible and there are a number of recreational facilities nearby. Facilities include picnic areas, restrooms, a bathhouse, a playground, tennis courts, watersport rentals and concession stands. ~ Located along Atlantic Boulevard between White and Reynolds streets.

FORT ZACHARY TAYLOR STATE HISTORIC SITE Though the chief attraction here is the excavated and restored fort, the park also contains one of the nicest little beaches, especially for sunset-viewing and boat-watching, in the area. A grove of trees provides some rare seaside shade. You can fish in the shipping channel. Swimming is good, but watch for drop-offs. There's excellent off-shore snorkeling. Facilities include picnic areas, restrooms and concession stands. Day-use fee, $1.50 per person (walk-in) and minimum $2.50 per car. ~ Located off the western end of Southard Street; 305-292-6713, fax 305-292-6881.

Key West Gay Scene

With so much to do concentrated on such an attractive little island, it's no surprise that Key West has become a popular destination. From its snorkeling trips and sunset cruises to its kitschy conch houses and trolley rides, Key West draws gay travelers from around the world. Even though it now appears that gay visitors are outnumbered by straights most times of the year, the gay community continues to have a strong presence in Key West. Gay visitors are welcomed everywhere and Key West's elected officials and business community continue to reach out to gay travelers. To see for yourself, check out Key West's excellent Web site at www.key-west.com/gaykw, where you will not only find practical information, but a warm Key West welcome to greet you through the cold hardware of modern technology.

The casual island atmosphere that prevails in Key West compels everyone who sets foot on its soil to let his or her hair down.

Its gay guesthouses set the standard for elegance, amenities and decor, while most innkeepers provide the kind of personal service that is unmatched by any hotel staff. Whether you are sampling its many superb restaurants, browsing its shops or cruising its nightspots, you will find people in Key West extraordinarily sociable.

If you can't wait to find out the gay happenings in Key West before you arrive, tap into *Southern Exposure*'s web site, which is updated every month with the same timely details as the magazine. ~ www. kwest.com.

Although tourists visit all times of the year, two events boast an especially large attendance of lesbians and gays. In September, women take over the island for **WomenFest Key West**, a seven-day get-together of sun-filled days and party-hardy nights. This week is filled with theme parties, specially organized women-only tours and events, a film festival and sporting events— including a tennis tournament and even a wet T-shirt contest! ~ P.O. Box 1601, Key West, FL 33041; 305-296-4238, fax 305-296-4238; www.womenfest.com, e-mail women1fest@aol.com.

The last week of October brings Key West's most popular event—**Fantasy Fest**. A Mardi Gras–style party that runs through Halloween, Fantasy Fest attracts all sorts of people in all types of costumes primed for a wild time. Just keep in mind that this small island can only hold a limited number of people, and during Fantasy Fest, it's advisable to make your reservations early if you hope to take part in the festivities.

The Key West Business Guild operates the **Gay & Lesbian Visitor Info Center**, where you can pick up its informative *Key West Map and Directory*. The guide is also available at gay guesthouses or by contacting the guild, which is the island's gay business association. Closed Saturday and Sunday. ~ 728 Duval Street; 305-294-4603, 800-535-7797; www.gaykeywestfl.com, e-mail key westgay@aol.com. The monthly publication, *Southern Exposure*, also offers information for gay travelers as well as timely listings of events and performances. ~ 305-294-6303; www.kwest.com, e-mail feedback@kwest.com.

Dedicated to Key West's homosexual population and culture, the **Gay and Lesbian Community Center** is open to anyone who supports its goals. This is a great, non-commercial place to become acquainted with the island's gay scene. The Hal Walsh Archives, created to document and preserve the island's gay heritage, contains photos, published materials, video interviews and profiles of early gay businesses. ~ 1075 Duval Street, Duval Square; 305-292-3223; www.glcckeywest.org.

LODGING   Gay visitors will find numerous guesthouses—many of which are exclusively for gay men and women. Several clothing-optional inns cater to young, single, party-minded males, while other, more intimate houses appeal to professional couples.

The famous purple-and-yellow-painted **Atlantic Shores Resort** is a gay party compound on the sea, complete with clothing-optional pool and pier, the Diner Shores all-night diner, and motel rooms with lilac-washed walls, wall unit ACs humming all night, and faux Deco headboards and nightstands. All in all, a little battered but generally clean, and not badly priced. Though rates begin in the moderate range, budget prices are sometimes offered to walk-ins. ~ 510 South Street; 305-296-2491, 888-414-4098, fax 305-294-2753; www.atlanticshoresresort.com, e-mail info@ atlanticshoresresort.com. DELUXE.

Papa's Hideaway is indeed hidden, its tin-roofed bungalows shrouded in dense garden down an Old Town sidestreet just two blocks from Duval. It's a popular destination for those looking for relaxation and quietude instead of a party scene. Check into the comfortable studios furnished with futons and kitchenettes; the conch-style cottage has two bedrooms, two baths, a full kitchen, sundeck and wraparound porch. Every room has a private porch, and there's a heated pool and jacuzzi set amid palms and orchids. Continental breakfast. ~ 309 Louisa Street, off Whitehead Street; 305-294-7709, 800-714-7709, fax 305-296-1354; e-mail papas kwf@juno.com. DELUXE TO ULTRA-DELUXE.

◄ HIDDEN

A 19th-century Victorian conch house, **Marrero's Guest Mansion** has 14-foot-high ceilings, hardwood floors and beautiful antiques. Bedrooms feature brass and wicker furniture, ceiling fans and, in some cases, balcony views of Old Town. A large clothing-optional pool is also popular at this 12-unit establishment. Continental breakfast and happy hour included. ~ 410 Fleming Street; 305-294-6977, 800-459-6212, fax 305-292-9030; www.marreros.com, e-mail marreros@aol.com. DELUXE TO ULTRA-DELUXE.

Two life-size bronze herons stand sentinel outside the high walls, and once inside the heavy wooden gates, frazzled travelers can see that **Heron House** is the haven of calm and relaxation they were looking for. The small courtyard is dominated by an attractive pool with a tiled heron at its bottom, and all is shaded and beautified by tall palms and fuchsia bougainvillea that runs riot to the second-story sundeck. Everywhere, orchids peep shyly or boldly from the foliage. The rooms are accessed through french doors topped by stained-glass transoms; inside are comfortable Caribbean-style furnishings, ceiling fans, mirrored walls and gray granite baths. Continental breakfast is spread by the pool each morning. Guests are mainly gay and lesbian, but everyone is welcome. ~ 512 Simonton Street; 305-294-9227, 888-827-9722, fax 305-294-5692. DELUXE TO ULTRA-DELUXE.

One of the most recent entrants in the gay-friendly guesthouse roster is the **William Anthony Guest House**, really two houses— a four-suite, circa-1895 structure now gleaming with pale blue clapboard, violet shutters, and lots of white gingerbread and picket fence; plus a conch-style cottage out back with two rooms. All rooms are nonsmoking, air conditioned and attractively furnished with colorful, comfortable furniture and lace curtains at the windows. All open onto an attractively landscaped courtyard that surrounds a jacuzzi and deck. An upper-level sundeck ties the two buildings together. Continental breakfast is served each morning, and each evening at happy hour, the owners invite guests to tell about their day's adventures. ~ 613 Caroline Street; 305-294-2887, 800-613-2276, fax 305-294-9209; e-mail aminore@aol. com. MODERATE TO ULTRA-DELUXE.

If you're looking for a relaxing house featuring a peaceful pool, jacuzzi and patio area, check into the **Curry House**. This 1890 Victorian home offers nine rooms, all furnished with antiques, and all with French doors that open onto a long veranda or a private deck. In the heart of Old Town, this three-story, white-and-green shuttered guesthouse is for males only. Rates include a full breakfast and poolside cocktails. ~ 806 Fleming Street; 305-294-6777, 800-633-7439, fax 305-294-5322. DELUXE.

At the **Oasis** you'll find an early 1900s mansion, two restored conch houses and a young, swinging, all-male crowd. All 20 rooms are spacious and comfortable; some have two-person jacuzzis. There are three swimming pools, two hot tubs and a spacious nude sunbathing deck. ~ 823 Fleming Street; 305-296-2131, 800-362-7477, fax 305-296-9171; www.oasiskeywest.com, e-mail oasisct@aol.com. DELUXE TO ULTRA-DELUXE.

The elegant **Coral Tree Inn**, located across the street, has classical music piped through the lush, palmy grounds, while art deco sconces give off a special glow in the halls. The turn-of-the-century building has been painstakingly restored, and all 11 guest rooms are sumptuously furnished with gleaming pine and oak furniture and mauve and lavender prints. Rooms here are slightly more expensive than the Oasis. This inn is also exclusively for men. ~ 822 Fleming Street; 305-296-2131, 800-362-7477, fax 305-296-9171; www.coraltreeinn.com, e-mail oasisct@aol.com. ULTRA-DELUXE.

With its worn wood floors and ceilings and contemporary furnishings, **Alexander's** blends old with new and gives the feeling of a very comfortable home. In the jungly courtyard, flaming bougainvillea dangle above a cobalt blue pool, and 17 rooms and suites are spread among three houses; a jacuzzi rounds out the amenities. Each room is decorated individually, though particularly appealing are the second- and third-floor treehouse rooms with their stained-glass windows and skylights. There's a primarily gay and lesbian clientele, but straight visitors are welcome.

Extended continental breakfast included. ~ 1118 Fleming Street; 305-294-9919, 800-654-9919, fax 305-295-0357; www.alexg house.com, e-mail alexghouse@aol.com. DELUXE TO ULTRA-DELUXE.

Catering to gays and lesbians, the **Brass Key Guesthouse** is a beautiful two-story, plantation-style house surrounded by verandas and tropical gardens. A lovely pool and a spiral staircase leading up to the sundeck make this bed and breakfast particularly inviting. Sixteen rooms are furnished with English antiques, ceiling fans and all amenities. Complimentary poolside drinks in the afternoon. ~ 412 Frances Street; 305-296-4719, 800-932-9119, fax 305-296-1994; www.brasskey.com, e-mail keywest@ brasskey.com. DELUXE TO ULTRA-DELUXE.

Newton Street Station, which bills itself as "a man's retreat in Key West," is an intimate, homey guesthouse exclusively for gay men, tucked away on a little-traveled street. The seven rooms, including one with private veranda and full kitchen, are simply but comfortably furnished, and a complimentary bicycle is reserved for each guest. Although the building, is less interesting than some (gingerbread is notably lacking), the lush landscaping and clothing-optional pool offer an attractive setting for each morning's continental breakfast. ~ 1414 Newton Street; 305-294-4288, 800-248-2457, fax 305-292-5062; www.newton-street-station.com, e-mail johnss@aol.com. MODERATE TO DELUXE.

The Newton Street Station, now a guesthouse, was once home to the station master of the short-lived Florida East Coast Railway.

Open to women only, **Rainbow House** offers nine suites and 29 rooms, some with private or shared kitchens. This Old Town inn serves an expanded continental breakfast poolside. Lush landscaping adds to the charm of the pavilion and veranda. Sitting areas are furnished with wicker and the tropical-style bedrooms feature print bedspreads. ~ 525 United Street; 305-292-1450, 800-749-6696, fax 305-292-8511; www.rainbowhousekeywest.com. MODERATE TO DELUXE.

Big Ruby's Guesthouse is *Out & About*'s favorite Key West guesthouse and received their palm rating in 1995. It's easy to see why. The 17 rooms, spread between three buildings, are tastefully decorated and have TVs, VCRs (with free movies), all-cotton bedding and extra-thick bath towels. The grounds are lushly landscaped and the pool is clothing-optional, open 24 hours and solar-heated in the winter. Every morning a substantial breakfast of eggs Benedict, breakfast burritos, french toast and the like is served poolside; the pool is also the place where guests gather in the evening for wine. Guests are mainly men, but women are always welcome. The staff will be happy to assist you in deciding on the island's various tours and activities. ~ 409 Appelrouth Lane; 305-296-2323, 800-477-7829, fax 305-296-0281; www.bigrubys. com. DELUXE TO ULTRA-DELUXE.

DINING

By day, **Diner Shores** attracts the vast spectrum of Key West visitors and inhabitants. But at night, especially late at night, the '50s-style diner is where gays and lesbians meet for after-club cocktails and cigarettes, and big breakfasts of eggs and hash, pancakes, and omelettes. There's a popular streetside terrace, and tables inside on the terrazzo. Open all the time. ~ 510 South Street, at Atlantic Shores motel; 305-296-2491. BUDGET.

The owners of Virgilio's bar can do no wrong with **La Trattoria**. Expect savory Italian fare dished out in a charming rustic setting decorated with statues and plants; its windows look out onto bustling Duval Street. Start with baked eggplant stuffed with ricotta and roasted red pepper. Then move on to the tortellini with cream sauce or crêpes filled with spinach, mushrooms and cheese. Also on the menu are veal, seafood, lamb and chicken dishes. Dinner only. ~ 524 Duval Street; 305-296-1075; www.la trattoriakeywest.com, e-mail italykw@aol.com. MODERATE TO DELUXE.

For intimate, elegant dining New York style, saunter over to the **Square One**, which is popular with gays and straights alike. The atmosphere is enhanced by soft piano music and, if you're seated outside, the courtyard garden. Try one of the different veal dishes, or perhaps the scallops, nestled on a bed of poached spinach. You'll also find steak, rack of lamb, duck and a variety of seafood prepared New American style. Dinner only. ~ 1075 Duval Street; 305-296-4300, fax 305-295-7160; www.keywest.com/themenu/ squareone, e-mail squareonerestaurant@yahoo.com. MODERATE TO DELUXE.

The flamboyant if not notorious guesthouse La Te Da seems a perfect backdrop for the famously popular **Alice's at La Te Da**. Chef Alice Weingarten's self-claimed New World fusion-confusion menu reflects Asian, Greek, Caribbean and American Southwest cuisine—and occasionally features kangaroo or some other exotic-game dish. Alice offers small and large plates, so order creatively. Favorites include spicy pink vodka conch bisque finished with Stolichnaya, vanilla pan-roasted chicken, Cajun spring rolls with hot-and-sour passion sauce and grilled mahi mahi with pineapple jalapeño salsa. Kalamata-studded potatoes typify the selection of sides. ~ 1125 Duval Street; 305-296-6707. MODERATE TO DELUXE.

Like sipping a cup of coffee in a neighbor's house, **The Coffee & Tea House of Key West** is cozy and welcoming. Couches, comfy chairs and local artwork decorate the rooms. Wind chimes clink on the front porch. And inside is a smorgasbord of international coffees, teas and an array of bagels and sweets for morning noshes. ~ 1218 Duval Street; 305-295-0788, 888-295-0788, fax 305-295-8810; e-mail chouse1218@aol.com. BUDGET.

SHOPPING

Key West offers a wide variety of shopping opportunities; you'll find many wonderful items tucked away in its boutiques and shops. As you would expect, all the stores in Key West welcome gay shoppers, but there are also establishments that cater specifically to the island's many gay visitors.

The best starting point for your shopping tour—and a recommended place to start any visit to Key West—is **Flaming Maggie's**. ◄ HIDDEN
Key West's alternative bookstore stocks mainly gay and lesbian literature. And if you can't wait to get home to begin your book, there's a friendly coffee bar and art gallery located in the store where regulars meet to chat. ~ 830 Fleming Street; 305-294-3931.

Slip on a handful of handcrafted rainbow rings or other gay pride jewelry for sale at **Goldsmith Jewelers**. One of the first jewelers to market products for same-sex unions, you can have them custom-make commitment rings for you and your significant other. ~ Hilton Hotel & Marina Shops, 71 Front Street; 305-294-1243, 800-771-1858, fax 305-296-6119; e-mail keysgold@aol.com.

And if you *are* shopping for commitment rings, perhaps you're ready to take it a step further by visiting the **Chapel By the Sea of Key West, Inc.** This commitment and wedding service offers "stress-free" wedding packages in a variety of settings for same-sex couples and is equipped to handle any—or all—details you can't attend to. ~ 205 Elizabeth Street; 305-292-5177, 800-603-2088; www.lazyway.com, e-mail chapel@lazyway.com.

A mask from **Maskerville Feathercrafts** probably won't go into ◄ HIDDEN
the closet after Halloween. This local cottage industry employs several master maskmakers who produce feather creations perfect for display as artwork on the wall. Working on the premises, artisans also craft durable, lightweight feather crowns, wings and boas, as well as whimsical hats, turbans and headdresses. Feathers come from non-endangered species such as ostriches, peacocks and pheasants, and all materials are obtained legally. ~ 309 Petronia Street; 305-292-3699; www.maskerville.com.

◆◆◆

WARM-WEATHER WONDERLAND

Key West's tropical maritime climate is the best year-round option among the gay resort towns. Its warm, sunny winters outshine Provincetown's unseasonably cold ones, and during the summer, when everyone in Palm Springs bakes in temperatures soaring above 100°F, cool ocean breezes keep Key West's temperatures bearable. In fact, its average summer and winter temperatures generally vary only 10°; Key West has never recorded temperatures colder than 41° nor hotter than 97°.

NIGHTLIFE   **One Saloon** is a popular gay dance bar that attracts the leather and denim crowd. Relax in one of the two bars, play pool or watch live dancers perform. The saloon patio is also a popular retreat on balmy nights. ~ 524 Duval Street; 305-296-8118.

Epoch is frequented by both gays and straights. The dancefloor, seemingly enclosed by rocky canyon walls, appears cavernous despite the number of bodies shimmying to the upbeat, high-speed dance music and breaking into a sweat under the state-of-the-art lighting. Take a breather upstairs in "celestial" surroundings and have the bartender mix you a drink before returning to the action downstairs. Cover. ~ 623 Duval Street; 305-296-8521.

For some reason, **Diva's Key West** is a favorite for local bachelor's parties. Straight folks adore the *thump-thump*, high-tech "dance club and show bar." Specializing in female illusionists, the lively right-on-the-street location pulls in a local crowd as well as a drag-curious tourists. Shows range from amateur cabaret to high-quality performance art. Occasional cover. ~ 711 Duval Street; 305-292-8500.

Generally speaking, the island's drag scene has reached an all-time high in both quantity and quality. Ranging from bawdy gigs to fine-art forms, the island's drag offerings dot Duval Street. The stage upstairs at the neighborhood **801 Bourbon Bar** presents nightly drag shows that are guaranteed to keep you amused. If you prefer to create your own amusement, mosey on downstairs and hang out with the local crowd of gays and lesbians who frequent this place. There's also pool tables and pinball machines to keep you in shape. ~ 801 Duval Street; 305-294-4737.

On Sundays, gay happenings start before nighttime with Key West's famous afternoon tea dances. For years the most famous of all tea dances has been **La Te Da**. Things heat up poolside with themed parties and disco music. For other entertainment at this laid-back and sophisticated spot, try the "Best in Drag" show six nights a week at the Treetop Bar. ~ 1125 Duval Street; 305-296-6706.

Near dusk, the party continues at the **Atlantic Shores Resort**, which has a bar and a clothing-optional pool side by side, and "Tea by the Sea" on the pier. On Thursday nights, there's a movie under the stars where a wall in the parking lot becomes the screen and everyone gathers on lounge chairs. Admission. ~ 510 South Street; 305-296-2491; www.atlanticshoresresort.com, e-mail info@atlanticshoresresort.com.

A neighborhood bar by day, **Numbers** transforms into a boisterous scene at night as male strippers take the stage. A mostly male clientele comprised of both locals and out-of-towners clamors in here in order to get the best view. ~ 1029 Truman Avenue; 305-296-0333, fax 305-292-9044; e-mail numbersbar@aol.com.

Amore Dive Resort
800·426-6729

Bay Harbor Lodge
800-385-0486

Gilberts
800·294-6701

Rock Reef Resort
800·843·5387

Bay Breeze Motel
937·5650

Kona Kai 800 365-7829

Billy O'Neil
Chihul

914 . 2898

www.od.com
800 . 822 . 1088

784 . 456 . 5000

800 . 433 . 7300

Danna

212 East Main Street, Ashland, Oregon, 97520
Phone: 541-488-1700   Facsimile: 541-488-1701   www.ashlandspringshotel.com

ATLANTIC SHORES 🏊 Neither beach nor park but a motel pool and dock on the Atlantic, it's absolutely the daytime destination of gays and lesbians looking for socializing and a suntan. The scene is a tawdry, gossipy one, with bodies all oiled up and close together on their beach loungers, lots of bloodshot eyes and talk of the night before. Some sunbathers wear swimsuits, but plenty prefer to bake in the buff. Techno music throbs from speakers. A blender grinds out piña coladas. Burgers hiss from the barbecue grill. The chair boy's well-honed muscles glint in tropical heat (everyone must have a chair, for which there is a charge). ~ 510 South Street.

HIGGS BEACH DOCK 🚴 🏊 Located along Key West's southern stretch of shoreline, Higg's Beach is popular with travelers for its fine beach and extensive park facilities (see the "Key West Beaches & Parks" section above). The dock, which juts out into the western end of the park, is active throughout the day with gay visitors enjoying the tropical atmosphere by swimming, sunbathing and socializing here. ~ Located at Atlantic Boulevard and Reynolds Street.

▼▼▼▼▼▼▼▼▼▼▼▼▼
Outdoor Adventures

SPORT-FISHING

From Key West you can fish in the Atlantic or on the Tortuga Banks. From December through April, **Yankee Fleet** has a two- or three-day trip on a headboat (complete with sleeping quarters, galley and on-board cook) for bottom fishing along the Tortuga. ~ Oceanside Marina, Stock Island; 800-942-5464; www.yankee-fleet.com, e-mail carol@yankee-fleet.com. For light-tackle, offshore or tarpon fishing charters contact **Sea Breeze Charters**. The half- or full-day trips include bait, tackle, license and drinks. ~ 25 Arbutus Drive; 305-294-6027. MV **Florida Fish Finder** has two- to three-day trips to the Dry Tortugas; common catches are dolphin, cobia, wahoo, kingfish, grouper and snapper. ~ 8262 Northwest 58th Street, Miami; 305-296-0111, 305-513-9955.

Owner/captain Karen Luknis worked the Ohio steel mills before falling in love with the delicate, mysterious marine environment surrounding Key West. Her friendly **Venus Charters** specializes in non-invasive, eco-friendly adventures inside the reef, including light-tackle fishing, backcountry tours, dolphin watching, snorkeling, and personalized excursions. These are fun, educational full- or half-day trips, emphasizing a no- or low-impact nature appreciation. The 20-foot Wellcraft open fishing boat accommodates four to six passengers; children are welcome. ~ Garrison Bight Marina, Palm and Eisenhower; 305-292-9403; www.venuscharters.com.

DIVING **Atocha Dive Expeditions**, run by Geoff Chapman and the Captain's Corner Dive Center, offers the only dive trips to the 1622 *Nuestra Señora de Atocha* wreck site. Treasure salvager Mel Fisher discovered the *Atocha* in 1985 and recovered $400 million in gold and artifacts—the most valuable wreck find of the 20th century. Located in about 55 feet of water, 35 miles southwest of Key West, the site contains cannon balls, tons of ballast, ship sections, and plentiful marine life. ~ 631 Greene Street; 305-797-3131; www.captainscorner.com, e-mail keywestque@aol.com.

Dive Key West Inc. books half-day reef and wreck dives. They also rent and sell diving gear. Certification classes—from resort to dive master—are available. ~ 3128 North Roosevelt Boulevard; 305-296-3823, 800-426-0707, fax 305-296-3823; www.divekey west.com, e-mail info@divekeywest.com.

Queen Conch Catamaran has daily four-hour snorkel trips out to the reef, and limits the number of snorkelers to avoid overcrowding. ~ Located at the Marriott Casa Marina, 1500 Reynolds Street; 305-295-9030.

For the experienced diver looking to further his or her skills, **Captain Billy's Key West Diver, Inc.** does advanced and technical instruction, including deep air and Trimox programs. Novice divers can join the twice-daily trips to reefs and wrecks, as well. ~ MM 4.5, on Stock Island; 305-873-4837, 800-873-4837.

BOATING If you don't know where to start in renting a boat, hie yourself to **Charter Boat Row** at Garrison Bight. Inspect the boats and chat up the captains before making a decision. Will it be the *Grand Slam*, the *Cha Cha II*, the *Relentless* or the *Can't Miss*? These and many other beauties are available most days. ~ Roosevelt Street and Palm Avenue.

The Flagship of the Conch Republic, the **Wolf**, a classic 74-foot topsail schooner, is Key West's own tall ship. Holding 44 passengers, she's available for day sails, sunset or starlight cruises, or custom charters. ~ Schooner Wharf at Key West Seaport; 305-296-9653, 877-296-9653, fax 305-294-8388; www.schooner wolf.com.

Boat rentals are abundant in Key West in places such as **Key West Boat Rentals**, which also offers jetski rentals and tours. ~ 617 Front Street; 305-294-2628. Powerboats, skis and hydroslides are available for half- or full-day rental at **Club Nautico**. ~ 717-C Eisenhower Drive; 305-294-2225.

For catamaran cruises out of Key West, call **Sebago**. They also offer snorkeling and parasailing. ~ 328 Simonton Street; 305-294-5687, fax 305-292-7788; www.keywestsebago.com, e-mail jsebago@ibm.net.

Yacht charters are available from **Witt's End Sailing Vacations**. ~ Summerland Key, Key West; 305-744-0022, fax 305-745-1476; e-mail captwitts@aol.com.

You and five of your mates can spend several days aboard the 60-foot *Playmate*, enjoying day and night dives along the Florida Keys or the Dry Tortugas, snorkeling, fishing, birdwatching and the fine cuisine provided by **Sea-Clusive Charters**. One-day charters are also available. ~ Key West; 305-872-3940.

Kayaking is terrific in the back country just north of Key West, and several outfitters will take you there from the island. **Mosquito Coast** takes kayakers up to Sugarloaf Key, where guides get into the nitty-gritty about coastal habitat, such as the vascular system of mangroves, which species absorb salt and how they dispose of it. The six-hour excursions include snorkeling and shore walking and substantial possibilities for seeing wildlife. ~ 1107 Duval Street; 305-294-7178, fax 305-292-2220; e-mail moscoast@aol.com.

KAYAKING

Adventure Charters & Tours advertises trips for "anyone seeking an alternative to the party boat/booze cruise atmosphere." Half-day trips go to Great White Heron National Wildlife Refuge, with kayaking through a maze of tidal streams and basins where one can look at sponges, starfish, sea cucumbers and sometimes conch. But best is the full-day adventure using the 42-foot *Island Fantasea* catamaran as a base—kayaks are launched upstream and met downstream by the *Fantasea*, awaiting with a grilled fish lunch. ~ 6810 Front Street, on Stock Island; 305-296-0362, 888-817-0841, fax 305-296-2574; www.keywestadventures.com, e-mail capt.tom@keywest-fl.com.

To rent kayaks, contact **Cayo Caribe**. ~ 1018 Truman Avenue; phone/fax 305-296-4115.

You can rent windsurfing equipment and Hobie Cats from several companies who set up shop at Key West's Smathers Beach on South Roosevelt Boulevard and Higgs Beach on Atlantic Boulevard. Located at both beaches, **Tropical Sailboards** rents windsurfers, Hobie Cats, sailboats, kayaks and snorkeling gear. ~ 305-294-2696, fax 305-294-2487. At Smathers Beach, **Sunset Watersports** offers windsurfers, parasailing equipment, Hobie Cats and kayaks. ~ 305-296-2554.

WIND-SURFING

On Stock Island, **Key West Golf Club** has an 18-hole course, spotted with lakes, palm trees and mangroves over rolling fairways, with public tee times. ~ 6450 College Road; 305-294-5232.

GOLF

TENNIS In Key West you can play for no charge at **Bayview Park**, on one of their five outdoor lit courts. There's also a pro shop and instruction available. ~ 1310 Truman Avenue; 305-294-1346. There are also public courts at **Higgs County Beach**. ~ Atlantic Boulevard between White Street and Reynolds Street.

BIKING Bicycling is a good way to explore Key West. Residents and visitors alike can be seen pedaling around on "conch cruisers," which seem to be any old bikes whose handlebars have been replaced with high-handled affairs that look just right in Key West. Biking path booklets are available through the Key West Chamber of Commerce.

Bike Rentals Places to rent bikes include **The Bicycle Center**, which has adult and kids' bikes. Rentals include helmets. ~ 523 Truman Avenue; 305-294-4556. **Adventure Scooter and Bicycle Rental** has three locations to rent from in Key West: Key Plaza, North Roosevelt Avenue, 305-293-9933; Hyatt parking lot at Simonton and Front streets, 305-293-9911; and Pier House, Duval Street, 305-293-0441.

▼▼▼▼▼▼▼▼▼▼▼▼▼
Transportation

CAR

Route 1, the **Overseas Highway**, leads directly over the bridge from neighboring Stock Island into Key West. You can reach Old Town by following Roosevelt Boulevard either to the right or left, along the Gulf of Mexico or the Atlantic Ocean. Once in Old Town, auto driving is difficult. Island traffic and parking run from frustrating to downright impossible, and city meters have insatiable appetites for quarters. It's clearly best to travel long distances via city bus, shuttle, taxi, or bicycle. Sightseeing is best done on foot or bicycle or via tour train or trolley (see "Key West Sights" in this chapter).

Visitors with vehicles should consider the city's **Park & Ride** garage, located near Land's End Marina. The covered garage is open 24 hours; the all-day $8 fee includes a shuttle ride downtown. ~ Caroline and Grinnell streets; 305-293-6426.

AIR Many visitors to Key West choose to fly to Miami International Airport (see Chapter Two for information). You can also fly into the small **Key West International Airport**, which is serviced by American Eagle, Cape Air, Comair, Delta Air Lines, Gulfstream International and USAir Express. However, a look at the map of Florida shows that by far the shortest distance as the crow flies from a major city on the mainland to Key West is from Naples. **Cape Air** has several regularly scheduled flights daily from Naples, Fort Myers and Fort Lauderdale. ~ 800-352-0714; www.flycape air.com.

X-Press to Key West schedules daily service in the winter from Fisherman's Wharf in Ft. Myers to Key West Bight aboard the *Atlantis*, with a five-hour layover in Key West. Return the same day, a different day, or travel one way. The trip is about four hours each way, saving about 12 to 14 hours of driving roundtrip. ~ 800-273-4496, 941-765-0808; www.atlantis.com.

BOAT

Greyhound Bus Lines services Key West. ~ 615 Duval Street rear; 305-296-9072, 800-231-2222.

BUS

Rental agencies at the Key West airport include **Avis Rent A Car** (800-331-1212) and **Dollar Rent A Car** (800-800-4000). Pick up at the airport can be arranged through **Alamo Rent A Car** (800-327-9633), **Budget Rent A Car** (800-527-0700), **Enterprise Rent A Car** (800-325-8007) and **Hertz Rent A Car** (800-654-3131).

CAR RENTALS

While potentially mistaken as giant Easter eggs, **Key West Cruisers** are brightly painted electric rental vehicles that require no gas. Shaped like eggs, the two- and four-seaters reach speeds of 25 mph. They offer a safe, comfortable and fume-free alternative to scooters or regular cars. ~ 1111-A Eaton Street; 305-294-4724, 888-800-8802.

The **City of Key West Port and Transit Authority** operates color-coded buses (that stop at same-colored bus stops) that run the entire length and partial width of the island. ~ 627 Palm Avenue; 305-292-8165, fax 305-292-8285; e-mail kwcdot@aol.com.

PUBLIC TRANSIT

Four Bone Island Shuttle buses circle the island from 9 a.m. to 11 p.m. daily. Spaced 30 minutes apart, two of the buses run clockwise and two run counter-clockwise. Each bus stops at four key locations: Key West Bight, Bahama Market, Ramada Inn and Casa Marina among them. This is a good way to move between Old Town and New Town. An all-day ticket for the privately owned ride is $4. ~ 305-293-8710.

Florida Keys Taxi serves the Key West airport. ~ 305-296-7777.

TAXIS

This fleet consists of cabs that seem to answer to different company names—**Five Sixes** is the most common—but a bubblegum-pink car will come when you call 305-296-6666.

Index

Aerial tours, 67, 122, 143
African Queen (boat), 74
Air travel, 66, 121–22, 166
Alligators, 52–53
American Indians, 7–9
Amtrak, 66
Anhinga Trail, 54
Animals, 16–19, 52–53. *See also specific animals*
Atlantic Shores, 163
Audubon House & Tropical Gardens, 130

Bahama Houses, 128
Bahia Honda Key: lodging, 111; sights, 108
Bahia Honda State Park, 116
Bartlum/Forgarty House, 128
Battleship USS *Maine*, 128
Beaches. *See* Beaches and parks *in area and town entries; see also specific beaches*
Bicycling, 63–64, 121, 166; tours, 127
Big Cypress National Preserve, 42, 48–49
Big Cypress Visitor Center, 43
Big Pine Key: dining, 113–14; lodging, 111–12; nightlife, 115; shopping, 115; sights, 108, 110
Birds and birdwatching, 18–19, 56, 110
Biscayne National Park, 50, 59–60, 81
Biscayne National Underwater Park Tours Inc., 50
Blue Hole, 53, 110
Boat tours, 42, 43–44, 45, 56, 97. *See also* Glass-bottom boat tours
Boat travel, 143, 167
Boating, 34, 62, 118–19, 164–65
Botanical Garden (Key West), 135
Bridge Tender's and Assistant Bridge Tender's Houses, 108
Bud N' Mary's Marina and Dive Center, 86
Bus travel, 66, 122, 167. *See also* Public transit

Calendar of events, 22–24
Camping, 33–34. *See also* Camping *in area and town entries*
Canoeing, 62–63, 119
Cape Sable, 56

Car rentals, 66–67, 122, 167
Car travel, 66, 121, 166
Charles "Sonny" McCoy Indigenous Park, 133
Chekika Recreation Area, 61
Children, traveling with, 27
Chokoloskee Island: lodging, 46; sights, 44
Christ of the Deep (statue), 72
Clothing, 24–25
Collier-Seminole State Park, 44, 49–50
Conch Key: sights, 96
Conch-style houses (Key West), 128
Conch Tour Train, 127
The Conservancy of Southwest Florida, 45
Coral Castle, 51
Coral reefs, 5, 18, 37, 68, 80–81
Corkscrew Swamp Sanctuary, 44–45
Crane Point Hammock, 97
Crocodiles, 52–53
Cudjoe Key: sights, 110
Cuisine, 28–29
Curry Mansion, 129

Dining, 26–27; price ranges, 26. *See also* Dining *in area and town entries; see also Dining Index*
Disabled travelers, 30
Diving, 62, 117–18, 164
Dolphin Research Center, 96, 100
Dolphins, 73, 96, 100–101
Dolphins Plus, 73, 101
Donkey Milk House, 129
Dragonfly Expeditions, Inc., 42
Dry Tortugas National Park, 142–43
Duck Key: dining, 102–103; lodging, 100; nightlife, 106
Duval Street (Key West), 130–33

East Martello Museum, 134
Eco Pond, 56
Eden of the Everglades, 43
Ernest F. Coe Visitor Center, 51, 54
Ernest Hemingway Home and Museum, 129–30
Everglades and Everglades National Park, 1–37, 38–67; animals, 16–19, 52–53; calendar of events, 22–24; cuisine, 28–29; geology, 4; history, 5–9; maps,

Lodging Index

Dining Index

HIDDEN GUIDES

Adventure travel or a relaxing vacation?—"Hidden" guidebooks are the only travel books in the business to provide detailed information on both. Aimed at environmentally aware travelers, our motto is "Adventure Travel Plus." These books combine details on unique hotels, restaurants and sightseeing with information on camping, sports and hiking for the outdoor enthusiast.

THE NEW KEY GUIDES

Based on the concept of ecotourism, The New Key Guides are dedicated to the preservation of Central America's rare and endangered species, architecture and archaeology. Filled with helpful tips, they give travelers everything they need to know about these exotic destinations.

Ulysses Press books are available at bookstores everywhere. If any of the following titles are unavailable at your local bookstore, ask the bookseller to order them.

You can also order books directly from Ulysses Press
P.O. Box 3440, Berkeley, CA 94703
800-377-2542 or 510-601-8301
fax: 510-601-8307
e-mail: ulysses@ulyssespress.com

Order Form

HIDDEN GUIDEBOOKS

____ Hidden Arizona, $14.95

____ Hidden Bahamas, $14.95

____ Hidden Baja, $14.95

____ Hidden Belize, $15.95

____ Hidden Boston and Cape Cod, $13.95

____ Hidden British Columbia, $17.95

____ Hidden Cancún & the Yucatán, $16.95

____ Hidden Carolinas, $17.95

____ Hidden Coast of California, $17.95

____ Hidden Colorado, $14.95

____ Hidden Disney World, $13.95

____ Hidden Disneyland, $13.95

____ Hidden Florida, $17.95

____ Hidden Florida Keys & Everglades, $12.95

____ Hidden Georgia, $14.95

____ Hidden Guatemala, $16.95

____ Hidden Hawaii, $17.95

____ Hidden Idaho, $13.95

____ Hidden Maui, $13.95

____ Hidden Montana, $14.95

____ Hidden New England, $17.95

____ Hidden New Mexico, $14.95

____ Hidden Oahu, $13.95

____ Hidden Oregon, $14.95

____ Hidden Pacific Northwest, $17.95

____ Hidden Rockies, $16.95

____ Hidden San Francisco & Northern California, $17.95

____ Hidden Southern California, $17.95

____ Hidden Southwest, $17.95

____ Hidden Tahiti, $17.95

____ Hidden Tennessee, $15.95

____ Hidden Washington, $14.95

____ Hidden Wyoming, $14.95

THE NEW KEY GUIDEBOOKS

____ The New Key to Costa Rica, $17.95

____ The New Key to Ecuador and the Galápagos, $17.95

Mark the book(s) you're ordering and enter the total cost here ⇨

California residents add 8% sales tax here ⇨

Shipping, check box for your preferred method and enter cost here ⇨

☐ BOOK RATE   **FREE! FREE! FREE!**

☐ PRIORITY MAIL $3.20 First book, $1.00/each additional book

☐ UPS 2-DAY AIR $7.00 First book, $1.00/each additional book

Billing, enter total amount due here and check method of payment ⇨

☐ CHECK   ☐ MONEY ORDER

☐ VISA/MASTERCARD _____EXP. DATE_____

NAME _____PHONE_____

ADDRESS _____

_____

CITY_____ STATE _____ ZIP_____

MONEY-BACK GUARANTEE ON DIRECT ORDERS PLACED THROUGH ULYSSES PRESS.

ABOUT THE AUTHOR

CANDACE LESLIE is a co-author of Ulysses Press' *Hidden Florida* and contributor to the *Texas Monthly Guidebook to Texas* (Gulf Publishing). Her work has appeared in *Reader's Digest*, *Coast to Coast*, *Chevron Odyssey*, the *Houston Chronicle*, *Texas Highways* and other publications. A member of the Society of American Travel Writers, Candace is also travel columnist for *Insite Magazine* and the *Bryan/College Station (TX) Eagle*. She was raised in Florida, a state she has "rediscovered" and writes about often.

ABOUT THE UPDATE AUTHOR

ANN BOESE, the update author, is an editor, essayist and free-lance writer whose work has appeared in *Newsweek*, the *Miami Herald*, *Tropic Magazine* and *Destination Florida* e-zine. Formerly editor/co-publisher of the literary journal *Bone Island Sun*, she has also written and/or edited numerous works on Cuban emigré culture. Boese is a long-time resident of Key West who co-owns Bone Island Press, publisher of the *Explore KW* travel guide. She is a member of the Society of American Travel Writers.

ABOUT THE ILLUSTRATOR

NORMAN NICHOLSON, a graduate of the Art Center College of Design in Los Angeles, has successfully combined a career in illustration and painting. His artwork has appeared in national ads, book and magazine illustrations and posters. His paintings have hung in important government collections as well as private and corporate collections throughout the United States. He currently teaches painting at the Academy of Art in San Francisco.